Trees

Questions and Answers

Trees

Questions and Answers

Bill Swain

CASSELL

Cassell Publishers Limited
Artillery House, Artillery Row
London SW1P 1RT

First published 1989

British Library Cataloguing in Publication Data

Swain, Bill
Trees
1. Great Britain. Gardens. Trees. Selection
and cultivation
I. Title
635.9′77′0941

ISBN 0-304-31680-6

Designed by Simon Bell

Filmset by Litho Link Ltd, Welshpool, Powys, Wales.

Printed and bound in Great Britain by Mackays of Chatham.

Contents

Acknowledgements

Good gardening is essentially a marriage of theory and practice. The theory can be taught and studied, but the acquisition of practical skills is very much a matter of learning by example. I was more than fortunate when I was young and impressionable to have had extremely good teachers, both of theory and practice, who were generous enough to share their knowledge and experience with me. There are many, like me, who owe a deep debt of gratitude to men like Ronnie Robson and Jimmy Clinker – and if any of them chance to read these words, I know they will murmur 'don't make 'em like that any more'.

Much of the influence of the lecturers and professors of London University and Wye College – Miles, Wains, Bagenall and many others – also comes through into this book. In addition to imparting theoretical knowledge, they demonstrated the all-important technique (perhaps more of a gift) of communicating and 'getting across' their various, sometimes extremely involved and difficult subjects.

Acknowledgements are due to friends and colleagues who have suggested and encouraged. Frances Kelly for her ideas and helpful comment, Barry Holmes of Cassell for his perception and expertise. Thanks are also due, of course, to the gardeners who have asked their questions, and so provided the raw material.

Finally – and by no means least – acknowledgement is due to someone who puts up with my long hours of silence when I am working (the effect on home life of a writer in the family is often underestimated) and who also helped with proof-reading the manuscript. Without the forbearance of my wife, this book could not have seen the light of day.

Very many other people have made a contribution over the years to the words that appear here in print. I may have written the words, but in doing so, my memory has stirred repeatedly and often with voices heard and faces seen again. I salute them all. It is their book as much as mine.

The photographs between pages 116 and 117 are by John Glover and Michael Warren.

List of questions

Problems of choice and identity

[ix]

Problems of cultivation

Problems of pest and disease

Legal problems

Miscellaneous questions

Introduction

Not only in aesthetic appearance, but also in a very real living biological sense, trees in this world are indispensable. Everyone with the space to do so should plant a tree of some kind, however small, because trees are the largest and most effective means of producing and injecting oxygen into the atmosphere of this planet. Because of their size and the total area of their leaves where the processes take place, trees produce significant amounts of oxygen and water vapour, and because of their sheer numbers in the world's land surfaces, the collective effect on atmosphere and climate is so vital that to say that life on Earth as we know it depends on trees is no overstatement. Not for nothing is the lush Amazon forest called 'the lung of the world'. In fact, without trees, the higher land-based life forms – including ourselves, could not have developed or be sustained. The effect of trees upon the fertility of soil is incalculable, and the expanding deserts of the world are sinister testimony to what happens when mankind strips away too many trees for crops. Tragically, and with who knows with what future consequences, the world's forest acreage is diminishing at an alarming rate every single day.

That trees affect the world's rainfall and climate is without doubt. Compared with their massed effect upon the environment, a tree, even a few in your garden, is right at the other end of the scale. Even so, whether it is only a single cherished specimen in a small garden, or hundreds of trees in so many acres, there is a contribution to be made towards redressing the world's declining tree population.

This book is intended to give you something to read and enjoy, to raise a few smiles and stir the imagination, to give you some commonsense advice and to help you avoid costly mistakes. It will, I hope, give you the urge to plan well and to plant trees – and in later years to stand back and admire and enjoy your planting as, like children, the trees grow to maturity.

From the experience of having answered thousands of gardeners' questions, both in conversation and the written word, I know that very many gardening problems are self-made and avoidable, often the result of impetuosity and a lack of understanding of the principles involved. Understanding puts the interest into gardening, and the success which follows leads to enjoyment.

Whether planting one tree, five, ten or a hundred, careful thought and selection are needed. Once planted, trees stay put, and you are going to live with them for a long time – they cannot be changed in the same way as annual bedding plants. The wise gardener chooses his friends carefully, gets to know them closely, and does all he can to help along what is going to be a long-term friendship.

This really is such an important point that it cannot be over-emphasized. I remember, many years ago, a very respected foreman in the London County Council Parks Nurseries at Avery Hill, saying: 'Planting a tree is like a wedding – it doesn't take long to do, but you have to live with it for the rest of your life. You don't rush into weddings, and you don't rush into planting trees. If you do, both can make you very sorry!' He could also have said that it is the next generation that often has to live with the consequences.

So sit down, relax, and do some armchair gardening with me – some say that it is the best kind! From a lot of experience, I can tell you it is the most important kind you will ever do.

Bill Swain
St Leonards

1

Choosing a tree

Whether you have a large gap, space for a group, or just enough room for a small single specimen, whether you are planting replacement trees or for the first time, you are laying up trouble for the future if you rush out and buy the first thing that catches your eye. The wise gardener always looks and thinks long and hard before he obeys all the entreaties to leap.

There are a great many beautiful trees, and as it is given to singularly few of us to be able to plant everything that we admire, there has to be a lot of discarding. You may be attracted to bloom, or spring or autumn foliage – some of the colours available are breathtakingly lovely – but there are other, more practical, points that must be considered first. Do you want evergreen all-year screening? Can you make a group of trees more interesting by introducing form or colour contrast? What size and shape of tree do you have room for, and how many? Is your soil acid or alkaline? Some subjects are very fussy and intolerant, some are only a little put out, while others thrive in any soil. These are just some of the questions you will have to ask, and which will restrict your potential choice.

If you have a sandy, quick-draining soil, you will not have much success if you plant willows, alders and similar wet- and damp-loving trees. It may also seem quite obvious that you will have serious problems one day if you plant a horse chestnut 'conker', a thumping great poplar, willow or oak – or even the kids' Christmas tree – in a small suburban garden, but it is amazing how regularly questions crop up asking how to move it, prune it, stop it getting too big – 'What can we do?'

[3]

Size, soil type, proximity to buildings are all fairly self-evident points to consider. Not so obvious – and therefore seldom considered – are factors such as the kind of leaves that will fall from a deciduous tree. Will they be hard, like oak, beech and hornbeam, so that they can be swept up easily from the lawn and paths, or will they crumble quickly like sycamore and chestnut, and produce a soft carpet that becomes slushy and slippery? When swept with a broom, gravel paths, level tarmac drives and patio paving have the same effect as a rasp; will the fallen leaves disintegrate under the broom into small particles that drop into cracks and crevices, imparting a degree of fertility for moss and weeds to gain foothold on an otherwise sterile surface? Would there be other problems, such as the winged seeds of sycamore which fly far and wide into flower beds and there give rise to a mass of seedlings, like the spiny husks of sweet chestnut that are so difficult to clean out of grass? Masses of conkers and acorns are nearly as bad, and pine needles build up into a thick carpet through which very little will grow.

There are so many things to think about, and the time to do so is before you plant. What begins as a long list of desirable possibles, has to be whittled down to a short one – but this is half the enjoyment. You can make up your mind while enjoying the delights of imagination and anticipation, in the same way as considering, comparing, and choosing where to go on holiday from great glossy brochures of inviting places – except that in your garden it will be a repeated annual holiday as your choice grows each year to maturity.

Where do you find this information? What is the best gardening version of the holiday brochure? The purpose of a mere list is to list what is available. Reference books should be something more and, like seed catalogues, the good are distinguished from the not so good by the amount of hard relevant useful information that is provided, the trouble taken to make the presentation interesting and readable, the quality of illustration, and so on. Terse description may be the soul of brevity, but it does little to inspire or inform.

The descriptive information in this book goes considerably further than in most, but this necessarily imposes a limit on what can be put between two covers. Just as we cannot grow everything, we cannot include everything here – there has to be a selection of the most attractive, useful and interesting. If you would like to refer to a longer list, possibly at the consequent cost of detail and interest, you will need to fall back on a more formal reference book, and you can do no better than refer to *The Hillier Colour Dictionary of Trees and Shrubs*. This has

[4]

been devised and developed from that nursery's stock list, and is a standard work of reference, worth its place on any gardener's bookshelf.

Just as important as book and picture reference is actual observation in gardens and parks, especially those in your locality. Gardeners living in or near London are fortunate in having two world-famous tree and shrub collections to visit. In addition to Kew Gardens and the RHS gardens at Wisley, Surrey, many locally administered parks and gardens also have fine collections and are worth a visit; some were originally private gardens and estates which their owners at one time landscaped and planted up with many fine and sometimes quite rare trees and shrubs. Unfortunately, very few subjects in local parks are labelled, and positive identification has always been a problem for the general public. Most towns and cities have parks and gardens – some, like Harrogate, are at least on a par with anything in London – but usually much better, both for identification and for the interest and information available for the asking, are the many private gardens that are opened from time to time in aid of charities.

Depending on the distance from your own garden, local parks and gardens are likely to have the same climate, possibly soil too, and can provide a useful indication as to what is likely to be happy with you. Apart from being enjoyable in its own right, walking round show gardens is invaluable in getting to know what shrubs and trees look like, both individually and in association with others to provide the maximum effect, and also quite often to see your 'possibles' as mature specimens. This is where and how you get ideas that you can adapt and copy in your own garden. Pictures are very helpful and those in this book are intended to be as informative as possible, but however good and explicit, no picture can tell you as much as the real thing. Get out and about, take this book or your copy of the *Hillier Colour Dictionary of Trees and Shrubs* with you for reference – and always carry a notebook and pen.

No doubt I shall not be very popular for saying so, but visiting garden centres is not such a good idea for our purpose at this stage of choosing and researching. A few, when attached to the nursery, may have mature trees from which propagation material is taken, but as a general rule, young immature specimens standing in nursery rows or huddled in groups waiting to be sold are no indication at all of what you may expect in years to come. Not a little circumspection is also needed in selecting a nursery or garden centre from which to buy, but we will turn to that in the next section.

2

Where and how to buy

The ubiquitous garden centre has become the major venue from which to obtain all manner of plants and garden requisites. There are two basic kinds of garden centre and you should be aware of the difference, knowing something about the place your trees and shrubs will come from.

The most common type of centre, including those operated by major food and DIY chains, buy in stocks of plants, shrubs and trees from the producing wholesale nurseries, and are no more than a gardening version of the supermarket. Like the rest of the operation, the trading technique relies on commodities having a fast enough sales turnover to justify the space they occupy on the shelves – or, in this case, in the walk-round serve-yourself plunge beds. Slow sellers do not pay for the space they occupy and are dropped. It is as simple as that, and consequently you cannot expect to find the unusual and less well-known varieties, which are not in such great demand. Well-known, common plants are available in abundance, but there is little choice for the more discerning gardener. The range of shrubs will be restricted, and that of trees even more so; after all, how often do you buy trees? The demand is less than that for shrubs, and this is reflected in the limited choice normally available. Furthermore, to keep prices down, it is not uncommon to find very immature 'whips' and specimens still in need of special care and training being offered for sale. By the same token, personnel are there primarily to look after the till. They cannot be expected to have the experience or the expertise to know much about plants, even less to give sound advice to those who need it.

The second kind of garden centre, and a better proposition, is the retail outlet of a nursery that actually propagates at least some of the plants it sells. Even here you need to be careful, however, because the hardwood propagation of shrubs and trees requires considerable space that may well need to be occupied for several years before the subjects are ready for sale. In a suburban area near a 'good point of sale' such space can be so expensive as to mean that the nursery centre, while producing its own softwood plants – bedding, pot and house plants – has to resort to buying in its hardwood shrubs and trees. However, since the staff are more directly involved with propagation, you can at least expect to find more feeling and pride in what they are handling, some expertise and care in the way the plants are looked after and, most important of all, be given good information and know-how if you ask for advice.

It is all part of the supermarket concept to encourage buying on impulse – a customer will see something in bloom, will like it, and plant it for an instant effect in their garden, whether it is suitable or not – and in fact there is a fast-growing tendency towards expendability, where a plant is enjoyed while it lasts and then thrown away to make room for the next. Off with the old and on with the new is no way to make and enjoy a garden, however.

Planting at any time is the modern approach, and for this purpose subjects have to be grown in pots or containers so that they can be popped into the ground with minimum fuss and grow away without check.

Some plants, especially evergreens, slow down during winter but do not actually stop and become dormant like deciduous subjects which lose their leaves in the autumn. While they are dormant most deciduous plants, including shrubs and even sizeable trees, can safely experience being uprooted and transplanted – provided, of course, the roots are not badly damaged in the process and are prevented from drying out. It is during this inactive period that they can be sold and transported free of soil or 'bare root'.

Evergreens do not become sufficiently dormant to be transplanted in this way and their root systems have to be kept intact and undamaged in a soil ball within a containing pot or bag. The crucially important part of the root – and this applies to all plants, deciduous or evergreen, trees, shrubs, herbaceous, seedling, young or old – is the vast number of extremely fine 'hair roots' which are so fine and numerous as to look like white fur or velvet. It is through this extremely fine hair root, technically called 'osmotic' root, that a plant assimilates both water and nutrients. The root hairs are so fine and fragile that any disturbance will break them, and even soil ball and pot-grown subjects have to be handled carefully. The removal of a pot or plastic bag when planting inevitably harms a great many osmotic hairs and immediate recovery therefore depends upon those that are left.

'Bare root' means that hardly any osmotic hairs can survive and new hairs have to grow before the plant can begin to absorb and begin to grow again. For this reason, evergreens have always been sold with an intact soil ball, and the modern method of growing in containers is merely an extension of that old method. While it may have been developed and become prevalent purely to facilitate all-year selling and planting, clearly it is beneficial even to dormant deciduous subjects to have their root systems kept intact.

You will most probably have to rely on the specialist nurseries for a really good comprehensive list from which to make your selection, and as some distance is quite likely to be involved (depending on where you live), visiting such nurseries will hardly be practicable for most. A few really good nationally known nurseries are mentioned on page 221, but there are a great many more nurseries around the country which are good and reliable, and quite possibly near enough for you to visit. It can be very helpful to have the benefit of the more localized knowledge of a nursery at no great distance from your garden, who will have closer acquaintance of your soil and climate conditions.

Make sure that your choice of tree is what you have decided that you want in your garden, and is not governed by the selection on offer locally. If your nearest nursery does not have what you want, you can always fall back on the national 'name' nurseries. Most of these are in the southern half of the country, and transport from distant nurseries incurs an inherent problem. Moist soil is heavy and transporting it is expensive, so you have a nice choice whether to choose from a restricted selection of pot-grown subjects at a local garden centre, or to select from the very much longer lists of the more distant specialist nurseries. These usually have retail centres for sales to their localities, but they still sell most of their trees and shrubs by the old and trusted method of 'mail order' and dispatch in late autumn, bare root in all suitable cases, but well wrapped, of course. No nurseryman worth the name dispatches plants with insufficient protection, but the superior are distinguished from the merely good by the trouble they go to in wrapping, protecting and packing with wet moss and sacking to prevent the root system from coming to harm.

The quality nurseries have experience and reputations. Both take a long time to build up and establish, and are not going to be jeopardized by anything less than good service and interest in their customers. If service is a measure of their quality, so are other indications, such as the trouble they take to make their catalogues descriptive and informative, and their presence and success at major horticultural shows like Chelsea and Harrogate. If you are completely unversed in these matters, take the weekly gardening journals, send for the catalogues advertised, watch the reports of awards made, and very soon you will be able to form your own judgements.

And so, finally, the truth of the old sayings 'you can't make a silk purse out of a sow's ear' and 'you get what you pay for' – which are other ways of saying 'don't buy cheap' – becomes apparent. You cannot expect a good mature specimen to develop from an ailing and misshapen start, and if you want quality goods, you have to pay the price. Seconds and misshapes can frequently be had from those who deal in them, but a cheap buy is seldom a good buy in the long run.

Propagating trees and shrubs is a highly skilled job, and a young tree can take several years from budding or grafting (it starts even before then) until it is ready for sale and transplanting. Skill, training into shape, careful transport: all cost money, and a good nurseryman is worth good money. Never begrudge paying it – in time, you will find it well worth the outlay.

3

Preparation and planting

This is the section where, if you will pardon the pun, we get down to earth. After all the thinking, deciding and selecting what to plant, this is the make or break. There is a lot of work to get down to, and it is tough, common-sense practical work.

Preparation

Before planting, the soil has to be prepared to ensure adequate availability of nutrients – your trees are not going to prosper if they are not fed well – and this is particularly important if you happen to be planting a replacement into ground that previously held a mature tree which was felled, since a large tree will have denuded the soil of nutrients. To be fair to the newcomer, you will have to restore the fertility bank balance. Straight chemicals are of very little use; they are unnatural, quick to dissolve and drain out of the soil, and do not last long. Organic manures, on the other hand, are much longer lasting and, if chosen carefully, will provide all three basic elements – nitrogen, phosphorus and potash – if not in exactly the right balance then nearly so.

The best manure I have ever used, and do not hesitate to recommend, is Humber Garden Compound Manure 1-1-1, that is, equal amounts of nitrogen, phosphorus and potash. Unfortunately, because it has a very strong smell, most centres will not stock it, and it

[10]

is difficult to find. Look around and enquire by all means, but do not waste too much time. Contact Humber direct; the address is on page 221. The mixture Blood, Bone and Fish, obtainable from Maskell's, is a good second best, and after that Growmore, which is readily available.

It is important to decide which manure you are going to use, and to persevere with it. This is particularly necessary with the first two mixtures. Time is required to build up soil bacteria populations in response to the organic source, and it is counter-effective to build up one bacteria chain and then turn to something else. A small handful, about 2oz (60g), roughly spread over each square yard (square metre) every two or three months, and lightly forked in, will go a very long way towards restoring fertility. If you can wait a year before replanting, this kind of preparation will give the new trees a much better chance to do well.

Heeling in

Once you have decided what to plant, where to get the trees and sent off your order, the very next job is to prepare for their arrival. The one thing that you cannot rely upon is the weather, and conditions may very well prevent planting for days or even weeks. It is important therefore to be ready with temporary protective accommodation for the new plants. Called 'heeling in', this consists of taking out a trench, as long as your estimate will accommodate all the plants ordered, a spit deep (a spit is the depth of the spade, about 10-11in–26-28cm) and two wide for shrubs, a spit deep and three wide for trees, throwing all the soil up on one side of the trench to form a ridge, against which, with roots in the trench, the plants can be laid – Figs. 1 and 2 make this clear. Laid at a shallow angle like this the plants are less liable to damage from fierce winds and from the arch enemy, drying out. The usual procedure is to turn another spit or two loosely over the roots, but if the weather has been cold the soil of the exposed sides of the trench will also be very cold for young roots. It is much kinder to have a good heap of compost, leaf mould or peat to cover the roots and as much of the above-ground parts as you can. With roots unable to absorb and replace moisture forcibly taken out of even bare twigs by wind, the big danger to plants in this state is wind scorch, so use

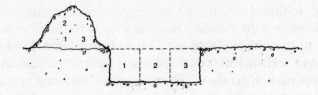

Fig. 1 *Heeling in: first dig a trench one spit deep, three spits wide (as long as you will need) and pile the soil on one side of the trench.*

Fig. 2 *Lay your trees in the trench at a shallow angle, resting on the ridge of soil.*

Fig. 3 *Cover the bare roots with compost, leaf mould or peat, if available, then turn over another spit of soil to cover them completely.*

[12]

anything to hand – cartons, straw, sacking – to deflect the wind, and cover and protect the plants.

Some dispatching nurseries are so confident of their packing that they suggest leaving a consignment intact until you are ready to plant. My advice is, simply, don't. Open the packing, check the contents, make quite certain of the root condition, soak the roots in tepid water if they are shrivelled dry, and get the plants safely tucked down in the heeling-in trench where they will be safe for a couple of weeks or so if need be. Now you are ready for planting.

Planting

Planting is not merely digging a hole and dropping a plant into it; there is a very great deal more to it than that, and if you value your plants, you will try to do the job properly. A tree, or a shrub, is going to stay in this soil for a long time, and this is your last chance to do anything about the soil underneath on which the new planting is going to rely for the first few years until the developing root system can reach further afield.

Let us assume that you have a bare root subject; invariably this will be bigger and more spread out than a containerized root ball. Take out a hole much bigger than the root spread, put the soil to one side. When you are sure that the hole is wide enough, take out another spit from the bottom and put this on the opposite side to the top spit. Fork over the bottom of the hole and work in plenty of compost or peat – remember, this is your last chance under the roots – and add a handful of the same manure that you have previously spread over the area. Tip in two or three full buckets of water as planting will begin the next day (see page 15).

Staking

A word or two about the stake is now appropriate. First, never mind what the so-called experts tell you – they may not have done the job for a living. A stake should be at least 18 inches (46cm) longer than

[13]

the *entire length of the tree from the top to the root*. This is to ensure that the top of the stake passes right up, into and through the head of branches, which are as yet no more than twigs (more about this on page 18).

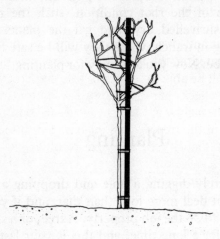

Fig. 4 Looping the branches of a young tree to a high stake avoids the possibility of neck break in high winds.

Secondly, all stakes are bound to rot and become weak. This can be delayed by giving the lower end two or three coats of a preservative such as Cuprinol. Better still, soak the stake end for 24 hours and drain it into an empty drum. Do not use creosote under any circumstances or you will surely harm your plants. The stake is most vulnerable at the soil surface, where moisture and air meet, so make quite sure that the protection extends well above this point. Clearly, this is a job that needs to be done in advance.

Trees and shrubs that have been standing a little too close in nursery rows often tend to fan out wide, and are a little thin where they have been growing into their close neighbours, with the result that they will often look better from one direction than from another. Offer up the subject to the hole, with the best side facing the direction from which it will mostly be seen – a path perhaps, or a window. Check that the size and shape of the hole are in order and decide just where the supporting stake will be positioned. Ideally this will be behind the tree, out of sight from where it will be viewed – but that is not so important as placing the stake where its top can comfortably pass

[14]

through the branches and twigs without risk of chafing, and where, if needs be, it can be used to pull a bowed stem straight. Decide if the stake position will be dead centre, left, right, back, or forward. Lay the tree to one side and, using a crow-bar, iron rod, or an old stake butt which will not matter if it splits as you hit it, make a hole about 18 inches (46cm) deep in the bottom of the planting hole to receive the point of the stake.

Work the stake in and tread it firm and offer up the tree again. It will need to be planted at the same depth as it was growing in the nursery, and you will be able to see a soil 'tide mark' at the base of the stem. However, do check that this allows any bottom-worked bud or graft to be clear of the soil by at least 2–3 inches (6–8cm). If you do not, the top 'scion' part of the tree may be encouraged to send out its own roots and ignore the 'stock' section. The result is always an unholy mess.

Holding the tree at the correct height, you can then judge whether it will help to make a small heap of soil on which you can sit the roots and spread them around. This is where you need three hands, one to hold the tree and two on the spade, so hold the tree upright with a string loop tied loosely around the stake.

The first out top spit, being more fertile than the second spit subsoil, is put back first, around the roots, and only one spadeful at a time. Shake the tree gently so that the soil crumb works down through and around the roots. Continue alternately to add soil and shake, add soil and shake, until it becomes safe to tread and firm without breaking the roots. Use your heel, not the sole of your feet, and do not stamp or kick – just gentle treading and firming, and no more than one spadeful each time. When you have used all the fertile top spit, finish off level with the other heap of second spit subsoil. Now bend down and grasp the stem of the tree, give a steady pull and try to pull it out! If there is any movement, you have not firmed enough and you will have to do the job again.

Tying in

You now have a stake and a newly planted tree a couple of inches apart. The next step is a vital part of the planting operation, one that is

[15]

so often ignored or done in a slipshod fashion, and which ruins and spoils more trees than any other – attaching the tree to its support. The first thing to appreciate is that the purpose of a tree tie is *not* to hold the tree up but to hold it firmly away from the stake without chafing. Plastic, weatherproof strap and buckle ties are readily available and widely used; I dislike them intensely, and you will see why. I was taught the correct way to make a tree tie, and it is worth taking the trouble to do it properly if you value your new tree.

This is how it is done: you will need some soft hessian sacking, some soft string, some thin rope or thick baler twine about ¼ inch (6mm) in diameter, and probably a bit of practice – but it is easy enough once you get the hang of it. Tear or cut a strip of hessian or sacking about 5 inches (13cm) wide and long enough to wrap around the tree twice to make two layers. Fold over the raw edges and wrap the sacking around the stem to form a collar about 3 inches (8cm) wide, and position it as near to the top of the stem as you can, just below the lowest branches and twigs that form the head. Arrange the wrapping so that the end comes between the stem and the stake where it will be hidden out of sight when finished. Tie it in position using the soft string, but not so firmly or tightly that it will strangle the tree as the stem swells in summer growth.

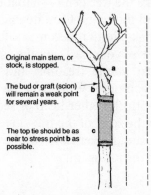

Original main stem, or stock, is stopped.

The bud or graft (scion) will remain a weak point for several years.

The top tie should be as near to stress point b as possible.

Fig. 5 Tying in: first wrap an edge – folded 3-inch (8-cm) band of hessian twice round your tree, securing it with soft string. Leave the cut end of the hessian between the tree and the stake.

Using the rope or thick string, make a hitch around the stake with the knot between tree and stake, leaving about 6 inches (15cm) for tying at the end. You will need a piece of wood about 2 inches (5cm) wide to form a distance piece between the stem and the stake. With this in position, take four or five turns around stake and tree, keeping the

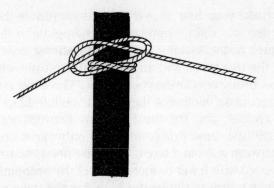

Fig. 6   Now tie the thick string to the stake, with the knot between the stake and the tree; leave 6–9 inches (15–22 cm) of string free at one end.

rope turns nicely centred on the hessian collar. On winding round the tree for the last turn, pass the rope between tree and stake, and as you begin wrapping the rope around itself, remove the distance piece – Figs. 7 and 8 make this clear. Wind as many wraps as are required to form a firm distance collar of rope, finishing off by tying to the original 6-inch (15cm) loose end, and tucking the ends out of sight.

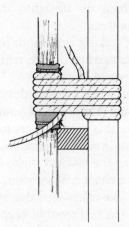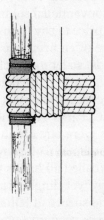

Fig. 7   Keeping the tree and the stake 4 inches (10 cm) apart with a block of wood, wrap the thick string around them four or five times.

Fig. 8   Make the flexible collar by wrapping the thick string across the loops between the tree and the stake; use as many turns as required to cover the distance. Tie the two ends together.

As you make your first tie, you should appreciate the purpose of it and 'feel' that it is right – tight, with no slipping on the stake, nicely in the centre of the sacking – a firm distancing collar between the stake and the tree stem, and all made with soft non-chafing material that will not bruise or scar the young bark. Three ties are required on a standard tree; make another at the bottom about 9–12 inches (23–30cm) from the ground, and the third midway between top and bottom, using exactly the same procedure. The only variation would be the distance between stake and tree if either are not quite straight, and this can be adjusted with fewer or more turns of the wrapping rope.

Let us now return to the matter of taking the stake up and through the head. Universal advice is to take the stake only to the top of the stem and to make the top tie just below the head. In my opinion – and all gardeners have their own opinions – this is wrong, because it allows the head to rock about in wind and concentrates all the stress at the top tie so that the stem breaks either at that point or at the implanted bud, from which the heads of roses, cherries and such like develop and grow out. Of course, when a young tree breaks its neck like this, there is no possibility of recovery. The precaution, therefore, is to take the stake up into the head and to tie in the leader and as many other branchlets as are needed to prevent it from rocking too much. An unconventional solution certainly, and perhaps also unsightly, but a small price to pay to ensure the safety of young trees.

I have often been questioned for advocating staking extra-high into the heads, so let me briefly tell you of an experience I once had, which has been worth more than all the theory in the world. A very heavy fall of wet, clinging snow set in one Easter week-end when I was on duty at the LCC Parks Nurseries in Avery Hill. Many hundreds of young cherries were already in bloom, and of course this greatly increased their catchment of snow. Realizing what was going to happen, I quickly called all hands to help in rushing along the rows to shake off the heavy wet clinging snow. We did not stand a chance. Very soon, in that eerie silence of falling show, came sounds like rifle shots: the first twigs were snapping under the weight. Then the real trouble began. Whole heads were turning over and breaking at the top ties. Hundreds and hundreds of prime young trees in full bloom were being destroyed, and all we could do was stand and watch, helpless, frustrated and angry at our inability to stop the carnage. Wet snow would still have taken a lot of twigs and branches even had the stakes been taken up, but a lot of broken necks would have been saved.

[18]

Experience a horror like that and you learn the hard way that it makes sense to put safety and protection before orthodoxy and appearance. Wind can have the same effect, so you will need to keep a watchful eye over your new young treasures.

Whether you are staking, repairing or renewing ties, finish off by lightly raking or scratching a tilth to knock out your foot marks. If you have done your work well, there is little else to do at this stage.

Half a bucket of water will help to settle the soil around the roots, but there is no need to 'water well' as is always advised. The three buckets of water the day before will have put moisture deep down, encouraging the roots to grow towards it, thereby enabling the plant to make new root and become established.

4

After-care

Although you have made ties using soft materials with a certain amount of give in them, this does not mean that, once made, they can be left and forgotten. One of the common disfigurements you are trying to avoid by going to this trouble to make ties properly is the strangulation scars that are caused by ties made too tight, by ties with no give in them, and by ties that have not been let out to accommodate the swelling stem. Plastic, wire and string can all cause this kind of serious damage, and although our hessian wrap ties are very much kinder, they too will need renewing. You will find that it pays to remake them every six months, but certainly not less than every year. The most important time to change them is in late autumn, both to allow for swelling of the stem that will have occurred with summer growth, and to destroy any pests hiding in the tie – a favourite place – and any eggs laid inside to overwinter. For this reason alone, do not try to save the material for re-use; put it all on the fire.

Re-staking

No matter how well you protect a stake point with preservative, its strength will deteriorate, particularly at soil surface level where air and moisture meet, where if a wind does snap it invariably the tree is killed by a greenstick fracture near the bottom tie. If a stake is going to go, better it does so deliberately under your control, than when it breaks under pressure and you lose your tree into the bargain. While replacing ties, with the tree stem unattached for a few minutes, it is a good opportunity to test that the stake will remain capable of doing its job until the next inspection. Give it a really good shove and try to break it! Push it hard and make quite sure that it is up to the job.

Natural decay is one thing, and although you may have gone to a lot of trouble to treat the stake with preservative, you can undo all the good work by neglect. Particularly with a new stake that has not been made firm enough, rocking to and fro in the wind can cause enough movement for a small cavity to form around the stake where it enters the soil. In reality, this is a collar of soil that becomes so compressed as to be able to hold water – clay and heavy soils are particularly liable to this – and the stake is therefore waterlogged at a point where it is most vulnerable. This is just asking for trouble – and if the ground freezes in cold weather, an ice collar forms which accelerates the deterioration. After strong winds, look at all your young shrubs and trees, especially those newly planted, and check the stakes for wind rock, water collars, loosened ties, and any other signs of trouble. Don't miss a single stake; they are there to hold the trees steady, not the other way round.

If the stake responds to your shoving and shows signs of weakness, cracking or even breaks, you have a repair and strengthening job to do. It will not be easy to remove the stump of a broken stake; it cannot be dug out because of damaging the treet roots. The best and safest method of extracting the stump is a two-handed job. Scrape away a little soil, enough to expose 2–3 inches (5–8cm) of the stump, and press a spade firmly into one side and another opposite as at B in Fig. 9. Position a piece of wood under each spade (A) to act as a pivot and depress both handles together. The stump should then lift without much difficulty. This can be done single-handed, but there is a knack to it and the job is much easier if you get someone to help you.

Taken out clean, you may be able to use the same hole to firm a new stake in position, but if this is not possible, do not try to insert another stake alongside the old one, as that can only cause root damage. By far the safest method is to proceed as for a weakened stake with the top part still in serviceable condition – by erecting a tripod. You will need three lengths of timber, long enough to reach from ground level about 2–3 ft (60–90cm) from the base of the stem to the top tie under the head. Nail or screw a piece of flat wood to one end of each length to make a firm 'T'-shaped base that will prevent the timber from

[21]

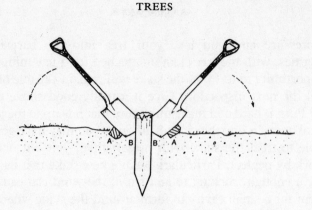

Fig. 9 *A broken stake is easily removed by levering it out with two spades biting into the stake and moving against wooden blocks on the ground.*

thrusting into the soil under wind pressure. Nail or screw the other end to the stake to hold it steady. Shorter lengths of timber across the bottom of each triangle will hold the stake firmly, and with it the tree. This may seem a lot of trouble to go to, but better to be safe than sorry.

You will often see illustrations in books and magazines – and the actual thing in orchards where it seems to be quite normal practice – of the 'crossbar' stake method of repair staking. Quick and easy – which is why it is popular – the risk of damage to the roots is avoided by keeping the two uprights well away from the stem. However, there is considerable risk in the concentration of stress at the

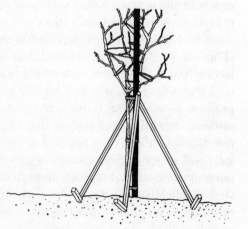

Fig. 10 *A weak or broken stake is best repaired with a tripod. This one has crosspieces on the feet to resist wind movement.*

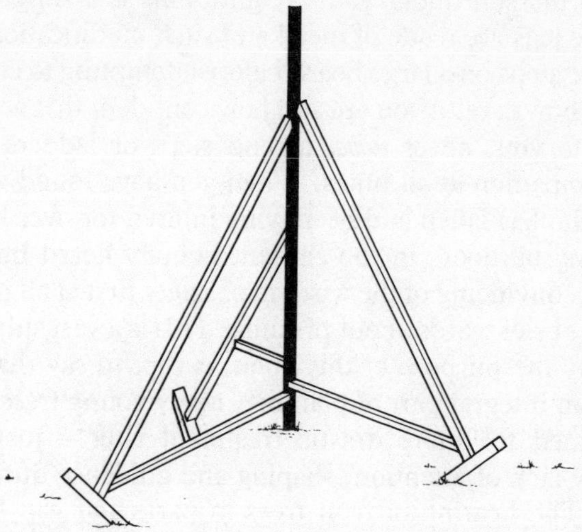

Fig. 11 For greater strength, three horizontal timbers are fixed from the legs to the original stake.

point where the stake is fastened to the crossbar. The tripod is more elaborate and takes a little more time to set up, but it is worth the trouble.

Of course, all this may draw your attention to stake maintenance and after-care that you have been neglecting for some time. It may also draw your attention – hopefully before it is too late to avoid a disaster – to the wisdom of extending all your stakes up into the heads. This will apply to other subjects throughout the garden – especially to standard roses – and not only to standard trained subjects. It is a relatively simple matter to tie or fasten stout canes to extend the stakes – but a word of warning! Making ties more than 6ft (2m) above ground of necessity means that you have to get up there to make them. A ladder is not much good with nothing substantial to lean it against, which leaves only a step-ladder. Unsteady at the best of times, on soft ground they can be lethal. The following points may seem quite obvious, but they are often overlooked and you are not looking for a tumble. It is more than likely that you will want to stand on the top step and reach as high as you can, so make very, very sure that any tendency to unsteadiness is not aggravated by the condition of the steps. Check them before use for condition, loose treads, loose screws or hinges and any other slackness, and if they are made of wood securely fasten cross pieces to the end of the legs to prevent them

[23]

pressing into the soil under your weight. This is a simple carpentry job, but if the legs are made of metal and such modification is beyond you, stand the steps on a large board before attempting to climb them.

No matter how careful you are and how confident that accidents will not happen to you, never *never* ascend steps or ladders in gardens without a companion at all times. When you have found somebody – as I have – who has fallen and been lying injured for over half an hour because, being outdoors in the garden, nobody heard him call, you will not need convincing of the wisdom of safety first at all times.

Next, a few brief words about pruning. This is a vast subject in itself and not really the purpose of this book, except to say that insofar as after-care is an integral part of planting, many young trees are spoiled and predestined for more drastic treatment later – just like some children – by lack of attention, shaping and guidance during the first early years. The bearing of fruit trees in particular can be seriously affected and you must always check the variety against the reference book. It is essential to know the identity, bearing habit and type of stock the variety is growing on before you can even begin to know what kind of pruning is required. An apple tree is not just an apple tree – it is a particular variety, growing on a particular stock and needing particular treatment, quite likely completely at variance with other apple trees alongside. I have had many queries like 'We prune every year without fail, but never get any fruit. Can you tell us why?' Indeed, when I point out that there are spur-fruiting and tip-bearing types, correspondence with this kind of questioner often reveals that they do not even know the variety of the trees concerned!

With ornamental and non-fruiting trees pruning is perhaps not quite so vitally important, but two basic rules, applicable to all trees are, first, try to avoid crossing branches and develop a balanced open framework, and second, take out anything unwanted while it is still young enough to be removed by thumbnail – 'nip it in the bud' before it becomes a bad habit. This is why the old gardeners used to say: 'the best pruners are not secateurs, but your thumbnail'. Resort to secateurs if you have to, but try never to let the problem grow to the stage of needing a saw.

While they are still young and immature, the stems of both top-budded and bottom-grafted subjects will often respond to being moved from the shaded crowding of the nursery pad to their new open position with plenty of light around by sprouting side shoots. If you want a nice clean standard stem, these should be rubbed away with thumb nail or fingers as soon as they are detected. To leave them till they have to be cut away is to leave a scar which can take years for subsequent bark growth to cover. Always keep a sharp look-out for side shoots.

Feeding

The importance of ensuring nutrient availability before planting was discussed on page 10, but a further reason for feeding before and under a new planting now becomes apparent. The first and absolutely vital task facing a new planting is for the roots to reach into the surrounding soil, searching for nutrients, and become 'established'. This is best achieved by working moisture-retentive organic matter and nutrient source into the soil underneath, where the roots will be encouraged to explore and develop. On the other hand, planting into soil that has not been fed is very little encouragement, and lavish feeding afterwards, perhaps as an afterthought, can actually attract root action towards the source of the food at the surface.

By and large, trees are deep rooted – and that is where the nutrient should be put, deep underneath. Provided that you do not make it the main source of supply, there is no reason why you should not be generous and helpful with a little top dressing after planting. Keep it light – 1 oz (30g) to the square yard (square metre), lightly hoed or scratched into the soil at three-monthly intervals, is ample – but use the same nutrient source as before planting in order to preserve and encourage the same bacterial chain. Trees are not a quick cash crop, and they do not want a diet of quick-acting tonics and pep pills any more than would be good for you.

To sum up: when planting trees, you should prepare well, plant well, stake well, renew stakes and ties regularly, and not just forget about your young charges in between periods of bloom, fruit or foliage. Young children need to be looked after all year round, not just on their birthday – so with trees.

Finally, remembering the enormous number of accident reports that followed the October 1987 storm damage, and the number of large trees that stand in private gardens, it is not inappropriate within the context of after-care to give some thought and attention to running repairs on large established trees and clearing fallen debris – and to safety first.

The overriding important fact that should be realized – but is so often overlooked – is that, as trees grow, they become big and heavy. They are up in the air, and even when apparently healthy they are potentially dangerous – and you don't have to increase the risk by being negligent or foolhardy. Whether picking fruit, pruning, removing and clearing broken branches, ladders up trees are lethal – think about it: narrow base, soft earth, movement, unaccustomed working positions, leaning to reach a bit too far, sharp tools and cut off branches to fall, children running about – it all spells danger. Even more dangerous are chain saws. In unskilled, untrained hands they are downright murderous, and in my opinion should be banned from all but trained, tested and licensed operators.

Don't try to use carpenter's saws either, they are not designed for pruning trees. The correct tools to use, especially when wood is sappy and 'green', are a logging saw for material up to 4 inches (10cm) thick, and a 36-inch Spear & Jackson bow saw for up to 9–10 inches (23–25cm) thick. For anything thicker than that, either obtain or hire a two-handed forestry saw, or arrange for insured tree fellers to do the cutting up.

Do realize also that even logs and trunks on the ground need support to prevent them rolling and crushing feet and legs. When a branch has broken and fallen, the first step is to see if this leaves the tree unbalanced, lop-sided – which means dangerous – and needing attention quickly. Does the point of breakage reveal deterioration, age, rotting or other sign of weakening? If so, all the more reason why you should not rely upon your own unskilled knowledge or abilities. A branch that has not broken away and is still hanging has to be roped up until it can be brought down under control, and that is fraught with many dangers. If a tree sheds anything of serious weight – if you have difficulty lifting a fallen branch – that is a fair indication of the unbalance that the tree is now left bearing. It is under stress, and you need skilled help.

Contact a firm of tree surgeons – the telephone directory yellow pages or your local newspaper should help you to locate one – but do make sure that the firm you use belongs to a professional organization like the Association of British Tree Surgeons and Arborists and so is insured in case anything gets out of hand. It will cost money, but it could cost a whole lot more if you do not have a damaged tree examined properly, and felled properly if it comes to that. You might even become a casualty yourself.

Any bared wood and wounds on a still standing tree should always be protected against infection by fungus or bacteria invasion by painting – not with creosote, which is lethal and can cause more trouble – with a special protective paint such as Arbrex. Just like your roses, don't leave spurs that can die back into the main trunk or branch. Cut clean, no snags and tears, and where the green cambium layer shows just beneath the bark, trim the edges of saw cuts smooth and clean with a sharp knife so that they heal more quickly, and paint over with protective.

Finally, if despite the warnings you are resolved to tackle a job yourself, and even if you are only clearing up, don't leave tools lying about, *and don't put them down on the ground*. Autumn leaf fall and storm damage inevitably means a lot of leaf and small debris which will quickly cover and hide tools. Obvious? – yes! but there is not a gardener that has not done it at some time.

We have all seen what severe winds can do – and been amazed at the immense size of some of the root boles that can be lifted out as big trees are blown over. It does not always take a storm of the severity of the one in October 1987 to topple a tree, and when it does happen, it is elementary wisdom to give attention to still standing trees, damaged or not, and particularly to those that are adjacent to where others have uprooted and loosened the soil, or that are within falling reach of buildings, roads and paths etc. If one tree falls, how many are left, still standing, but in a less than safe condition? The removal of a sizeable tree, whether wind blown or for any other reason, exposes its neighbours to wind stress through the gap that they have not had to face before. This should always be borne in mind, and large trees in such positions have to be regarded as suspect. Further winds, not necessarily strong gale force, may make them realize their age and weakened state.

Such a calamity may take longer than a year to show, and rather than rush in in too much hurry, it is more prudent to make haste slowly, let the soil settle, and use the time to look around at the options. Think things over carefully, and see if you can put back something better than what came out. Take a wander through the tree list and descriptions that follow – and let your imagination be excited.

5

A glossary of botanical terms

At one time plants were called by local 'common' names, which varied widely from region to region. This inevitably led to utter confusion until, in the eighteenth century, the Swedish naturalist Linnaeus devised the system of nomenclature now used throughout the world for the naming of plants.

The code for all plants, internationally and rigidly applied, is that the name by which a plant is first described botanically – and the choice normally is the prerogative of the original describer, who may have been, but was not always, the discoverer – is the name by which it shall be known, unless and until it is accepted at international conference level that it is not accurate, or that another name is more satisfactory. For example, plants have often been named and grouped with others, and this has sufficed until later science has shown that they are distinct. So the name has to be changed. Another reason for changing, even after a plant has been known under a name for many years, is the discovery that it had in fact been described and named earlier by somebody else, in which case the earlier name takes precedence.

Not unlike Esperanto, the universal botanical 'language' derives from the ancient languages of learning and civilization, for the most part Latin, Greek and Arabic. These provide the basic roots from which are built up the generic and species names. Sometimes, the origin and meaning of the generic name is obscure. It could be descriptive, it could be named after an individual – the discoverer, perhaps, a king or queen, or even a friend. Some plant names even derive from characters in Greek mythology.

[28]

The second or species names, many of which are listed here, do tend to be more distinct and descriptive, always meaning something, and fall by and large into four basic categories. First, they may describe a particular prominent feature of the plant such as its size, its form and shape, the shape and colour of foliage or flowers or the season in which these are borne. Secondly, the species name can indicate the natural habitat, for example mountains, woods, meadows, rivers, swamps and deserts. Thirdly, species names may indicate locality, country or continent of origin – or even a particular garden where the plant was first raised or found growing – and fourthly, as with the generic name, the species name may commemorate the discoverer, some other person, royalty or other notable. A third, or even a fourth, name progressively indicates further differences and distinctions from near relatives such as double-flowered, colour, shape and so on.

A complete list would be an enormous dictionary in itself. The following is therefore an alphabetical selection of the more frequently used and their meanings, which should be helpful in selecting features and attributes that are attractive to you, and which render a subject suitable or unsuitable for your purpose. The majority – those marked with an asterisk★ – may have the alternative endings -um or -us. Other alternative endings are indicated in brackets.

affine(is) having an affinity with, related to another species
alata★ winged (usually referring to seeds)
alba white
alpina★ alpine, from the Alps or similar mountainous regions
alternifolia★ leaves borne alternately first one side then the other
altissima relating to high origins
amabile(is) lovely appearance
ambigua★ ambiguous or doubtful origin, or identity with others in same genus
amoena★ pleasant, agreeable
angustifolia★ narrow leaves
aquatica★ associated with water, in or by ponds, rivers and streams
arborea★ tree-like (more usually applicable to shrubs)
argentea★ silvery
arguta★ sharp-leaved
armata★ armed (usually thorns or spikes)
aromatica★ aromatic, scented
arvense(is) of cultivated land, fields and meadows

[29]

atlantica★ from the Atlas Mountains of north Africa
aurantica(aca)★ orange
aurea★ golden
australe(is) from a southern region
avia★ bird-like

bella pretty, prettiest
betulens★ birch-like
bicolor flowers of two colours
biflora twice flowering
bignonioides bignonia-like
boreale(is) from a northern region

caerulea★ blue
californica★ from California and western North America
campanulata★ bell-shaped flowers
campestre(is) from fields, plains and flat areas
capense(is) from the Cape area of South Africa
carnea★ pink flesh colour
chinense(is) from China
cinera★ grey, dull silver; ash-coloured
citriodora★ citron, lemon-scented
coccinea★ scarlet red
commune(is) commonly found, occurring in profusion
concolor self- or same-coloured
confusa★ confused origin and identity
controversa counter to the usual
cordiformis heart-shaped
coriacea★ tough, leathery leaves
crassifolia★ thick fleshy leaves
crenata★ shallow round-toothed edges to leaves

decidua★ deciduous, drops leaves (opposite to evergreen)
delavayi commemorates the Abbé Delavay
discolor two-coloured
dulce★ sweet

edule(is) edible
elata elated, angelic

[30]

elegans elegant
europaea from Europe

fastigiata★ erect, upright pointing growth
ferruginea★ brown, rust-coloured
flava★ pale yellow
flore-pleno double-flowered, many-flowered
floribunda free-flowering, florid
foetida★ fetid, unpleasant, strong-smelling
formosa★ handsome, beautiful (not from Formosa)
fragrans fragrant aroma
fragrantissima★ very fragrant, most fragrant
fruticosa★ shrub-like habit

glabra★, *glabrescens* glabrous, without hairs,
glauca★ glaucous, green-grey waxy surface
glutinosa★ glutinous, sticky
grandiflora★ large-flowered
graveolens unpleasant smelling

henryii(ana) commemorates Dr Augustine Henry
heptalobum many-lobed foliage
heterophylla★ variable leaves
himalaica from the Himalaya region
hippocastanum large seeds
hirsuta★ hirsute, hairy
hispanica★ from Spain
hookeri commemorates Sir Joseph Hooker
horizontale(is) horizontal spreading habit
humile(is) low-growing
hybrida★ a hybrid

incana★ grey, downy, velvety leaves
insigne(is) outstanding
integerrima without teeth
intermedia★ intermediate between other species

japonica★ from Japan
jasminea(oides) jasmine-like

[31]

Kewensis raised at Kew Gardens

laciniata★ narrow deep-cut foliage
lactea★ milk-white
laevigata★, *laevis* polished smooth leaves
lanceolata★ lance-shaped leaves
latifolia★ broad-leaved
lilacina★ lilac-like
lilliflora★ lily-like flowers
litorale(is) from the seashore
lusitanica★ from Portugal
lutea★ yellow flowers

macropetala★ many lower petals
macrophylla★ large leaves
maculata★ spotted, blotched
major(us) greater
marginata★ margined
maritima★ from maritime and seaside areas
media★ middling, mid-way between other species
microphylla★ small-leaved
minor(us) lesser
molle(is) soft-leaved
montana★ from mountainous regions
moschata★ musk-scented

nana★ dwarf habit
nigra★ black
nipponica★ from Japan
nitida★ shiny-leaved
nudiflorum★ flowers borne naked without leaves
nutans nodding habit

occidentale(is) from the west
odorata★ sweet-scented
odoratissima★ sweetest-scented
officinale(is) used as a herb
orientale(is) from eastern regions
ovalifolium oval leaves

ovata★ egg-shaped leaves
oxyacantha coloured thorns

palmatum palm-like
palustre(is) from swamps and marshes
paniculata★ flowers borne in panicles
parviflora★ small-leaved
pauciflora a paucity of flowers, few flowers
pedunculata★ leaves having a peduncle (foot)
pendula★ pendulous, weeping
picta★ as though painted, coloured
pinata★ small pointed and divided leaves
platanoides like platanus (plain tree)
platyphylla★ broad-leaved
plumosa★ plume-like leaves
polyantha★ many-flowered
praecox early into leaf or flowering
procera★ very tall, high-growing
procumbens procumbent, creeping, ground-hugging
pseudoplatanus false platanus (plain tree)
prostrata★ prostrate, close to the ground
pulchella★ beautiful
punica★ crimson red
purpurea★ purple

racemosa★ flowers borne in racemes
repens creeping and rooting
reticulata★ net-veined leaves
rivulare★ from rivers and streams
rosea★ rose-red colour
rotundifolia★ round-leaved
rubra★ red
rupestre(is) from rocks and cliffs

salicifolia★ willow-like leaves
sanguinosa★ blood red
sativa★ sown, planted or otherwise cultivated
sempervirens always green, evergreen
serrata★ serrated, saw-toothed leaves
sinense(is) from China

[33]

soulangeana from the garden of Mgr Soulange-Bodin
speciosa★ showy
spicata★ flowers in spikes
spinosa★ carries spines, thorns
slendens shining, glistening
stellata★ star-shaped flowers
suaveolens sweet-scented
suffruticosa★ hard and woody base of stems
sylvatica★ from woodlands

thunbergii commemorates Carl Thunberg
tomentosa covered with short hairs, downy
tremula tremulous foliage
triacantha(os)★ thorns or spikes borne in threes
tricolor leaves of three colours
trifolia★ flowers in clusters of three
tulipifera★ tulip-like flowers

umbellata★ flowers in embels and whorls
unedo bitter tasting, inedible
uniflora★ single-flowered
utile(is) useful

variegata★ varied, variegated colours
veitchii commemorates the sponsor and nurseryman Veitch
velutina★ velvety surface to leaves
vernale(is) having a springtime season
versicolor variously coloured, changing colours
violacea violet colour
virida(is) green
vitifolium grape-like leaves
vulgare(is) common type

williamsiana commemorates J. C. Williams
willmotiae★ commemorates Ellen Willmot
wilsonae commemorates the collector E. H. Wilson

6

The tree list

This chapter is intended to be more than just a dreary list. On the contrary, it should be something to enjoy reading, to stir the imagination and to inspire the will to plant a tree. You will find plenty of old friends, of course (sometimes with a new slant), and some that are new. Large trees and small are included, familiar trees and neglected ones – and a fair sprinkling of unusual and perhaps surprising ideas.

Unless mentioned otherwise, all species are hardy – although it should be appreciated that hardiness is an imprecise term, and is usually taken to mean resistance to cold temperatures. This can be baffling however, because experience shows that such resistance can be variable and uncertain; there are no absolute guarantees. This normally results from the vagaries of the British climate, such as mild winters followed by sharp frosts or piercing cold winds. The more susceptible then are those subjects that hail from milder climes and which by their nature are encouraged into early sap movement and growth, making them vulnerable to late severe conditions. In fact, if you plant with understanding and sensibly applied protective measures, it is often surprising just how many doubtful or suspect subjects can be grown quite successfully.

Obviously, northern counties can be expected to have colder temperatures and more severe conditions than in the south, although this is not always so. The many almost exotic subjects at Inverewe Gardens in Wester Ross, Scotland, show that the warm Gulf Stream can play surprising and welcome tricks, particularly in the western coastal area. Hills, forest belts, prevalent wind direction – such factors all play an important part, and point to the wisdom of looking around at neighbouring gardens, parks and estates, and noting the subjects that are happy with, or merely tolerate, local conditions.

A further guide to all-round excellence are the awards made by the Royal Horticultural Society. The abbreviations AGM and FCC refer respectively to 'Award of Garden Merit' and 'First Class Certificate', each followed by the year in which the award was made.

The eventual height of a tree depends upon many factors, such as local conditions, soil and climate, as also will the number of years to attain that height. Unless more clearly stated, the following descriptions are a fair indication: small, 12–25ft (3.5–7.5m), medium, 25–50ft (7.5–15m), large, over 50ft (15 m).

Broad-leaved species

Acer

The 'Maples', a large genus that can vary in size from small shrubs to large trees, are not too fussy about soil types and generally easy to grow. Flowers are usually quite inconspicuous, but the genus contains some of the most striking and brilliantly coloured autumn foliage of all trees. Although excellent when standing alone as solo specimens, they are seen at their best in association with other and larger trees where colour contrast and shape are thrown into relief. Seen in a woodland glade, with sunlight shafting and glinting onto them, many of the maples are literally breathtaking. Just one point to bear in mind however – fallen leaves usually make a soft wet mush on paths and drives.

A. cappadocicum A medium-sized tree from the Caucasus and western Himalayas. Two varieties are worthy of note:

A.c. 'Aureum' Makes a variable 20–40ft (6–12m) spreading tree. Early foliage is a striking deep red, turning brilliant golden yellow in autumn. AGM 1969.

A.c. 'Rubrum' Makes a slightly larger tree, with a similar spreading habit. Early spring foliage is brilliant red, turning green during summer, and back to red and gold by autumn.

A. griseum The 'Paperbark Maple' is a medium size tree but has a more upright habit than *cappadocicum*. It is known mainly for the curious peeling bark that reveals bright red underbark. Autumn foliage turns fiery tints. AGM 1936.

A. japonicum Usually reaching the stature of large spreading shrubs or small 20–25ft (6–7.5m) trees, these Japanese maples need shelter from cold winds – a woodland setting is ideal. There are half a dozen varieties, of which the best is:

A.j. **'Vitifolium'** A small spreading grape-leaved tree, some 20ft (6m) high with foliage turning an incredibly brilliant red in autumn. FCC 1974.

A. negundo The common and so-called 'Box Elder' from North America. Bright green and fast growing, three varieties are notable:

A.n. **'Auratum'** This will reach 30ft (9m) or more eventually, for it is slower growing than the type. It has bright golden foliage.

A.n. **'Elegans'** This will grow to 30–40ft (9–12m), and has leaves margined bright yellow, turning cream. FCC 1898.

A.n. **'Variegatum'** A well-known and very popular medium-size tree, 'Variegatum' will make 40ft (12m) in favourable spots. It is lightly coloured and attractive, with leaves margined white.

A. palmatum The true 'Japanese Maples' and the largest group of the entire genus with more than 20 varieties commercially available. Most are no larger than shrubs, seldom over 15–18ft (4.5–5.5m) high, but nonetheless desirable for that. The following are the most tree-like:

A.p. **Heptalobum** (previously known as *septemlobum*) **elegans'**. The large 6-inch (15-cm) deeply lobed bright green leaves turn brilliant scarlet red in autumn.

*A.p.***'Heptalobum, Osakazuki'** Generally regarded as the most spectacular of all the maples, this has slightly darker colours than 'Heptalobum elegans' and is a smaller tree of some 15–20ft (4.5–6m) high. AGM 1969.

A. platanoides This group of about half a dozen sub-species are the 'Norway Maples'. All are fast growing with striking foliage – clusters of yellow flowers in April seen against the green leaves, which themselves turn buttercup yellow in autumn, make it an outstandingly attractive 50–60ft (15–18m) tree. AGM 1969. All the *platanoides* varieties are worth investigating if you have room for a collection – especially *A.p.* **'Crimson King'**, which, with its deep crimson purple foliage throughout summer, makes a fine colour contrast with its neighbours.

A. pseudoplatanus The 'Sycamore' – native to Europe, and quite often reaching 40–50ft (12–15m), this species has half a dozen varieties of which *A.p.* **'Brilliantissimum'** is regarded as the best. It has slow growing, pale pink springtime foliage, turning bright yellow/green. AGM 1973.

A. *rubrum* The 'Red' or 'Canadian Maple' is a large 80–100ft (24–30m) tree in its native habitat, but reaches nowhere near that height here. The dark green leaves turn scarlet red in autumn. It does not give its best on chalky soils. AGM 1969. Still only suitable for the largest gardens, the two clones **'Scanlon'** and **'Schlesingeri'** – if you can find them – are somewhat smaller at about 40ft (12m) with even more spectacular colouring.

Aesculus

These are the familiar 'Horse Chestnuts' or 'conkers' so beloved of schoolboys – and for edging around village cricket grounds. Typically English – but they originated in south-eastern Europe! Mostly large trees needing lots of space, there are many forms in addition to the common 'conker'. The most notable of these are:

A. *californica* One of the smallest of the genus, this species comes from western North America, where it reaches about 25ft (7.5m) and has a dense cover of white/pink fragrant bloom.

A. × *carnea* The common red-flowered chestnut, often called the 'red buckeye', this is not as large and spreading as *A. hippocastanum* alongside which it is often seen. **A. *carnea* 'Briotii'** is a darker and more richly coloured form.

A. *hippocastanum* The common white-flowered 'conker' is one of the best-known and loved trees. A word of warning: it can make an exceptionally large tree, and its roots have been known to be particularly efficient at working their way into drains. Definitely not for planting near buildings.

A.h. 'Baumannii' (previously known as **'Flore Pleno'**). This is a double-flowered form that does not set seed – so no conkers. White-flowered, equally as attractive as the type, it avoids the attention of little boys!

Ailanthus altissima

(Previously *glandulosa*) The Chinese 'Tree of Heaven', elegant and very fast growing, tolerates most soil conditions and even town pollution. It has striking leaves up to 3ft (1m) long that colour well in autumn, hence its popularity. In its native China, it can reach 50ft (15m) high and although nowhere near so tall here – 20ft (7.5m) is about its maximum – it is very spreading in habit, has invasive roots which throw up suckers where they are not welcome, and really needs far more space than the suburban gardens where it is most often seen. Caution is needed!

Alnus

The 'Alders' are useful because of their liking for damp situations that are resented by many other subjects. They are tolerant of most soil conditions except dryness and chalk.

A. glutinosa The 'Common Alder', native to Britain, Europe and Asia can reach 60–70ft (18–21m). It has yellow catkins in March and shiny green foliage that is often retained until very late autumn.

A. incana The 'Grey Alder', so called because of greyish undersides of leaves, is widespread throughout the temperate regions of the northern hemisphere. Its chief claim to our attention here is its fast growth up to 50ft (15m) and its extraordinary hardiness in cold, exposed, wet conditions.

Amelanchier

The 'Snowy Mespilus' and 'June Berry' – a small group of three or four species. All are very attractive with masses of white flowers in spring, and pink-red early foliage. They are not shrubs, although often described as such. Our stock tree of A. lamarckii at Avery Hill was well over 25ft (7.5m) high forty years ago when I worked there, and is probably well above that by now.

A. laevis This is a beautiful tree from North America, with white fragrant bloom and richly coloured autumn foliage. Somewhat less than the 30–40ft (9–12m) it reaches at home, this species deserves to be better known and more widely grown.

A. lamarckii This is often confused with and erroneously labelled as A. canadensis, which is quite distinct – so be careful! A. lamarckii has millions of small starry white flowers, just like a sprinkling of snow, contrasting with early red foliage that turns scarlet in autumn. Beautiful is a word that scarcely does it justice.

Apricot

– see *Prunus*

Aralia elata

The 'Japanese Angelica Tree' is reasonably hardy in the south of Britain, but even there benefits from the protection of other trees near and around it, or buildings 'around its shoulders'. It does best in full sunlight, and can reach 30ft (9m) in height. The huge 3ft (1m) long leaves are topped by great plumes of creamy-white bloom in early autumn – a time when there is not a lot of other tree bloom about. It is very spectacular indeed.

Arbutus unedo

The 'Strawberry Tree' is a small genus of evergreen trees rejoicing under the common name because of the similar appearance of the red fruits borne in summer and autumn. Although belonging to the same botanical order as heathers, rhododendrons and other acid-loving subjects, it is tolerant of all but the most chalky soils. Native to southern Europe – and to Ireland, where it is also called 'The Killarney Strawberry' after the district where it grows profusely – it reaches 35ft (10.5m) with little difficulty. FCC 1933 and AGM 1969.

Some confusion arises over the precise meaning of the species name, opinions being divided between 'unedo' meaning 'un-' edible, and 'un' as in the French number one, meaning that you will only ever try to eat one fruit – they are that bitter!

Ash

– see *Fraxinus*

Aspen

– see *Populus tremula*

Beauty Tree

– see *Kolkwitzia*

Beech

– see *Fagus*

Betula

The 'Birches' are noteworthy for attractive stems and branches, and for the beauty of their yellow/green foliage in autumn – not for nothing is their other common name 'Queen of the Woods'. Thriving best in the thin woodlands of sandy lime-free heaths, they are often read, therefore, as indicators of local acid conditions. Their origins are very widespread – birches grow naturally throughout the northern hemisphere.

B. jacquemontii From the western Himalayas, this has paper-white peeling bark, and reaches 30ft (9m) or more. Excellent, and worth looking out for. AGM 1969.

B. pendula (previously *verrucosa*) The 'Common Silver Birch' with white bark and rough grey-black markings is one of the most beautiful of our native trees and good enough for an AGM in 1969. In favourable woodland conditions it can make 75ft (23m).

B.p. 'Youngii' 'Young's Weeping Birch' forms a flat-topped small tree, seldom over 30ft (9m) as upward growth quickly turns over to curtain down to the ground. AGM 1969. This is magnificent as a specimen on a lawn, and nice to sit under in the dappled shade.

Bladder Nut

– see *Staphylea*

Buddleia

The 'Butterfly Bush' is a well-known spectacular flowering shrub that almost became regarded as a weed during World War II due to the astonishing speed with which it colonized bomb sites. One plant at least is worth considering as a small tree by training it up as a single main stem to 7–8ft (2–2.5m) and then allowing the pendulous habit to take over and shower long fragrant flowering branches to the ground. It is too brittle to stand entirely alone – the stem will need staking until the tree is very mature – but the effect achieved is well worth the trouble.

B. alternifolia From China, this has masses of fragrant lilac-purple bloom in June and July. AGM 1924. The 'standard' treatment makes an unusual and beautiful small tree for anyone with a small garden.

Carpinus

The 'Hornbeams' are native to Britain and Europe; five or six varieties are commercially available.

C. betulus The 'Common Hornbeam' can reach over 60ft (18m). It is a wide-spreading tree with strongly ribbed leaves which resist breaking and mushing, making them easier to clear from lawns and paths.

C.b. 'Fastigiata' This has similar dimensions to the species type, but makes a narrower compact tree when young. It tends to lose the fastigiate form with age and merge into its close neighbours. AGM 1969.

Carya

'Hickory' hails from North America, and has large compound leaves that turn a bright yellow in autumn providing fine colour and form contrast, especially against evergreen conifers.

C. cordiformis The species usually planted in Britain, this makes a large tree of up to 100ft (30m) and needs plenty of room.

C. ovata The 'Shagbark hickory' is shorter and smaller with a more upright habit and rich yellow autumn colouring.

Castanea

The 'Sweet Chestnut' is a generally long-lived and drought-resistant tree thriving on light dry soils and tolerant of chalky conditions. Flowers are smaller and less conspicuous than those of the 'horse chestnuts'. The spiny husks of the nuts are a problem to clear from grass.

C. sativa The 'Spanish Chestnut', fast-growing to 60–70ft (18–21m), is a native of southern Europe and the Mediterranean littoral (hence the clue to what is needed here for a good crop of nuts: a warm dry summer). Sometimes it takes several years before bearing a worthwhile yield – the variety 'Marron de Lyon' begins cropping when young but is not easy to find in the nursery lists.

[42]

Catalpa

The 'Indian Bean Tree' from the USA is a large tree of some 60–70ft (18–21m), not unlike the horse chestnut in shape and form, with similar large panicles of bloom in late June and July. It tolerates most soil conditions and atmospheric pollution – several fine specimens stand in London squares and parks.

C. bignonioides The individual foxglove-like flowers are creamy white, flecked with yellow and purple, and are followed not by nuts, but by long seed pods like runner beans. Unusual and handsome, this tree should be better known and more widely grown. AGM 1960.

C.b. 'Aurea' The golden-leaved form is somewhat smaller in stature and has large velvety soft leaves.

C. fargesii Much more rare, but one of the very best of all summer flowering trees, with lilac pink flowers shading yellow with brown and red spots. This makes 30–35ft (9–10.5m) and is very eye catching.

Cercidiphyllum japonicum

One of the most beautiful deciduous trees that have come to us from Japan, this has an upright 50ft (15m) form, with slightly pendulous branches. The bright green foliage turns yellow, pink and red-tinted in autumn – and has a pleasing aroma of scorching sugar! The flowers are insignificant, but what does that matter – the autumn colouring is out of this world. If you have a deep moist soil and a nice glade to provide a little protection and background, here is the perfect foil in colour and form. It is hard to understand how such a beautiful tree can be so rare.

Cercis siliquastrum

The 'Judas Tree', a small rambling deciduous tree from southern Europe and the eastern Mediterranean, is smothered during May and June with rosy purple flowers. Although only making some 20–25ft (6–7.5m) maximum in this country, it needs plenty of space because it is so liable to flop about that it often has to be propped up. AGM 1927. This is the legendary biblical tree from which Judas hanged himself.

C.s. Alba A white-flowered form, rather rare.

C.s. 'Bodnant' A derivation with deeper purple flowers. FCC 1944.

[43]

Cherry

– see *Prunus*

Chestnut

– see *Aesculus* and *Castanea*

Cornus

The 'Dogwood' or 'Cornelian Cherry' is a genus of some 30 or more species, mostly shrubs of varying stature, with a few large enough to be regarded as small trees.

C. controversa A magnificent small tree from China and Japan, with branches clothed throughout late spring with large clusters of creamy white flowers. It bears small black fruits in autumn as foliage turns purple-red.

C.c. 'Variegata' This is a slower growing variety with silver variegated foliage. It is seen at its best against a dark background.

C. mas The 'Cornelian Cherry' is a small tree and one of the first into bloom each year, with small yellow flowers on naked twigs and branches from early February. It has bright red cherry-like edible fruits in autumn as the foliage turns red. AGM 1924. There are at least half a dozen variable forms.

Corylopsis

A genus of nine or ten species of Asian origin, with masses of drooping tassel-like fragrant primrose-yellow blooms conspicuous before the leaves appear in spring. It is easily grown on all but shallow soils.

C. glabrescens From Japan, this makes a 15–20ft (4.5–6m) spreading tree – and is guaranteed to make even experienced gardeners whistle and wonder what it is! FCC 1968 and AGM 1969. There is a glorious specimen at Nymans Gardens, Handcross, Sussex.

Cotinus coggygria

Previously and widely known as *Rhus cotinus*, it is now a separate genus, still known commonly and variously as 'Sumach', 'Smoke Tree' and 'Venetian Sumach'. Native to central southern Europe, it is usually grown as a shrub, but will make the stature of a small tree (I have measured it at 18ft (5.5m) in a woodland setting near Southampton) and is much too useful to be left out of this collection. Round green leaves of the type are surrounded by fawn-coloured plumes of bloom inflorescence in June and July, gradually turning to smoke-grey by late summer and autumn and giving an impression of smoke, hence the common name. AGM 1969. The varieties **'Foliis Purpureis'** (AGM 1930), *purpureus* (AGM 1969), **'Royal Purple'** (AGM 1969) and particularly **'Flame'** (AGM 1969) all have shades of purple foliage turning to brilliant autumn colouring which enhances the smoke effect. Indispensable for contrasting colours – there should be a space in all gardens for at least one.

Cotoneaster

This is another subject usually – and erroneously – regarded only as a shrub. Several species are sufficiently vigorous to reach small tree stature with ease, even as standards, when the autumn display of berries, for which this large genus is well known, are held high and seen to best advantage. The choice is wide: cotoneasters can be evergreen as well as deciduous, are variable in habitat and happy in almost any soil. You cannot grow them all, so here are some of the very best.

C. **'Cornubia'** Semi-evergreen, this spectacular species has heavy crops of large red berries that drag down the branches. It reaches 15ft (4.5m) as a shrub or trains well as a standard. FCC 1936 and AGM 1969.

C. frigidus Another semi-evergreen, *C. frigidus* is from the Himalayas where it reaches 20ft (6m) or more. It has large leaves and clusters of crimson berries. Train it as a half standard 3–4ft (1–1.2m), or a full 6–7ft (1.8–2m) standard, then let the spreading habit take over. AGM 1925.

C. **'Hybridus Pendulus'** A glossy evergreen with prostrate branches carrying an abundance of brilliant red fruits during autumn and winter. Grown on a stem this makes a magnificent weeping tree.

C. **'Rothschildianus'** A hybrid raised at Exbury, near Southampton, this is also suitable for running up as a standard to spread its pale evergreen foliage and masses of creamy white berries above other shorter subjects around it. Unusual, very eye-catching, and handsome when trained as a solitary standing specimen.

C. watereri This is really a group of hybrids with variable parentage. All have strong vigorous growth, ideal for working up as standards, and profuse crops of orange-red berries.

Crab Apple

– see *Malus*

Crataegus

'Maythorn', 'Quickthorn', 'May', 'Hawthorn'. There are upwards of 60 species and varieties commercially available of this very large genus originating throughout the whole of the northern hemisphere. Flowers, ranging from white through pink to deep red, and orange-red fruits, from the size of small berries to almost cherry size, are normally borne in profusion. Tolerant of almost any soil and notable for their ability to withstand winds and coastal conditions, all are worth looking at, but the following are among the best.

C. crus-galli The 'Cockspur Thorn' is a small tree from central and eastern North America. It has a spreading habit and berries that last over winter, but beware – its thorns can reach 3 inches (8 cm) long!

C. monogyna The 'Common Hawthorn' or 'Quick' is native to Britain, Europe and Asia. Fast growing, it is used extensively for clipping and forming into thick, impenetrable hedges. If allowed to have its head, it will get up to 35ft (10.5m) or more. It has strongly fragrant white bloom (the fragrance is not to everyone's liking) and masses of 'haw' berries.

C.m. **'Biflora'** A smallish tree, sometimes called 'Praecox' because it is so early into flower. The 'Glastonbury Thorn' clone regularly blooms before Christmas. (See also question 125.)

C. oxyacantha **'Coccinea Plena'** Often listed simply as 'Paul's Scarlet', this is probably the most widely grown hawthorn of all. It seldom exceeds 20ft (6m), and has double scarlet blooms. FCC 1867, AGM 1969.

C. pruniflora A small tree with glossy leaves that turn brilliant fiery shades in autumn, and with very persistent berries. AGM 1969.

Crinodendron hookeranum

(Previously called *Tricuspidaria lanceolata*) This is one straight out of the bandbox – imagine hundreds upon hundreds of crimson rose lantern-like blooms hanging all over the tree from top to bottom! It comes from Chile, South America, and does best if protected from severe conditions – a woodland glade is ideal – and grown in a lime-free soil, with plenty of accumulated leaf-fall around its roots. Spreading and shrubby, I have seen it growing in a wood near Southampton (from which I used to collect material for propagation) in a thicket 20ft (6m) high – so it really is more a tree than a shrub. Magnificent for bottoming and underplanting large trees. FCC 1916.

Davidia involucrata

'Dove Tree', 'Ghost Tree', 'Pocket Handkerchief Tree'; the common names show the effect that the appearance of this tree has had on imaginations. It is a hardy tree from China, tolerant of all but extremes of soil conditions. The actual flowers, which appear in May, are quite small and hardly noticeable, but two large bracts hang from each and flap in the breeze like pocket handkerchiefs. It can reach 40–50ft (12–15m).

Elder

– see *Sambucus*

Elm

– see *Ulmus*

Escallonia

The 'Chilian Gum Box' is originally from Chile, South America. There are 20 or so species and varieties in this genus of flowering evergreens that not only tolerate almost every soil type, but also – surprisingly for a South American shrub – can withstand salt-laden sea winds, as their frequent use in seaside promenade gardens clearly demonstrates. They are invariably grown as shrubs, even as hedging, but one or two are vigorous enough to be run up as 7–8ft (2–2.5m) standards. If they are then 'topped' to encourage a head of side shoots and pruned hard for a couple of years, the response is a curtain of long semi-pendulous branchlets 3–5ft (1–1.5m) long smothered end to end with bloom. Particularly good and recommended is:

E. 'Donard Seedling' This is a very vigorous hybrid raised at the Slieve Donard nursery in Northern Ireland, with long arching wands bearing glossy leaves, and pink buds opening white. AGM 1969. I have grown this variety exactly as described above, and can vouch that it is a wonderful sight in full bloom. Another very good and unusual idea for a small garden.

Eucalyptus

These are very fast-growing trees from Australia, indeed, arguably the fastest growing in Britain, but not generally regarded as fully hardy. Notable mainly for their attractive blue/grey foliage and stems, eucalyptus are normally tolerant of all soils except strong alkaline and chalk. They resent root disturbance, so only ever plant young pot-grown specimens.

E. gunnii This is probably the most commonly planted species of eucalyptus in Britain – and the hardiest, having withstood a recorded 19 degrees of frost in a small nursery at Camberley, Surrey. It has made 50–60ft (15–18m), but can be kept coppiced and will then produce a mass of young shoots that are in great demand by florists for bouquet work.

There are several other varieties, some with curious bark markings, but more of curiosity value than intrinsically beautiful.

Fagus

The 'Beech' is one of the most glorious of all large trees. A genus of nearly two dozen species, it has a distinct preference for chalk soils – indeed, the presence of beech trees is often interpreted as an indication of soil alkalinity and chalk conditions.

F. sylvatica The hard timber of the native 'Common Beech' is beloved of furniture makers, hence the establishment of that industry around High Wycombe and nearby towns of the chalky Chiltern Hills, which at one time were thickly clad with beech. The trees are long since felled and gone except in a few preserved beauty spots like Burnham Beeches. Large, spreading, and one of the longest living of our native trees, the rich golden browns of beech woods in autumn are legendary. Much too big for all but the largest gardens, but the following varieties could be a little more acceptable.

F.s. 'Dawyck' (synonymous with and often listed as 'Fastigiata') This is still a largish tree but, as the synonymous name describes, it is a very upright growing form that therefore occupies less ground area than the species type. AGM 1969.

F.s. purpurea The 'Purple Beech', as well known as its species type, also has remarkable autumn colouring.

F.s. 'Purpurea Pendula' Much less common, and seldom more than 25–30ft (7.5–9m) high, this tree has a flat-topped and very weeping habit, with dark purple leaves turning gold in autumn. It makes a splendid solitary specimen for lawn or glade planting.

Flowering Crabs

– see *Malus*

Fraxinus

The origins of the 'Ash' are very widespread, from North America through Europe and Asia to the Himalayas. Fast-growing, these trees are very tolerant of all soil conditions, wind, atmospheric pollution and salt-laden coastal wind.

F. excelsior The native 'Common Ash', with conspicuous black buds during winter is a large and valuable timber tree.

F.e. 'Pendula' The 'Weeping Ash', also called 'Garrelous Ash', is nothing like so large as the type, but often makes 30ft (9m) and more, with long hanging branches reaching to the ground. If you have the space, it makes a magnificent subject for a solitary planting in a lawn or glade where it can be seen unobstructed.

F. pennsylvanica The 'Red Ash' from eastern North America has a very attractive variation, *F.p.*'Variegata' with bright silver-grey leaves, margined and mottled cream-white. If you have room for a 45-ft (14-m) beauty, this is different, interesting, and well worth looking out for as you tour around gardens and parks. You usually know what to expect with the well-known large trees, but with these lesser-known beauties it is always better to have sight of a mature specimen before committing yourself to planting.

Garrya elliptica

From the far west of North America, this is most often grown in our gardens as a large shrub, although it can easily make 20ft (6m). With

[49]

grey-green evergreen foliage, the male form also has masses of long decorative paler-coloured catkins in January and February, which provides interest when much else of the garden is still sleeping off winter.

Gleditsia triacanthos

The 'Honey Locust' from the eastern USA is probably best known for its vicious barbed spines, but is worth growing on its merits as a handsome solo specimen tree eventually making some 35–40ft (10.5–12m). It has delicate, feathery green-gold foliage, and long shiny brown seed pods on mature trees. It grows well in all soils and is remarkably tolerant of atmospheric pollution.

Golden Rain Tree

– see *Koelreuteria* and *Laburnum*

Halesia

This is a small genus of half a dozen species and varieties from North America.

H. carolina The aptly named 'Snowdrop Tree' is a delightful 20ft (6m) tree which produces masses of white snowdrop-like flowers before the leaves appear in spring, and small winged seeds in autumn. AGM 1946. Beautiful as a solo specimen, it is even better when planted as a small group of three or four.

H. monticola Taller and larger than *carolina*, this has correspondingly larger flowers and seeds. It has two varieties:

H.m. 'Rosea' The flowers are pale pink.

H.m. vestita This has larger 1-inch (2.5-cm) flowers, sometimes tinged rose-pink.

Hamamelis

The 'Witch Hazels'. For the most part scarcely more than large shrubs, this small genus of three or four species and a dozen or so varieties are among the first into bloom each year, and a welcome portent that spring is not far off. All bear fragrant yellow to orange-red spidery flowers from December to March on bare twigs and branches before the leaves appear, and which amazingly are able to withstand snow and the most severe weather conditions. The following are among the best:

H. intermedia 'Diane' A coppery red-flowered hybrid first raised in Belgium, this has fine autumn colouring.

H. mollis The 'Chinese Witch Hazel' has clusters of strongly scented golden-yellow flowers followed by bright yellow autumn foliage. AGM 1922.

H. vernalis From central parts of the USA, the 'Ozark Witch Hazel' is small in stature, with small pale orange flowers during January and February. The flowers are very heavily scented.

Hawthorn

– see *Crataegus*

Hippophae rhamnoides

The 'Sea Buckthorn' has grey-green foliage that contrasts with the clusters of bright orange berries of the female form – a male is also needed for good pollination. Remarkably tolerant of sea winds, this is a first-rate wind break, and a substantial thorny barrier. AGM 1944. It is most often grown as a shrub but can reach 20ft (6m).

Ilex

'Holly' is a large genus of evergreen and – perhaps surprisingly to those who only think of holly in terms of Christmas decoration – deciduous shrubs and trees. There is even a greenhouse species! Their origins are literally worldwide and they have a variety both of leaf colour and shape (not always spiny) and of berry colour. They are generally dioecious (male and female flowers borne on separate plants), which means that at least one of each will need to be in close proximity to ensure that berries are borne by the female plant. This often gives rise to confusion because varietal names like 'King' and 'Queen' are not an indication of the sex of the tree and its ability to bear the sought-after berries.

There has also been a great deal of natural hybridizing which, because it has taken place outside human control, has resulted in a great many hybrids of uncertain parentage, and in some cases multiple. The effect of this on many nursery catalogues is utter confusion, and the effect upon customers who order, guided by the too often very brief catalogue descriptions, can be a great disappointment. This is why it is best to buy hollies from a sales outlet at gardens and nurseries where you can see the mature specimens growing, or at least to order from a catalogue that is clear and specific in its naming and description details, including sex.

To positively identify the sex of a holly, you will need to examine the flowers very closely when they are borne about May (you may need a magnifying lens). If the small white flowers have four tiny stalks (stamens) in the centres, the tree is male – unless it is one of the few bi-sexual varieties. However, if the flowers only have one club-headed stalk in the centre, this is the pollen-receiving female pistil and the tree is a berry-bearing female.

I. altaclarensis 'Golden King'. This has broad, almost spineless green leaves with bright yellow margins. Despite the masculine name, it is female and, planted in a favourable position, reliably bears heavy berry crops that last well through Christmas. AGM 1969.

I. aquifolium The 'Common Holly' will easily make 60ft (18.5m) tall in favourable positions. It has both male and female forms, and there are many varieties in cultivation.

I.a. **'Argentea Marginata'** The 'Broad-leaved Silver Holly' has both male and female forms – so be careful! The leaves are margined white. AGM 1969.

I.a. **'Argentea Pendula'** 'Perry's Silver Weeping Holly' is rare, and only the very top class nurseries are likely to offer it. It has strongly weeping branches, white-margined leaves, and usually carries a heavy crop of berries.

I.a. **'Christmas Cheer'** This is perhaps the best variety for Christmas berries because they are very persistent and not so ready to drop from cut branches taken indoors.

I.a. **'Ferox'** The 'Hedgehog Holly', seldom much more than a small tree, is grown mainly for its curious leaves, the upper surfaces of which have numerous sharp spines even sharper than those at the edges, and which make an impenetrable hedge. The fallen leaves resist decomposition for a long time, and the many spines form a carpet over which cats, dogs, foxes, badgers and similar soft-footed creatures will not cross.

I.a. **'Golden Queen'** A striking tree with large spine-edged leaves, dark green with a broad yellow margin, this may have a feminine name, but it is male! AGM 1969.

I.a. **'J. C. van Tol'** A variety with dark green glossy leaves, almost devoid of spines, this bears reliable abundant crops of red berries for Christmas. AGM 1936.

I.a. **'Silver Queen'** This has dark green leaves with cream-white margins and marbling. Again, it is a male.

I.a. **'Pyramidalis Fructuluteo'** The botanical name describes this variety well; it is a nicely shaped pyramid, actually a tall cone, with plenty of bright yellow berries. AGM 1936.

Judas Tree

– see *Cercis*

Juglans

Although making large handsome trees with large leaves, the 'Walnut' is generally grown not for appearance but for the nuts – which frequently leads many gardeners to disappointment and frustration when they do not appear. The main reason for a tree's failure to produce nuts is its reluctance to be fertilized by its own pollen. Walnuts should, therefore, always be planted in groups of three or more, which at once excludes them from all but the very largest gardens. If you want nuts, the three most commonly grown species are the following.

J. **nigra** The 'Black Walnut' from North America, has large leaves and large round nuts, often in pairs. If you want this particularly for the nuts, make sure that you buy only a named fruiting clone from a reliable nursery.

J. **regia** The 'Common Walnut' is not native to Britain as is often supposed, but originates from the Caucasus regions of Iran. It is often grown from seed, but this leaves the tree's nut-bearing abilities very questionable and doubtful for many years – a wait of thirty years is by no means uncommon. Make certain that you only buy plants certified as having been propagated vegetatively, for example by grafting, or cloning from a known early-fruiting variety.

J.r. **'Laciniata'** This is known as the 'Cut-leaved Walnut', and also as the 'weeping' or 'pendulous' walnut because of its tendency to do just that.

Kalmia latifolia

If we may allow ourselves a little licence to include what is really a shrub, albeit a large one, the 'Calico Bush' from North America is a rhododendron-like subject that thrives in the heavy leaf fall and dappled sunlight of a woodland glade. It does not like chalk, and requires the constant moisture of deep accumulated leaf mould. Masses of conspicuous rosy-pink flowers, like closed corrugated saucer lanterns in the bud, form large dense clusters of bloom as they open and merge in June and July. AGM 1946. This glorious plant is another subject ideal for bottoming and underplanting large trees.

Koelreuteria paniculata

The common names 'Pride of India' and 'Golden Rain Tree' describe this subject well enough – although, despite the 'India', it actually comes from China. It can make 50ft (15m) or more with long leaves and showers of small yellow flowers during July and August, after which bladder-like fruits form as the foliage turns bright yellow. It will do well in any soil and makes a magnificent solo standing specimen for a large lawn.

Kolkwitzia amabilis

'Wilson's Beauty Bush' is from the Hupeh region of China. I knew and propagated this as a most attractive shrub or small tree until invited to visit the garden of a good friend at Bramdean, in Hampshire, where it stood trained as a 6ft (2m) standard, with its branches pulled down and trained into a weeping position, completely smothered with small soft pink flowers with yellow centres. What a picture! My opinion of it changed at once, because grown like this it has to be one of the all-time beauties. There are times when even a hardened old cynic is lost for words. Don't miss out on this glorious small tree – for even the smallest garden it can have very few rivals – and it is not all that well known. The forms 'Rosea' and 'Pink Cloud', FCC 1963 and AGM 1965, are slight variations.

Laburnum

'Golden Rain' is very well known and hardly needs any description. Native to Britain and Europe, it grows well on any soil, including chalk.

L. anagyroides (previously *vulgare*) is the common type and, being vigorous, serves as the stock upon which other less vigorous varieties are often grafted.

L.a. 'Aureum' The yellow-gold-leaved form. FCC 1875.

L.a. 'Pendulum' This 'Weeping Laburnum' has long, slender, drooping branchlets.

L.a. 'Vossii' The one big drawback with laburnum is that all parts are poisonous, particularly the seeds. However, this very free-flowering variety, with longer and markedly deeper yellow racemes of bloom, sets much less seed and, to the extent that inquisitive little fingers pick them up and put them in little mouths (there are several cases every year) that much safer.

Pergolas are a familiar construction in many gardens and are perhaps most often associated with roses, honeysuckles and similar climbers and ramblers that are trained and tied in to produce flowering tunnels. A practice that was popular in Victorian times, and practised extensively in French gardens, was to form a tunnel of iron hoops, and on this frame train apples and pears with the fruit hanging down inside the tunnel.

Several years ago, when visiting an old friend, Charles Puddle, the then Head Gardener at Bodnant Gardens, North Wales, we walked through a laburnum tunnel in full bloom – and that was a gardening experience not to be forgotten in a hurry! If the idea appeals, and you would like to plant such a tunnel, laburnum 'whips' are easily obtained, or you can grow your own from seed. They are fast-growing and you can thus form an unusual garden feature quickly and at remarkably low cost. Set the hoops or arches 3ft (1m) apart and, when the saplings become big enough to reach each other comfortably – about 3–4ft (1–1.2m) – cut and graft them together, first to the neighbour on one side, and then, in another few feet, to the other side, then back to their own hoop, so that many plants become in effect one long single living plant. The French called this process *plêching*. They achieved much heavier fruit cropping this way, and the technique can be applied to many other subjects; the effect on the laburnum is to produce more bloom than ever. What a glorious way to welcome visitors to your front door, having them approach through such a tunnel!

Lilac

– see *Syringa*

Lime

– see *Tilia*

Liquidambar

If ever the name of a tree was a literal interpretation of its appearance, this is it! From North America, this tree has leaves not unlike maples (it is in fact related to the witch hazels). The flowers are insignificant, but the autumn colouring is like liquid amber as the tree moves in the breeze.

L. styraciflua The most commonly grown of the half-dozen or so kinds available, this has an additional interest in the long horny ridges of bark that form along the branches. It makes a narrow columnar tree of some 30–40ft (9–12m). All the named varieties available are remarkable for autumn colour and make handsome solo specimens.

Liriodendron

The 'Tulip Tree' from North America has the flowers similar in shape to the magnolias, and in fact it belongs to the same botanical order. It is fast growing and tolerant of all soils including chalk.

L. tulipifera This can become a large spreading tree of some 100ft (30m) or so. It carries greenish-yellow flowers in June and July, which are not very conspicuous against the large leaves. Some trees can take years to come into flower bearing. AGM 1973.

L.t. 'Aureomarginatum' A smaller tree, this might be more acceptable to gardens with limited space. The leaves are margined a lighter pale green.

L.t. 'Fastigiatum' A very upright form, this is almost like the familiar poplar and requires even less space than 'Aureomarginatum'.

Lombardy Poplar

– see *Populus nigra* 'Italica'

Magnolia

A well-known spectacular tree having many evergreen and deciduous species, the beauty of magnolias has led to a great deal of hybridizing and crossing, and there are a vast number of varieties. Although reckoned to prefer acid conditions most are tolerant, if not entirely happy, in slight alkalinity – indeed, an internationally known and respected magnolia specialist nursery is situated on chalky soil on the outskirts of Canterbury, Kent. Tolerant also of clay and atmospheric pollution, it is no wonder there are so many to be seen parading their glory every spring. Magnolias are generally hardy, but the early flowering kinds need protection from wind and frost to prevent damage to the buds. Most often seen exposed in draughty suburban front gardens, a semi-woodland setting is much better – there are some outstanding specimens at Nymans Gardens, Handcross, Sussex. Seeing how popular the magnolia is, it will no doubt surprise many people to learn that, in botanical and evolutionary terms, it is one of the oldest trees still extant on this planet, and is indeed almost a 'fossil tree'!

M. acuminata This vigorous species from North America can get up to 50–60ft (15–18.5m). It has metallic blue and yellow flowers during May and June, followed by rather conspicuous cucumber-like fruits that give the common name 'Cucumber Tree'.

M. campbellii The 'Pink Tulip Tree' is from the Himalayas, where it is reputed to get up to 150ft (46m), but it reaches nothing like that here. It has large pink water-lily-like flowers early in February–March (one of the varieties that needs protection for its buds) and is sometimes slow to reach flowering maturity. FCC 1903.

M. denudata (previously *conspicua*) The 'Yulan' and 'Lily Tree of China' grows up to 30ft (9m). It has pure white, fragrant cup-shaped flowers in early spring. FCC 1968.

M. grandiflora An evergreen species from the south of the USA which, not surprisingly, appreciates the protection of a wall or building behind and around its shoulders. It often makes 30ft (9m) or more. It has huge blooms, nearly 1ft (0.3m) across, mostly in spring but continuing intermittently all year – a venerable specimen in the despatch yard of factory buildings at Bridport, Dorset, usually contrives to have at least one bloom at Christmas! Three varieties are commonly available:

M.g. **'Exmouth'** This has creamy yellow blooms, usually starting when the tree is still quite young. AGM 1969.

M.g. 'Goliath' Probably the very largest flowering kind. FCC 1951, AGM 1969.

M.g. 'Purple Eye' More rambling and spreading than the above forms. The flowers are fragrant, coloured white with a purple base inside.

M. soulangeana A hybrid between two Chinese species, *M. denudata* and *M. liliiflora*, this has large cup-shaped flowers, white with purple staining at the base. AGM 1932. This is unquestionably the most loved, well-known and widely planted of all magnolias. It arose in the early years of the nineteenth century, and was first noticed as a chance seedling – bearing a bloom at that early age – in the garden at Fromont, near Paris, of Mgr Soulange-Bodin, after whom it was named. During the many attempts to identify the parentage, and to intentionally repeat the cross, very many variations have occurred – just like human children of the same parents! In the 1940s when I was a student, there were 83 named and registered variations of *M. soulangeana*! My tree, a vegetative 'pup' of the stock tree at Avery Hill, which is reputedly vegetatively descended from the original in Paris, still has the distinguishing ability to produce bloom on its infantile offspring, and thrives so well in London clay and where the domestic water supply is notoriously limy, that it has to be kept cut back to restrict its overall dimensions. The secret – that might well be copied by anyone with lime problems – is to water only in times of drought, with the dregs of the teapot, and to mulch around with spent tea leaves and tea bags, so that rain and earthworms can take down the acid humus.

M.s. 'Brozzonii' This has larger and later flowers, and is generally regarded as the finest of the *M. soulangeana* varieties. AGM 1969.

M.s. 'Lennei' Not quite so vigorous and large as the type, but this will still make 20ft (6m) or more, and has large goblet-shaped rose-purple blooms in April–May with the white restricted to the inside base. AGM 1969. It is thought to have originated in much the same way as *M. soulangeana*, in a garden in Lombardy, Italy.

M.s. 'Rustica Rubra' A vigorous form with bloom best described as midway between the previous two. AGM 1969. It is charming in the dappled light of a woodland setting.

M. stellata Japan's contribution to the magnolias is a smaller and slower growing 15ft (4.5m) tree that has fragrant white, narrow-petalled, starry flowers in March and April. FCC 1878, AGM 1923.

M.s. 'Water Lily' This form has much larger flowers, each having many more petals, which completely smother the tree.

[58]

Maidenhair Tree

– see *Ginkgo biloba* in the conifer section.

Malus

The 'Crab Apples' and 'Flowering Crabs' are a very large genus of attractive trees, grown variously for bloom from late March to early June, for highly coloured and often heavy crops of edible fruits, for dramatic autumn foliage colours, and for combinations of all three! Selection is almost invidious – there are so many, and all are very good. Choice is really a matter of personal preference, and this is another reason for visiting gardens and getting to know the names of those that you particularly like. Seldom higher than 30ft (9m), among the finest are the following.

M. floribunda From Japan, this smallish tree is literally weighed down by the immense crops of red and yellow fruits that follow crimson buds and open white flowers. AGM 1923.

M. hupehensis A Chinese species of distinctly upright habit and abundant fragrant bloom, opening white from crimson red buds. The fruits are red and yellow. AGM 1923.

M. 'John Downie' A hybrid, this is probably the most widely grown crab because, by general consent, it is the best fruiting. White flowers are followed by massive crops of large orange-red fruits for making the much-vaunted crab-apple jelly. AGM 1969.

M. tschonoskii A narrow, upright-growing 30ft (9m) conical tree from Japan, with white-pink bloom followed by yellow-tinged purple fruit, and multi-coloured yellow, orange, scarlet and purple autumn foliage. This is an absolute beauty for planting in small gardens and restricted spaces.

Maples

– see *Acer*

May

– see *Crataegus*

Mespilus

– see *Amelanchier*

Morus

Alas, the 'Mulberry' is not so widely grown as it used to be, and should be, if only for the most superb jam of any fruit – if you don't know mulberry jam, you don't know jam! The three varieties normally grown are:

M. alba The 'White Mulberry' from eastern Asia and China has only small white fruits which turn pink with ripeness. This is the species used for feeding silkworms.

M.a. 'Pendula' Very weeping habit, with vertical curtains of fruiting branches. AGM 1973.

M. nigra The 'Black Mulberry', also from Asia, is the best kind for fruit and jam. It makes a magnificent stately solo standing tree. The 'black' refers to the dark purple that the fruits should be allowed to become as they ripen, sweeten, soften – and fall. They are astringent if picked while still firm, red and easy to handle. Fruit should be allowed to fall into netting (old net curtains) suspended like hammocks below. Rather messy and 'squashy', it is the only way, and well worth it. This tree is happy in all but wet soils, and tolerant of town pollution and sea air. If you have the space for a productive 40ft (12m) tree, plant a mulberry – you won't be sorry.

Mountain Ash

– see *Sorbus*

Nyssa

A very small genus of deciduous trees from North America and Asia. The bloom and fruits are insignificant, but the rich colouring of the autumn foliage is quite extraordinary. Intolerant of lime and chalk, they prefer wet soggy soils and are therefore valuable for planting into areas that might otherwise remain under-utilized. They are highly resentful of having their roots disturbed, so make quite sure that when you plant it is in the right place, and will not be moved.

N. sinensis A small Chinese tree with narrow 6-inch (15-cm) leaves. Young foliage growth is bright red and remains so throughout the summer, changing in autumn to every shade of fiery red imaginable.

N. sylvatica The 'Tupelo' from southern North America is a magnificent tree. Slow growing, it eventually makes 50ft (15m) or so.

The dense foliage is dark glossy green, which turns a startling mixture of scarlet, orange and yellow in autumn. FCC 1968, AGM 1969. In a glade, seen against other trees, the colours are unbelievably beautiful.

Oak

– see *Quercus*

Oxydendrum arboreum

The 'Sorrel Tree' from eastern North America is one of the few subjects to receive separate awards for different features – AGM 1947 for the brilliant colouring of autumn foliage, and AGM 1957 for its bloom – plus FCC 1972, so this tree has to be something quite extraordinary. It has slender racemes of white flowers at the shoot tips in late summer and autumn, and the most brilliant yellow autumn foliage.

Pagoda Tree

– see *Sophora*

Photinia

A genus of about ten species of evergreen and deciduous small trees from China and Japan. They belong to the same botanical order as our European hawthorns, and are sometimes called the 'Chinese Hawthorn'. Except for the extreme south-west of Britain, they are regarded as only half hardy and will therefore need the protection of light wind-deflecting woodland.

P. beauverdiana A small 15–20ft (4.5–6m) tree. The young foliage is pink, contrasting in May with white hawthorn-like flowers. By autumn, the fruits have turned dark red, and the foliage brilliant hues.

P. fraseri This is evergreen and, being a hybrid, it can be rather variable. Early foliage is coppery red, becoming dark glossy green.

P.f. 'Red Robin' A reliable clone first raised in New Zealand, the brilliant colour of its young foliage is reckoned to be better than *Pieris* – and that is saying something!

P.f. 'Robusta' An Australian clone similar to 'Red Robin' but more robustly upright in habit.

P. serrulata A Chinese species, with 6-inch (15-cm) long evergreen leaves appearing very early in the year and, remaining remarkably resistant to frost and cold, staying coppery red for almost the whole of their long growing period. White flowers in April and May are followed by bright copper-red haw-like fruits. Lime tolerant, this does not mind chalky soils.

P. villosa A small deciduous tree from China, Japan and Korea. White hawthorn-like flowers in May are followed by bright red fruits, and brilliant autumn foliage of scarlet and gold. AGM 1969. Not for chalky soils.

Pieris

The 'Lily of the Valley Tree' is too wide and spreading to be thought of as a conventional tree, but the more vigorous kinds will attain heights of 20ft (6m) or more in favourable positions, and it has to be included here because of the outstanding beauty of the bloom and young foliage. All are evergreen and dislike lime.

P. 'Forest Flame' A hybrid between one of the forms of a species from the Himalaya border region of Burma and China – *P. formosa forrestii* 'Wakehurst' – and the beautiful but more shrubby *P. japonica* from Japan, this was raised in the 1950s at Sunningdale in Surrey – one of the better results of enforced international co-operation! It is very hardy, with large panicles of drooping lily-of-the-valley-like flowers seen against the brilliant scarlet red of the young foliage, which gradually changes through pink and creamy white to its eventual green. AGM 1973. Hardy enough to stand exposed without protection, to see this in a spotlight of sunlight shafting through the branches of trees overhead is stunning – just like a flame in the forest.

P. formosa forrestii 'Wakehurst' One of the parents of 'Forest Flame' and, as you would expect, rather similar, having passed on many of its own qualities. It is more vigorous than its offspring. AGM 1957.

P. japonica 'Variegata' A variegated form of the second parent of 'Forest Flame', this has leaves that mature with creamy-white margins after the young red-pink stage, and an even greater abundance of the same creamy-white flowers. AGM 1969. Although the species type is regarded as being shrub-like in habit and stature, this variegated form seems to be more vigorous when conditions are to its liking – there is a large thicket of it at Nymans Gardens, Sussex, that is well over 20ft (6m) high.

Platanus

Great numbers of the 'Plane Tree' have been planted along the roads and streets of London and other towns for three main reasons. First, it is remarkably tolerant of town and traffic pollution (the trunks of older trees flake their bark and do not develop the dirty corky bark like other trees); second, and equally remarkable, is its tolerance of the unnatural ill-treament of having its moisture supply impeded by covering the soil with pavement and tarmac, and third, it survives the periodic drastic removal of its top growth – 'pollarding' – carried out along roads to allow light through to traffic and reduce the quantity of leaves that fall and create hazard to traffic and pedestrians. However, that said, and despite the numbers still growing in and around towns, this genus of three or four species has little to commend it for garden or estate planting.

Plum

– see *Prunus*

Pocket Handkerchief Tree

– see *Davidia involucrata*

Populus

The 'Poplars' are fast-growing trees for all soils except deep chalk. Most are not unhappy in moist and even wet soils, which is not surprising when you consider that they belong to the same botanical order as the willows. Several have scented foliage, and one at least is so fast growing, and so easily propagated and therefore cheap, that it is often regarded as 'expendable' and planted to achieve quick screening and wind deflection for a few years until the other slower-growing subjects have grown sufficiently for the purpose.

P. balsamifera From North America, this makes a large 60-ft (18.5-m) tree. The leaves have a distinct scent of balsam, particularly when brushed and bruised.

P. berolinensis A hybrid of *P. nigra* 'Italica' and often called 'The Berlin Poplar', this is a large vigorous tree that inherits much of the upright growth of its parent, but is broader. Grown extensively along roads and streets in European towns, it is the continental counterpart of the 'London Plane'.

P. nigra **'Italica'** The 'Lombardy Poplar', one of the fastest growing of all trees in Britain, is a very familiar landmark on the skyline in the countryside, being extensively grown as a windbreak screen.

P. **'Serotina'** This is a very vigorous open-branched tree, the leaves of which, appearing later than most in spring, are coppery red before turning green, and are accompanied by coppery-red catkins 4 inches (10 cm) long.

P. **'Serotina Aurea'** The 'Golden Poplar' is even more attractive than the species type, having clear golden yellow foliage in spring, before becoming pale green in summer and returning to golden yellow in autumn. A handsome large tree with just the right amount of colour contrast to make it stand out from its neighbours.

P. tremula The 'Weeping Aspen' becomes very attractive during winter when laden heavily with purple-grey catkins that enhance the hanging habit. It is a good solo specimen for lawn planting.

Prunus

This very large genus includes the stone fruits, such as cherries, plums, damsons, apricots and almonds. Very popular indeed, the extensive number of species from all parts of the world has been vastly increased by the enormous amount of hybridizing and crossing that has taken place. Mostly smallish trees, up to 30ft (9m) or so maximum, all are worth describing – this is an impossibility, but the following selection cannot be denied from this book.

A cultural point must come first, however. It is not generally appreciated that all ornamental flowering *Prunus* species are liable, to a greater or lesser degree, to 'peach leaf curl' which is a major scourge of fruit trees. It is a wise precaution, therefore, to include all flowering types in a routine lime-sulphur or other anti-peach curl measures; with flowering almonds and peaches, this is imperative. All the stone fruits prefer a chalky limy soil, and benefit from light lime dressings every six months or so.

P. amygdalo-persica **'Pollardii'** This form of a hybrid between the peach and almond species has glowing rich pink bloom. It can make 25ft (7.5m). FCC 1935, AGM 1937.

P. avium The 'Gean' or 'Wild Cherry', native to Britain, easily makes 40ft (12m). It has clusters of white flowers in April followed by small stony red-purple fruits. The autumn foliage turns crimson red.

***P.a.* 'Plena'** (previously 'Multiplex' and 'Flore Pleno') The 'Double Gean' – has masses of dazzling white double bloom that completely obliterates the branches. An extraordinary sight in sunshine, this is one of the very finest of all flowering trees.

P. blireana A hybrid between a purple-leaved cherry from the Caucasus and a Japanese apricot, this small tree has red-purple foliage and rose-pink double bloom. FCC 1923, AGM 1928. A charming tree to grace even the smallest garden.

P. mume The 'Japanese Apricots' are small trees with almond-scented flowers carried very early in spring – so early it is almost winter. Probably the best form is:

***P.m.* 'Beni-shidon'** This has very strongly fragrant rich pink double flowers.

P. sargentii (previously *serrulata sachalinensis*) From Japan, Korea and the Sakhalin Peninsula, this is one of the most beautiful – many argue the very best – of the flowering cherries. Flowers are single pink in March and April and, seen against the young copper-red foliage, are astonishingly lovely. They are followed by glorious autumn colouring. The tree makes 25ft (7.5m). FCC 1925, AGM 1928.

P. subhirtella The 'Spring Cherries' from Japan are a small group of smallish trees, thought by some authoritative opinion to be a hybrid, which is probably true because the several forms are quite variable. The pendulous form, *P.s.* 'Pendula Rosea' – the 'Weeping Spring Cherry' – is particularly attractive, forming a small 15-ft (4.5-m) flat-topped umbrella shape with curtains of pale pink flowers in March–April. A fine solo specimen for a small garden, it is undeservedly overshadowed by the too-popular 'Cheal's Weeping'.

P. triloba A very popular beauty from China, this is often grown as a short standard on a 3–4ft (1–1.2m) stem which hardly does it justice. It is seen much better on a 6–7ft (2–2.5m) stem from which the double peach-pink bloom, borne in extraordinary profusion just as the leaves begin to appear, can hang above eye level from the upright growing branches. AGM 1935.

P. yedoensis The 'Yoshino Cherry' is a hybrid of *triloba* with a strong almond scent. It makes a graceful medium-size tree of about 25ft (7.5m) with arching, but not drooping, branches, and has blushed-white flowers in March and April. AGM 1930.

***P.y.* 'Shidare Yoshino'** A smaller weeping form.

[65]

Japanese Cherries

Japan is the legendary land of the flowering cherry and, as one would expect, the number of varieties that have originated there is vast. Most are hybrids, with the identity of the original parentage lost in the history and traditions of ancient Japanese culture. There are far too many for them all to be described in catalogues – in fact, I doubt whether there are more than half a dozen catalogues in the country that offer more than a cursory few varieties. However, they are very worth every effort to find and see in gardens during the prime months of February, March and April. Those listed here are under their anglicized Japanese names with, where appropriate, the anglicized Latin names in brackets.

Prunus **'Amanogawa'** *(P. serrulata erecta)* Well-known with a narrow fastigiate habit up to 25–30ft (7.5–9m). It has profuse clusters of fragrant blush-white flowers in April. AGM 1931. It takes little space and is particularly suitable for small gardens.

P. **'Kanzan'** (syn. *P.* 'Sekiyama') *(P. serrulata purpurascens)* Often confused with and incorrectly called 'Hisakura' (which has single flowers), this has large double deep purple-pink flowers, borne in profusion on stiffly upward-pointing branches which leave space underneath for pedestrians and traffic – hence its popularity for roadside planting. A vigorous growing tree – 30–35ft (9–10.5m) is not uncommon – this is probably the most frequently planted cherry of all.

P. **'Kiku-shidare Sakura'** *(P. serrulata rosea)* Originally and incorrectly known as 'Cheal's Weeping Cherry', this rivals 'Kanzan' as the most popular cherry because, being a small tree it is so suitable for small gardens. It has clear pink double flowers on long drooping branches that curtain to the ground. However, this is not a long-lived tree and very liable to attack by canker, leaf-curl and other diseases that gain entry through the abrasion of the drooping branches against paths and other hard surfaces. Never prune it unless absolutely necessary, but if you do always protect with Arbrex at once.

P. **'Shimidsu Sakura'** *(P. serrulata longipes)* The large double flowers, pink in bud and pure white when open, hang in long stalked clusters. This flowers later than most – late April into May – and therefore is useful in a collection for extending the flowering season. AGM 1933.

P. **'Ukon'** *(P. serrulata grandiflora, P.s. luteovirens)* A medium-size spreading tree of 20–25ft (6–7.5m) with – unusually for the cherries – pale yellow bloom tinged with green, freely borne and conspicuous against the brown-bronze young foliage which turns purple-red in autumn. AGM 1969.

Pyracantha

The 'Firethorns'. In the same way that some of the *Cotoneasters* are vigorous enough to be thought of and grown as standard specimens, so too are the firethorns. Usually seen against walls, in shrubberies, and slaughtered as hedges, these thorny evergreens can make spectacular solo specimens on lawns and in groups where the various berry colours can contrast and enhance each other. Although prolific, the bloom is not special in itself, but the masses of berries are another matter.

P. coccinea 'Lalandei' This has a vigorous erect habit, with a nice conical form and can make 25ft (7.5m) high. Large orange-red berries are borne in great profusion. AGM 1925.

P. 'Orange Glow' A hybrid of uncertain parentage, this is vigorous, with enormous crops of bright orange-red berries each autumn persisting long into winter.

P. rogersiana This has deeper orange-red berries, but is nowhere near so vigorous as *coccinea*.

P.r. 'Flava' Rather more spreading, when the sheer weight of masses of bright yellow berries bears branches down, or they are pulled and trained down from a standard; it makes a fine weeping specimen. AGM 1969.

Pyrus

The 'Pears'. Most of the ornamental pears have greyish or silvery leaves, which is a clue to the species' liking for well-drained dryish soils, making one in particular very suitable as a substitute for a weeping willow when that subject's liking for a wet soil, and the space it needs, cannot be provided.

P. salicifolia 'Pendula' The 'Willow-leaved Pear' from Asia Minor is a graceful small tree worth growing on its own account. Flowers are creamy white and very attractive against the long silvery leaves. It is charming as a solo standing specimen weeper in the lawn. AGM 1969.

Quercus

The 'Oak' is a large genus of both deciduous and evergreen trees, with a wide variation from small shrubs to very large trees. Most are reasonably lime-tolerant, but on chalky soils the root system does not develop so vigorously and achieve a good 'hold' or 'grip' in keeping with the above-ground size. This can make them rather vulnerable when exposed to strong winds, as was amply illustrated by the number that went down in Kent and Sussex during the October 1987 gale.

We are concerned here primarily with planting for appearance and amenity purposes, not for commercial value and timber production. Oaks can become very big and will therefore only interest those who have a lot of space, and who may well have lost trees and be replanting. The following selection contains suggestions for introducing variety, and one or two that are more suitable for limy chalky soils than the common so-called 'English Oak'.

Q. alba The 'White Oak' from eastern North America makes 50–60ft (15–18.5m), and is definitely not one for chalk. Foliage is tinged red when young, turning green in summer and deep crimson in autumn.

Q. cerris The 'Turkey Oak', a large tree originating in southern Europe, is probably the fastest growing in this country of all the oaks and will make 80–100ft (24–30m) with ease. More tolerant than most of chalk, it also withstands sea and coastal conditions.

Q. coccinea The 'Red Oak' or 'Scarlet Oak' from eastern North America, like many other subjects from that part of the world, has not evolved to be tolerant of chalk or alkalinity, but does have the American propensity for brilliant autumn foliage colours. Where it can be grown, it makes a striking 50–70ft (15–21.5m) tree with deeply lobed shiny green leaves, and a distinct bristle to each lobe, the whole turning a glowing red in autumn.

Q. frainetto The 'Hungarian Oak' (from Hungary) is a magnificent large fast-growing tree, having large 8–9-inch (20–23-cm) leaves, and quite at home on chalk. It is superior to the 'Common Oak' or 'English Oak' in most respects.

Q. ilex The 'Evergreen Oak', 'Holly Oak' or 'Holm Oak' from the Mediterranean area thrives in all soils provided they are not poorly drained. Will make 50–70ft (18.5–21.5m) and, although tolerant of coastal conditions and wind, does not like the extremes of inland exposure to cold. It is regarded as the most majestic evergreen tree grown in Britain, excluding the conifers.

Q. robur (syn. *Q. pedunculata*) The 'Common Oak' or 'English Oak' is native not only to this country but also to the whole of Europe and Asia Minor as far as the Caucasus. A very well-known large tree, this often makes 80ft (24m) or more.

Q.r. **'Fastigiata'** The 'Cypress Oak', with its narrower, more upright form, could be a more suitable replacement in the gaps where those that were left standing may try to 'come in' and take advantage of the vacant space and light. The shape contrast also makes for more interest.

Q. rubra The 'Red Oak' is another fine coloured tree from eastern North America, that, like its compatriots, does not like chalk. A large tree of about 90–100ft (27.5–30m), it was widely planted at one time for its fast growth and toleration of town pollution. The foliage turns ruby-red before autumn leaf fall. AGM 1973.

Quick, Quickthorn

– see *Crataegus*

Rhododendron

So well known as to need no description here, their sprawling, spreading habit means that they are invariably regarded as shrubs. However, in the woodland settings and deep accumulated leaf litter that they love, some will get up to 30ft (9m) and more, so they cannot be dismissed on grounds of size. Indeed, in 1975, in that neglected wood near Southampton, I personally measured a lead-labelled but unidentifiable hybrid at 48ft (14.5m)! They are usually regarded as lime-hating, but this also is not universally true, because some are remarkably adaptable and tolerant.

With a genus already worldwide in its origins, probably no other has been more crossed, hybridized and experimented with – there are literally hundreds of species and uncountable numbers of varieties and forms, far more in fact than a specialist book could possibly contain, and quite out of the question here. This is not to dismiss the genus, however; these beautiful shrubs and trees must have a place in any garden, park or estate that can offer suitable conditions, whether as underplanting or as a main feature.

One, few, or many, inevitably and essentially, choice is purely a matter of personal taste and preference – but I would recommend that at all times you thoroughly investigate a potential species in a reference book or a fully descriptive and detailed nursery catalogue

[69]

before buying and planting. The range is vast, and the points to consider are endless. This is a case where the *Hillier Colour Dictionary of Trees and Shrubs* is a boon – no serious gardener should be without a copy.

Rhus

The 'Sumach' from North America, was previously grouped with *Cotinus* (see page 44). Small shrubby trees grown principally for their ornate foliage which colours brilliantly in autumn in shades of yellow, orange and red, they are tolerant of all soil conditions. The flowers are inconspicuous – the foliage is the main attraction.

R. glabra 'Laciniata' This has a wide spreading habit, and is invariably grown as a shrub. However, it can be trained up as a half or full standard to make an imposing solo specimen. In this variety, the leaves differ from the type in being finely divided and fern-like, turning a fiery orange-red in autumn. The female plants have scarlet fruits. FCC 1867.

R. typhina The 'Stag's-horn Sumach' is another spreading shrubby habit that can be run up as standard, but it tends to sucker. It has brown felt-covered stems, and closely resembles *Ailanthus* in appearance. Foliage and fruits as for *glabra*.

Robinia

Surprisingly, these are members of the pea family! These large and medium-sized flowering trees with ornamental foliage originate from the USA and Mexico. Hardy, fast growing, and thriving in all soil conditions, they have a tendency for suckering, inquisitive and invasive roots, particularly for the larger **R. pseudoacacia** – and, only needing half a chance to get into drains, they are not for planting near buildings.

R. hispida The 'Rose Acacia', a small tree with bristly thorny stems, has dark rose-pink pea-like flowers in May and June. It is rather brittle and will need careful staking when young if run up as a standard.

R. pseudoacacia Variously called 'Common Acacia', 'False Acacia' and 'Black Locust', this is a large 70–80ft (21.5–24.5m) open tree from eastern USA with long conspicuous racemes of slightly scented yellow-white bloom in June that is very attractive to bees.

R.p. 'Frisia' A much smaller 30ft (9m) tree with rich yellow-gold foliage from spring to autumn. Invaluable for colour contrast. AGM 1969.

Rosa

The 'Rose'. Invariably thought of as bushes and standards, or as climbers and ramblers over fences, pergolas and walls, roses could be used to greater effect if only we would be a little more adventurous and imaginative with our gardening! Some species and varieties are sufficiently vigorous and tall-growing to clothe buildings with more beauty and interest than the more mundane ivies and creepers – and if over the walls of a building, why not up and through the branches of trees? Using flowering climbing plants for this purpose, and to climb into and through hedges, was a widespread garden feature at one time. In a neighbouring neglected and run-down estate at Chislehurst, Kent, through which I used to wander, was an ash tree whose old age had been made glorious by the masses of scented bloom of a Banksian rose climbing through it, fully 30ft (9m) up. Beauty in the midst of neglect. A house wall, a tree – having such dimensions, can we not then think of roses as trees? And could we not therefore suggest reviving an old idea, and consider a few suitable varieties, able to expend their considerable energies in this way?

R. banksiae Almost thornless and semi-evergreen, this has dense groups of strongly violet-scented white flowers. It was discovered in a garden in Canton, China, in about 1800.

R.b. 'Lutea' The 'Yellow Banksian Rose' has masses of double yellow flowers. It is a marvellous sight in full bloom over a house or in a tree.

R. brunonii The 'Himalayan Musk Rose' is even more vigorous than the Banksian. There was – and, hopefully, still is – a specimen in that neglected wood near Southampton, 45 feet (14m) up in a *Robinia* tree, smothered in white flowers, and so strongly scented as to quite pervade that part of the wood.

R. filipes 'Kiftsgate' From western China, this is perhaps the most vigorous rose of all. The young foliage is richly copper red, with incredibly large panicles of sweetly scented white bloom with bright yellow centres – I have frequently counted over a hundred separate blooms in a single drooping panicle. It is an absolute must wherever the opportunity exists to grow a rose of this size.

R. 'Wedding Day' Raised in the 1940s at Highdown, Sussex, this is the result of self-crossing a hybrid of two Chinese species. It is a very vigorous climber that can reach 30ft (9m) with little trouble. Large trusses of strongly scented flowers, deeply yellow in the bud, open creamy white with vivid orange-yellow centres, fading to pink. It can be difficult to find, but is well worth searching for.

R. wichuraiana A vigorous semi-evergreen from Japan that can send out trailing shoots from the main stem as much as 12–15ft (3.5–4.5m) long. The flowers, which can be 2 inches (5 cm) across, are white, richly scented and borne rather late in summer. AGM 1973.

Rowan

– see *Sorbus*

Salix

The 'Willows' form a very much bigger genus than is often supposed, with a great variety of size and form. They generally prefer damp and wet positions, and have male and female flowers on separate plants. Young stems are often colourful in winter, and some varieties grown for this purpose are invariably pruned hard each year in order to promote such growth.

S. alba The 'White Willow', widespread throughout Europe and Asia, is a large, elegant, slender tree of some 50–60ft (15–18.5m), having pale green leaves with silver reverse. Excellent for wet positions and exposure to wind.

S.a. 'Chermesina' (previously 'Britzensis') The 'Scarlet Willow' is a familiar tree, capable of making 60ft (18.5m) when allowed to have its head. Most often seen along river banks, it is cut back hard to produce bright red stems in winter.

S.a. 'Vitellina' The 'Golden Willow' is a smaller tree than the type, with bright yellow young growth.

S. chrysocoma A form often incorrectly listed as a weeping variation of the White Willow *S.a.* 'Vitellina pendula', this is regarded as the finest weeping willow. Of medium size, 30ft (9m) wide-spreading, with curtains of long golden stems to ground level, this has attractive catkins, both male and female on the same tree. However, it is just a little liable to attack by scab and canker diseases, and unless you want to expose other vulnerable subjects nearby, you would be wise to carry out a routine fungicidal spraying every year. AGM 1931.

S. *caprea* 'Pendula' Commonly known as the 'Kilmarnock Willow', this is a small tree, rarely much more than 10ft (3m) high. It is eminently useful for those wanting a weeping willow in a small garden.

Sambucus

'Elder'. The black berries of the common wild elderberry are familiar enough as shrubs of the hedgerows, but other varieties have more pronounced ornamental value and can be run up as half and full standards in much the same way as *Rhus* (see page 70) to make attractive specimens. The wood is rather brittle, and the standard forms will therefore need careful staking. All the elderberries are happy on chalk.

S. *nigra* The common elderberry has some most attractive variations:

S.*n*. 'Aurea' 'Golden Elder' with golden-yellow leaves.

S.*n*. 'Laciniata' 'Fern-leaved Elder' with finely cut, fern-like leaves. There is also a fine golden-leaved form, but unfortunately it is hard to find.

S. *racemosa* The 'Red-berried Elder' differs from the common black-berried elderberry in having conical heads of more creamy-yellow bloom and scarlet red berries.

S.*r*. 'Plumosa Aurea' This is much smaller growing but worth trying the 'standard' training. It has deeply divided, plume-like golden leaves and rich yellow flowers. This is one of the very finest of all golden-leaved plants.

Snowball Tree

– see *Viburnum opulus* 'Sterile'

Snowdrop Tree

– see *Halesia*

Sophora

The 'Pagoda Tree' makes 50–70ft (15–21.5m) in its native China, but much less than that in Britain. A handsome flowering tree, it requires full sun and well-drained soil and is not suitable for damp situations.

S. *japonica* The 'Japanese Pagoda Tree' originates in China! It has large leaves 1ft (72cm) long, with creamy-white flowers in long panicles at the branch ends in late summer. It flowers prodigiously in the long hot sunny summers of Mediterranean and south-eastern Europe where it is widely planted. It grows to 30–40ft (9–12m) and is very distinctive.

S.j. 'Pendula' This is the weeping form, but the branches have a more stiff and rigid habit than most weeping subjects, forming a large space to sit under. It is sometimes called the 'Arbour Tree' for this reason. It makes a fine solo standing tree for a lawn.

S. tetraptera 'Grandiflora' The 'New Zealand Kowhai' is a small tree seldom much more than 20–25ft (6–7.5m) with drooping branches and clusters of unusual tubular yellow flowers during May. It needs protection from cold winds.

Sorbus

The 'Mountain Ash', 'Whitebeam', and 'Rowan'. These are very familiar trees, with their orange-red berries alongside roads, in suburban gardens, and wild in hedgerows. There are between 50 and 60 forms available, from shrubs to 40ft (12m) trees. Most thrive in chalk soils except the group that concerns us here.

S. aucuparia The 'Rowan' or 'Mountain Ash' section contains 10 or 12 varieties. Notable for toleration of acid soils, it is the one group of the genus that is not happy – or long lived – in chalk.

S.a. 'Asplenifolia' (syn. 'Laciniata') An elegant small tree with deeply cut fern-like leaves. AGM 1969.

S.a. 'Fastigiata' Stiff upright habit, big dark green leaves and large bunches of bright red berries. AGM 1969.

S.a. hupehensis From China, but closely related to our native forms, this very distinctive small tree has upright branches, blue-green leaves and clusters of white-pink berries that hang on late into winter. AGM 1969.

S.a. 'Joseph Rock' A smallish tree from China, seldom over 25ft (7.5m), this has fiery autumn foliage colouring of orange, red, purple and bronze contrasting with clusters of creamy-yellow berries. FCC 1962, AGM 1969.

S.a. kewensis This is a 30ft (9m) hybrid with dark green ornamental fern-like foliage turning red-purple in autumn. It has vermilion red berries. AGM 1969, FCC 1973.

S.a. pohuashanensis A splendid 30–35ft (9–10.5m) tree, this is regarded as the best of the Chinese rowans with attractive foliage and the heaviest crops of orange-red berries, which normally cause the spreading branches to bow under their weight. Very hardy and reliable. AGM 1969, FCC 1973.

Staphylea colchica

The 'Bladder Nut' from the Caucasus is a small genus of half a dozen species and varieties of which *S. colchica* is the most widely grown and best known. It is a small 12–15ft (3.5–4.5m) tree with panicles of conspicuous white flowers in May, followed by bladder-like seed capsules. FCC 1897.

Strawberry Tree

– see *Arbutus*

Sweet Chestnut

– see *Castanea*

Sycamore

– see *Acer*

Syringa

The familiar 'Lilac' is a large genus ranging from small shrubs to others with the vigour and stature of trees. Most originate in Tibet and China, but a few came from Europe. The 30 or 40 named cultivars contain all colour shades from white through lilac to deep purple, both single and double, and have been developed from *S. vulgaris* the 'Common Lilac' from the mountainous regions of eastern Europe. They are all well known and readily available, but there are many more species and hybrids that are different, equally as attractive, and which deserve to be more widely known and grown. The following is a small selection of the most outstanding.

S. chinensis The 'Rouen Lilac', named after the French town where it was raised, is a hybrid and one of the most strongly fragrant of all the lilacs. It has a shrubby bush habit, but the stock tree used for

[75]

propagation where I worked at one time had become 15ft (4.5m) high, so we know it can become tree-like. It is smothered each year with drooping heads of lavender blue. AGM 1969.

S. josiflexa A hybrid between *S. josikaea* from Hungary and *S. reflexa* from China, this was raised in Canada! As often happens with hybrids, there can be wide variation, and it is advisable therefore in this case to obtain plants that have been propagated vegetatively from a parent that has 'settled down' to produce offspring that remain reliably true to the clone type. A nursery that describes and offers plants raised in this way can be regarded as one that knows its job.

S.j. 'Bellicent' This form has very large and long panicles of fragrant rose-pink bloom that hang and festoon the tree. This different and interesting lilac is vigorous enough to reach the proportions of a small tree – I have seen it run up as a 3ft (1m) half and 5–6ft (1.5–2m) full standard. Both make ideal solo specimens. FCC 1946, AGM 1969.

S. sweginzowii This is a vigorous but elegant species from China. The form *S.s.* 'Superba' has very large panicles of fragrant flesh-pink bloom during May and June.

These are just a few of the species outside the lists of the popular cultivars. A perusal through a really good nursery catalogue will reveal many more in a walk off the beaten track that is well worth taking.

Thorn

– see *Crataegus*

Tilia

The 'Limes' or 'Lindens' are a genus of a dozen or so species, widely distributed throughout Europe, Asia and North America and notable for the clusters of small yellow-green fragrant flowers during summer that are beloved of bees. They grow well in all soils, are tolerant of town and traffic pollution and stand hard pruning ('pollarding'), qualities that have resulted in their widespread use for roadside planting, especially in European towns. Unfortunately, some are more than liable to be infested with aphids, which drop sticky 'honeydew' on anything left under the tree.

T. euchlora A medium-sized hybrid, this is notable for its freedom from the aphid attack that plagues many limes. However, its flowers have a narcotic effect on bees, which can often be seen staggering around on the ground near the trees unable to fly, but still capable of stinging. This may be a problem where children play. FCC 1890, AGM 1969.

T. europaea When not pollarded the 'Common Lime' makes a large 80–100 ft (24.5–30 m) tree. It is long-lived and the form usually used for roadside planting.

T. petiolaris (syn) *T. americana* 'Pendula') The 'Weeping Silver Lime' is considered to be one of the most attractive of the large weeping trees. The leaves are white-felted underneath, held on long leaf stalks, and turn in the lightest breeze giving the tree its 'silver' appearance. The flowers are strongly scented but narcotic to bees. AGM 1969.

Tree of Heaven

– see *Ailanthus*

Tulip Tree

– see *Liriodendron*

Ulmus

The 'Elms' are hardy and fast-growing, tolerant of most soil conditions and of atmospheric pollution. At one time a very common tree in the English countryside and towns – despite a somewhat dangerous tendency to drop a branch without warning – planting of elms has virtually ceased due to the devastating 'Dutch Elm disease'. It is sometimes claimed that the 'Cornish Elm' *U. stricta* has a marked resistance, but a great deal of work has to be done before a reliably resistant or immune form can lead the way for elm planting to begin again.

Viburnum

If we can justify the inclusion here of vigorous tree-like shrubs such as *Cotoneasters* and *Pyracanthas,* two or three of the *Viburnums* also justify a mention. A genus of at least 50 commercially available species, some are evergreen, the deciduous types often have fine autumn colouring, and many have brightly coloured berries. However, it is flower and scent that are the main attractions – indeed, the fragrance of some varieties is among the most pervading in the garden.

V. bodnantense This strong upright-growing hybrid was raised at Bodnant Gardens during the 1930s.

***V.b.* 'Dawn'** Perhaps the best-known clone, this carries dense clusters of very strongly fragrant, pale rose-tinted, remarkably frost-resistant flowers from October through winter. AGM 1960.

V. carlesii From Korea, the species type is less vigorous than *V. bodnantense*, FCC 1909, AGM 1923.

***V.c.* 'Diana'** This clone is strong growing with red buds opening pink and very strongly fragrant. AGM 1969.

***V. opulus* 'Sterile'** The 'Snowball Tree' is possibly the tallest growing of the genus – 15ft (4.5m) is by no means uncommon, especially in a damp boggy situation, and I have measured it at 18ft (5.5m). Being spreading in habit, it needs rather more space than a small tree. The sterile flowers are gathered into globular heads of brilliant white; with the sun on them, they look just like glowing snowballs. One of the most attractive and popular flowering subjects, it can suffer the most hideous attacks by black aphid, and is in fact an overwintering host plant for the pest. Inclusion in the garden's routine winter wash spraying programme is advisable to keep the pest under control, and to prevent migration to other plants in the garden. AGM 1964.

***V. opulus* 'Xanthocarpum'** This has large bunches of yellow berries, which become almost glass clear as they ripen. It is a strong growing and very attractive plant. FCC 1966, AGM 1969.

Walnut

– see *Juglans*

Willow

– see *Salix*

Witch Hazel

– see *Hamamelis*

Conifer species

Conifers are so distinct and varied in form and colour from the broad-leaved trees as to warrant not only their own classification or section in most catalogues and books, but also their own sections within arboreta and gardens. Indeed, at Bedgebury in Kent, just off the A21, an entire large estate is devoted to conifers and very little else. Here, however, we have to think of them in association with other trees and in the context of a private garden or small estate, providing distinctive form and colour contrast.

Conifers have the most incredible diversity in size, from dwarfs whose mature height is measured in inches or centimetres to skyscraping monsters on nodding terms with airline pilots. The basic problem in a selection like this is what to include.

Sheer rationality dictates that we have to exclude the 'rockery dwarfs', trees though they may be, and select the most attractive that can add something to our gardens. We are looking for intrinsic beauty, of course, but as with the broad-leaved species, we are also looking for subjects that are 'different' and interesting – and if they have a story to them that we can tell to our friends, well, that all adds to the enjoyment.

The range of shape and colour offered by conifers is so wide that there is something suitable for inclusion in any garden setting, however small. The vast majority are evergreen, but the deciduous species are no less valuable and contain some of the most beautiful and majestic of all trees. Some conifers are so very fast growing that money, investment and such factors have led to them being planted in the serried ranks of Forestry Commission and landowner. We shall be looking more for aesthetic beauty.

Abies

The 'Silver Firs' are mostly conical trees. Their narrow needle leaves have white undersides which impart the silver appearance. The cones in some species are blue, violet or purple when young.

A. *concolor* The 'Colorado White Fir' from Colorado, Arizona and New Mexico has a form 'Candicans' in which the silver effect is accentuated to contrast with the long pale green cones. In its native clime, it makes 100 ft (30 m) without difficulty; in the UK 80ft (24.5m) is more like its limit.

A. magnifica The 'Californian Red Fir' makes 200ft (61m) at home in Vancouver, Canada. It is a narrow, slender tree with young bark showing white. The grey-green leaves are curved, and the 10-inch (25-cm) long cones coloured purple. It does not like chalk one little bit.

A. pinsapo The 'Spanish Fir' is from the mountainous area of southern Spain, where it reaches 100ft (30m). Here in the UK it makes 60ft (18m). It has dark green foliage and 6-inch (15-cm) long purple cones. Contrariwise, both this species type and its glaucous grey-leaved form *A.p.* 'Glauca' are notably tolerant of chalk soils.

A. sachalinensis This is from Sakhalin, to the north of Japan, in the extreme east of Siberia. It has dense and short light green-grey leaves with conspicuous blue-white resinous buds in winter. The 4-inch (10-cm) cones are olive-green.

Araucaria araucana

(Previously *A. imbricata*) The familiar 'Chilean Pine' or 'Monkey Puzzle Tree' is from South America where it easily reaches 100ft (30m). Several varieties are known, but only one can be considered as really hardy in Britain. The Victorians were curiously fond of this tree; presumably they planted it for its curiosity rather than for its beauty. It needs plenty of all-round light, which is not possible in confined spaces like suburban gardens, and the result is the many spoiled trees that have lost their lower branches. If you want to be a Victorian, give it plenty of daylight and plenty of space, and it can become a very large tree.

Calocedrus decurrens

(Previously *Libocedrus decurrens*) The 'Incense Cedar' is a tall-growing tree from California, USA, quite capable of reaching 100ft (30m) in this country, and unmistakable for its very narrow column-like shape, a contrast and breaking of skyline that adds variation and interest to any collection of trees. It really needs to be seen from a distance across an expanse of lawn for its sheer majesty to be appreciated, which means only large gardens can handle it.

Cedrus

The 'Cedars' are a genus of mostly large-growing evergreen trees from arid regions of North Africa through Asia Minor to the Himalayas, and containing some of the most stately and handsomely beautiful of all trees.

C. atlantica The 'Atlas Cedar' from the Atlas Mountains region of Algeria and Morocco has two even more magnificent forms:

C.a. glauca The 'Blue Cedar'. The glaucous surface of each needle-shaped leaf imparts a silvery-blue appearance to the whole tree. It can reach 100ft (30m), and needs a lot of space and clear viewing from a distance to be fully appreciated. To see this tree covered in hoar frost, just on the point of thaw and glistening, is sheer magical fairyland, and will defy the efforts of any poet to describe. If you have room for a large specimen tree, make this your first choice. FCC 1972, AGM 1973.

C.a. **'Glauca Pendula'** If *C.a. glauca* is majestic dignity, then the beauty of its weeping form is impudence, for it is a much smaller tree, scarcely ever more than 20–25ft (6–7.5m) high. It has the same silver-blue appearance, but hanging in curtains to the ground from branches that tend to droop so much that they sometimes need a judiciously placed prop to support them and allow the curtains to hang. I have marvelled at this tree as a solo specimen on a lawn, and seen it against a back-drop of red-coloured foliage. I knew one at Headley, Surrey, standing as a centre-piece in a bed of a hundred Zambra roses with bronze foliage and flame-orange bloom. I have seen it with the frost thawing – but to see it draping over the white and black of a Westmoreland water-worn stone rockery, reflecting in a pool, is to make one wonder how nature can be so beautiful.

C. deodara The 'Deodar' or 'Fountain Cedar' is from the western Himalayas, where it is reputed to reach 200ft (61m) – that must be a fantastic sight! It is a large, broadly conical-shaped tree, dark green but with brightly glaucous and pendulous young shoot tips, so that the whole tree looks as though it is dripping like a fountain! Absolutely commanding all around when standing as a solo specimen, it needs a wide open space and can reach well over 100ft (30m) in Britain.

C. libani The familiar 'Cedar of Lebanon' from Asia Minor can be recognized from afar when its unmistakable flat top and horizontally held branches break a skyline. It is not generally realized that young trees are more conventionally conical in shape until they become tall enough to begin developing the horizontal branches and flat top. This takes many years, so you will definitely be 'planting for posterity' with this tree.

Chamaecyparis

This is not a large genus, but it contains an immense number of varieties and forms from small shrubs to large and tall trees, and from darkest green through yellow to blue-grey. They are very tolerant of most soils, town pollution, and hacking with shears to confine them to shape. Before the advent of the ubiquitous 'Leyland Cypress', these were some of the most widely planted subjects for hedging and screening.

C. lawsoniana The 'Lawson Cypress' has literally dozens of variations from dwarfs to large trees, and in every shape and colour. The type was used extensively for hedging and as an alternative to the universal privet. Its one drawback is a ready tendency to abandon growth in its lower branches as they run into and merge with neighbouring foliage, thus obstructing light, so that it becomes green at the top and bare at the bottom – an effect all too common in suburbia. There are so many forms and variations that selection is quite impossible, but here are a couple that are outstandingly good.

C.l. 'Pembury Blue' This is often offered as a dwarf grower for rockeries and heather gardens, but it is definitely not suitable – mine is 18ft (5.5m) high. Given all-round light, it retains lower branches well and makes a narrow columnar tree. It is the best of the grey-blue 'Lawsons'. AGM 1969.

C.l. 'Stewartii' The conventional conical habit of this tree is made more elegant by the golden-yellow young tips seen against the green of the older growth. Erect growth without being fastigiate, it is one of the best and most reliable of the 'Golden Lawsons'. It makes a nice solo specimen and can reach 30ft (9m).

C. nootkatensis I shall always remember walking through a very exposed Forestry Commission plantation, not far from Ullapool in Wester Ross, which was planted with various conifers to 'test their hardiness', as a nearby notice stated. Some were happier than others, some were definitely miserable – but this one was clearly quite unconcerned. As the saying goes about the pudding, 'the proof is in the eating', and this species is as tough as they come – which is not surprising, as it comes from Alaska! It makes a bright green conical tree of 60ft (18.5m) or more and is one of the parents of the intergeneric hybrid popularly known as the 'Leyland Cypress'.

C.n. **'Pendula'** Smaller in stature, 40ft (12m) or so, and more spreading than the type, the branches of this variety are slightly upcurving near the main stem, but the young tips are long and hang like the 'Deodar'. Seen with light snow on it, this is the stuff of fables.

Christmas Tree

– see *Picea*

Cupressocyparis leylandii

The 'Leyland Cypress', an intergeneric hybrid between *Cupressus macrocarpa* and *Chamaecyparis nootkatensis*, has become exceeding popular as a hedging and screening plant – completely replacing the previously all-powerful Lawson cypress. Very fast growing, it is only surpassed in terms of feet or metres per annum by one or two eucalyptus species and the lombardy poplar. Grown as an individual specimen, it makes an upright, almost fastigiate tree, quite capable of reaching 60ft (18.5m). It has proved to be tolerant of sea winds and, somewhat surprisingly, chalk soils. AGM 1969.

The hybrid first occurred in 1888 in Wales (6 seedlings) and for the first 30 years of its existence propagation was virtually impossible because further seed (and then only two) did not occur until 1911. Vegetative propagation by cuttings is very difficult, and the know-how and equipment had not been developed. As the original seedlings had grown, variations had become apparent – which is quite natural, like human identical twins with slight differences. Later seed also threw up more widely varying differences – like brothers and sisters from the same parents. When the full and massive hedging and screening potential became possible to exploit by the development of mist propagation and other techniques to propagate vast numbers, the rush began to glue roots to *C. leylandii* cuttings as fast as possible. The demand for something better than *Chamaecyparis lawsoniana* was enormous, and so was the opportunity to make a great many fast bucks – regardless of the gaping fact that at one time there were 14 distinctly identifiable and named variations of *Cupressocyparis leylandii* being grown and sold!

The situation was little short of being a racket with *C. leylandii* being offered left, right and centre by all and sundry. When clipped as a hedge, much of the variation did not show so much, but when allowed to have its head and grow as a tall screen, it was another matter entirely. If you plant for a uniform-looking screen, you expect uniformity, not something with one ear.

Several years ago, and quite near to where I used to live, the local Parks Department planted a row of *C. leylandii* to screen the exposed open side of a nursery. Three were near a slow leak in a gas main and died, but the remainder got away fine. The following year, replacements went in. The only feasible explanation for what has happened is that the people responsible did not know as much as they should have done, because now, some twelve years later, a fine uniform screen 20ft (6m) high is ruined by replacements that have grown differently to the others, and which stick out like a sore thumb!

So, a word of warning! If you plant a screen of *C. leylandii* –and there is nothing quicker or better – take a few precautions. Don't buy cheap, and don't be palmed off. Buy only from a nursery that knows what you now know, knows that there are differences, and can give you a copper-bottomed assurance that any number you order will all have come from the same identical clone. Ask them how they can be so sure – if they propagate themselves, that is something – but if they buy in rooted cuttings for 'growing on' (the usual procedure) they have only a wholesaler's word. Having been in the trade, I know what that is worth. Unless you are absolutely confident in your supplier, don't risk it, but go to one of the nurseries listed on page 221.

C.l. 'Castlewellan' The 'Golden Leylandii' is almost a repeat story of the above. Appearing first as a quite natural variation or 'sport', it had the equally natural tendency for several years (as do all natural sports) to 'sport back' or revert to type. It is quite natural for such a sport to take several years and generations to settle down and become reliably 'fixed', and this is no exception. But has this worried the fast buck brigade? Not a bit! Only recently, I saw several rows of this variety in a very well-known and reputable garden centre, all in plastic pots with nicely printed plastic labels bearing the same name and the same hefty price, and with more variations and mongrels than you would find in Battersea Dogs' Home!

I can only repeat: be on your guard.

[84]

Cupressus

This is also a large genus with many species and varieties, from which I have selected just one or two extra-special varieties.

C. macrocarpa The 'Monterey Cypress' from California has two very nice golden forms:

C.m. **'Goldcrest'** A medium-sized tree of narrow conical shape, this has dense foliage, with young growth which is feathery and bright rich yellow.

C.m. **'Golden Pillar'** As the name suggests, this has a narrow columnar habit. There are not many really reliable golds which are long and narrow, but this is very good and, of course, more than useful for its colour and shape contrast.

C. sempervirens The 'Italian Cypress' or 'Mediterranean Cypress' is familiar to all who holiday in the Mediterranean. It is very upright, with almost perpendicular branches, and a tall, long slender shape gradually tapering to a single point or two or three small lead tops. Dark green and very distinctive as it breaks the skyline, it will make 40–50ft (12–15m) in this country.

Deodar

– see *Cedrus deodora*

Fir

– see *Abies*

Ginkgo biloba

For a long time the 'Maidenhair Tree' was thought to have been the sole survivor of the tree types that grew some 150 million years ago, and which form much of the coal deposits throughout the world. It is 50–60ft (15–18.5m) tall, with an open, sparse habit. The leaves are fan-shaped and two-lobed like the maidenhair fern, hence the common name. Deciduous, the foliage during summer is a light green turning in autumn to clear buttercup yellow. AGM 1969. It is hardy, and tolerant of most soil conditions (except dryness) and town pollution.

Juniperus virginiana

The 'Pencil Cedars' are a group of slow-growing, generally small to medium-sized trees originating from Virginia and neighbouring states in the USA. The variety that has our attention here is 'Skyrocket'. A chance seedling found growing in the wild, this has the distinction of being one of the (if not the) very narrowest and upright-growing of all trees. The blue-grey foliage and extremely slender form make it useful and popular for form contrast but beware, for it can reach 15–20ft (4.5–6m) tall.

Larix

The 'Larch' is vigorous, fast-growing in most soils except extremes of wet and dry. The small fine needle leaves are deciduous, which means a thick carpet of fallen needle debris to be cleared up each autumn – a very difficult job on a lawn! Most often regarded as a commercial timber tree, there is, however, something special to gain our attention for planting in the garden, and we find this in the following forms.

L. griffithii The 'Sikkim Larch' from the Himalayas is a 30–40ft (9–12m) tree with long drooping branch tips that turn red-brown with age, and which are clearly visible as the bright green leaves fall in autumn.

L. kaempferi (syn. *leptolepsis)* The 'Japanese Larch' is a large tree, making 80–100ft (24.5–30m) in Japan, and not much less here, where it is planted extensively for afforestation. Two forms interest us in the garden.

L.k. **'Blue Haze'** This has glaucous grey-blue leaves.

L.k. **'Pendula'** A flat-topped tree, with very long pendulous branches, this is one of the largest and most spectacular weeping trees.

Lawson Cypress

– see *Chamaecyparis*

Leyland Cypress

– see *Cupressocyparis*

Maidenhair Tree

– see *Ginkgo*

Metasequoia glyptostroboides

This has been given several common names in its short modern history, but 'Dawn Redwood' is the name that is enduring. It has an astonishing story. Like the coelacanth fish that scientists had for long thought to be prehistoric, fossil remains were the only clue to forming an impression of what the giant ferns and trees looked like that grew 100–200 million years ago, and which have formed the layers of coal found all over the world. In 1941, living trees remarkably similar to the fossilized remains were found in a remote part of Hupeh, China. More were discovered in 1944, when their significance was recognized and specimens and seeds were collected. In 1945, with the end of the Second World War, the sensational news broke that a living fossil, thought to have been extinct for 150 million years, had been discovered.

Seeds and young plants rapidly found their way round the world and one of the first specimens into this country was planted in the RHS gardens at Wisley, Surrey. As the first seedlings have grown, they have developed into trees almost exactly as scientists had predicted from the fossilized remains. However, something that the scientists could not have foretold has been the beauty of the tree. Deciduous, the colour of the new young foliage in spring is a delicate pink before turning darker and then bright fresh green. Mature trees in China are 120ft (36.5m) high, and it seems they may eventually reach that height here for they are fast growing and quite hardy. AGM 1973.

Monkey Puzzle

– see *Araucaria*

Pencil Cedar

– see *Juniperus virginiana*

Picea

'Spruce', 'Norway Spruce', 'Christmas tree'. This is a large genus of evergreen trees with a wide variety of shape, form, colour and size, ranging from dwarf shrubs to very tall trees, as Trafalgar Square well knows with its annual Christmas tree from Norway. The trees do not have a particularly good root hold and should not, therefore, be planted in shallow, sandy, dry, and chalky soils, or in exposed windy positions.

P. abies The familiar 'Christmas tree', native to northern Europe, will reach 100ft (30m) with ease. There are a dozen or so forms of the type, with the widest possible diversity of size.

P. brewerana 'Brewer's Weeping Spruce' from California and Oregon, USA, has a tall, slender, most elegant form with very long drooping branches bearing shiny leaves, blue-grey on top with white undersides. Making some 30ft (9m) high, it is generally regarded as the most striking and beautiful spruce of all. FCC 1974.

P. glauca The 'White Spruce' is a large conical tree from Canada, with dense branches and foliage. The young growth is upturned and glaucous white. It is very hardy and useful for planting in cold exposed conditions, and most effective as a wind deflector.

P. omorika The 'Serbian Spruce' has a graceful, slender form, growing to 70ft (21.5m) tall, and with short slightly drooping branches curving up at the tips. It grows well on chalk, coming as it does from the limestone rocky valley of the River Drina in Yugoslavia. AGM 1969.

P. orientalis From the Caucasus, and not unlike the Serbian Spruce, the 'Oriental Spruce' has the same dense dark green foliage, but it is a little more spreading.

P.o. 'Aurea' This is an interesting golden variation with creamy yellow young growth which turns gold and contrasts against the mature green. It makes a medium-sized tree of 30–35ft (9–10.5m). FCC 1893.

P. pungens 'Koster' One of the most intensely silver-blue of all conifers, the 'Silver Colorado Spruce' makes a fine 30ft (9m) solo specimen, and is striking as a colour contrast to other conifers. It has a neat conical habit similar to its much larger Christmas tree relative.

Pinus

The 'Pines' are another large genus with extremes of size, colour, shape and habit. They are not tolerant, however: all dislike shade and atmospheric pollution.

P. cembra The 'Arolla Pine' comes from the mountains of eastern

Europe and northern Asia. It has a 30ft (9m) chunky columnar form, and long dark green needle leaves with whitish undersides. The large dark blue cones remain closed until they rot to release seeds. It is different, interesting and very imposing.

P. montezumae The 'Montezuma Pine' from Mexico and Central America is hardy only in the mild south-west and those parts of Britain exposed to the warm Gulf Stream. This is a most exotic-looking tree: the dark blue-grey leaves, 10inches (25cm) long, give it a distinctive shaggy appearance contrasting with the orange colour of young shoots. It is a magnificent and unusual tree for those who can offer it the right conditions.

P. ponderosa The 'Western Yellow Pine' is from western North America. At 100ft (30m), it is taller than *P. montezumae* but, coming from further north, is quite hardy here, and the nearest in exotic appearance to *P. montezumae*. Tall and stately, it has rather short branches and 10-inch (25-cm) needle leaves.

P. sylvestris The 'Scots Pine'. With so many illustrious trees from overseas, it is not easy to be patriotic with one of our own natives in matching the opposition of its own merits. The widely planted common Scots Pine, which can reach 100ft (30m), has a short 20-ft (6-m) form 'Aurea' which turns a glorious golden yellow in winter. In dappled sunlight with snow on the ground it makes a perfect picture.

P. wallichiana The 'Bhutan Pine' or 'Banana Pine' is a large 100-ft (30-m) tree from the Himalayas. This exotic tree has long 9-inch (23-cm) blue-grey needle leaves, older branches lower down developing drooping tips, and long blue-grey cones like bananas! It can be an incredible sight when frost and snow covered, and makes an outstanding specimen tree, not unlike the Deodar Cedar.

Sequoia sempervirens

The 'Californian Redwood'. Although very few will have the space we can hardly omit the world record-holder for height at over 370ft (113m)! The tallest tree in Britain stands in an estate in north Devon and is 150ft (46m) tall. A majestic tree and guaranteed to break any skyline, it does need a lot of room. It is also very long lived – several specimens in the Humboldt State Redwood Park in California are over 2,000 years old.

Sequoiadendron giganteum (syn. *wellingtonia)*

This is not quite as tall as the Californian Redwood, but what it lacks in height it makes up for in bulk, and it is generally accepted as being the world's largest tree (although some will argue that the Banyan is bigger) and also the longest living, having been authenticated at 3,200 years. Specimens in Britain at 100ft (30m) are not uncommon. The record-holder in Devon is 175ft (53.5m) high. It makes a regular tapering cone densely clothed with bright green needle foliage, but needs so much room to be grown and seen that only the largest gardens can accommodate it.

Taxodium distichum

The 'Deciduous Cypress' or 'Swamp Cypress'. The second common name reflects the affinity of this tree for swampy, wet soil conditions, but it will in fact grow well, reaching 50–60ft (15–18.5m) in all but chalk and dry soils. Deciduous (as the first name indicates), the delicate frond-like foliage imparts a feathery appearance to the tree. From the southern USA it is the dominant tree in the famous Everglades Park, Florida, and, in keeping with so many subjects from the American continent, the bright green foliage turns a most brilliant orange-bronze before autumn.

Taxus

'Yews' are slow-growing, very long-lived trees with widespread origins from Europe to Siberia. All foliage parts are poisonous, especially to cattle, and particularly the pink fleshy fruits and seed, which is why it is often confined to churchyards, away from browsing animals. It was in great demand in medieval times when the long-bow was the principal weapon of war. It accepts most soils and conditions except deep chalk.

T. baccata The familiar 'Common Yew' will eventually make 60ft (18.5m) and has very small dark green flattened leaves. The type is the most tolerant of chalk but it is not happy. There are many forms, all of much shorter stature, mostly with spreading habit, and perhaps more properly regarded as shrubs.

T.b. **'Fastigiata'** The 'Irish Yew' is unmistakable for its several vertical upright leading shoots arising from a broad dense base. Very dark green, it is scarcely ever more than 20ft (6m) high. FCC 1863, AGM 1969.

***T.b.* 'Fastigiata Aureomarginata'** The 'Golden Irish Yew' is similar in every way to its type, except that it has a broader base, a more statuesque form, and the leaves have a yellow margin, imparting an overall golden effect. It is even more deserving of an award than the type.

Thuja

The 'Arbor-vitae' is a genus of half a dozen or so species with over two dozen varying forms from the dwarfest of shrubs to big specimen trees of 50–60ft (15–18.5m). All have evergreen and, some more than others, scaly aromatic foliage. The genus contains some of the most brilliantly coloured of conifers, but sadly most are small and dwarf.

T. occidentalis As the name implies, this is the 'Western' or 'American Arbor-vitae'. The branches turn up at the tips, and the dark green foliage usually takes on a bronze hue in winter. There is nothing particularly outstanding to commend it except that it has a form that is quite outstanding.

***T.o.* 'Rheingold'** This is invariably listed as a shrub, and indeed is often and erroneously sold as a 'rockery dwarf'. I have taken cuttings for propagation with a 10-ft (3-m) pole pruner, and could scarcely reach the top. Slow-growing, it makes a broad cone shape of deep golden amber. It is wonderful for colour contrast; a conifer garden is not a conifer garden without 'Rheingold'. AGM 1969.

T. orientalis The 'Eastern' or 'Chinese Arbor-vitae' has about half a dozen forms and the least aromatic foliage of the genus. The species type is a narrower conical, almost columnar, shape compared to the Western Arbor-vitae, and the foliage is much more dense and closely packed.

***T.o.* 'Conspicua'** This is another shrub with tree-like ambitions. It is light, upright, almost fastigiate with bright golden-yellow young growth against just a little older green showing through, and positively glows in sunlight.

T. plicata Just to show how contrary and diverse plant life can be, this form, previously called *T. lobbii,* is the 'Western Red Cedar', which in its native homeland of North America frequently excedes 200ft (61m) whereas a form of it, *T. p.* 'Cuprea', has a struggle to reach 3ft (1m)! This, the type, has bright green evergreen foliage, is

[91]

strongly aromatic, and has been offered widely for hedging. Fast-growing and quick to develop a hedge 'face', it just as quickly grows through its useful phase, outgrows its dimensions and becomes difficult to constrain as a hedge. Hedging apart, *T. plicata* needs a lot of room if it is to develop into a good solo specimen, so where space is at a premium, the narrower form becomes more than merely useful.

T.p. **'Fastigiata'** This long, slender, tapering form has an effect like *Calocedrus* and the Italian cypress, with the narrow tops breaking the skyline.

T. standishii (previously *T. japonica*) The 'Japanese Arbor-vitae' is one of the most aromatic trees of the entire genus. It has a loose spreading habit with upturning branches and drooping ends and tips. The yellow-green foliage smells strongly of lemon, especially when brushed or bruised.

Tsuga

'Hemlock'. There are a dozen or so species and as many more varieties of mostly evergreen large trees, and just a few dwarf shrubs to prove the rule of extreme diversity. One species in particular – the type – is worth looking at: – *T.* **canadensis.** The 'Eastern Hemlock' from eastern North America is a large tree, often distinguished by its main trunk being forked, sometimes into several forks, from near the base. Of course, this gives the tree a distinctive shape, but its important attribute here is its relative toleration of chalky conditions. The rest of the genus is notably intolerant.

Yew

– see *Taxus*

7

Questions and answers

Problems of choice and identity

1 Conker in the drains

We had a large horse chestnut blown down in the storm. Fortunately for us it was growing from the pavement 20 yds (18 m) from the house and fell in the road. However, its removal has revealed that the roots had entered drains from our house and next door, and thus forestalled a serious blockage later. The loss of this and other trees nearby has meant that we have lost our screen that hid a factory complex. The local council are not replanting, and we and our neighbours would like to plant replacements inside the front boundary that will be as nice to look at as the chestnut in bloom but which is not cursed with the conkers. We would be pleased if you could suggest something.

First, ensure that the drain repairs are very thorough and, because you want to replant with trees, encase the exposed drain run in concrete. Some trees are worse than others, but you cannot blame any tree for trying – especially if you invite it to help itself to moisture and nutrients. As the blown-down victim was large, you will be looking for something similar. It will take time to plug a gap that size, so why not think of two or three fast-growing fastigiates that also provide more varied form contrast? Or, if it has to be the same shape and size as the conker, have a look at *Catalpa* and the evergreen conifers. Read through the tree lists in this book and let your imagination do some walking.

2 Holly that isn't

We thought that a shrub in our new garden was a holly, but it now has orange tubular flowers. Can you tell us what it is please and something about it?

Even without the sample enclosed, the short description is sufficient to identify *Desfontainea spinosa*, a handsome evergreen shrub that can get up to 8–10ft (2.5–3m), and is a native of Chile and Peru in South America. It is not generally regarded as hardy beyond the mild south-west in this country, so your plant is a good example that shows that hardiness depends on complex factors. In fact, there is a luxuriant thicket of this shrub – as there are very many other exotic and sub-tropical subjects – at Inverewe Gardens, on the coast of Wester Ross in the far north-west of Scotland, several hundreds of miles further north than they have any climatic right to be.

This is the result of the effect on the climate of the western coastal area of Britain – even as far north as northern Scotland – of the warm Gulf Stream that flows across the Atlantic from the Caribbean and South Atlantic to our shores. Inland areas do not feel the full effect, but without the Gulf Stream the climate of the British Isles as a whole would be very different, and many trees and shrubs from other climes would be unable to survive at all.

3 The wrong eucalyptus

How shall I grow-on the eucalyptus tree which I have grown from seed? They are the variety globulus. *Have I grown the correct variety to get the lovely circular leaves that my wife wants for her flower arranging? I heard someone on radio say that the variety* gunnii *should be cut down hard in early spring for this foliage and I am now in a quandary.*

Of the several eucalyptus species that can be grown in Britain, only one, *E. gunnii*, has a really good claim to be regarded as hardy. Many get through mild winters, but it only takes a hard one to cut them down, and unfortunately for you *E. globulus* is one of these. The leaves of mature growth are different to juvenile foliage in some varieties, and again, *E. globulus* is one of the 'wrong 'uns', whereas *E. gunnii*, kept coppiced hard to 18 inches (46cm) from ground level, throws up long shoots with just the foliage you are looking for.

4   Tulip tree risks

I wonder if you could give me some information about the tree Liriodendron? *I have a specimen planted near the house and I would like to know if the roots could affect nearby drains and house foundations.*

In the eyes of any tree, a drain run is a potential source of moisture and nutrients. How important that is will depend upon the tree's needs, its size, whether the soil adequately supplies those needs, and whether the root system and inclination to search is merely inquisitive or downright invasive. All trees vary in these respects, but given the chance of a crack or a leak, however small initially, you cannot expect any tree to ignore the opportunity completely.

A good rule of thumb is to regard the spread of a tree's root system to be a fair approximation of the above-ground spread or bulk of its trunk and branches. Of course, you have to vary this concept on rock-hard soil such as chalk, and a tall spindle-like tree does not put down a deep spindle root. However, you should not let your conception of root spread be governed by the size of the root boles that lift out when a tree topples over in a storm. Roots break, and the spread is far beyond the impression given by the unearthed portion.

Liriodendron can become a very big tree, with a large total leaf area evaporating considerable quantities of moisture every day, which has to come from somewhere. Moisture absorbed from the soil causes it to shrink, and in soils like clay the shrinkage factor is very considerable. So you have to consider whether a potentially large tree with a large root spread is near enough to your drain run to search for and find a weakness, and whether its expanding roots could cause pressure on and fracture the drain, or perhaps whether soil shrinkage could have the same effect. Your dilemma is not confined to the situation today, however; you always have to look well ahead with trees and consider what may happen as they get bigger. Regrettable as it may be, removing the tree now will always be less expensive than after it has done the damage.

5   Ornamentals – not for fruiting

I have a ten-year-old flowering peach, Prunus persica *'Klara Mayer'. The tree was selected for its decorative bloom but also for the edible fruit which we were given to understand it would bear. So far, although it has bloomed very profusely, it has not borne a single fruit. Could you please say why – does it have to have a pollinator?*

Many flowering trees and shrubs owe their extra attraction to factors such as double flowers, or some other genetic reason, that renders them sterile, or at least very reluctant to set seed and fruit. By the same token, many heavy fruiting subjects bear bloom that is more efficient at pollination and less so at making lots of coloured petals. Of course, some subjects contrive to have it both ways, but 'Klara Mayer' is not one of them. It is a flowering peach, and even if you did find a fruit one day, it would be nothing like the juicy thing that you evidently have in mind. For that, you will need to grow a fruiting type like 'Peregrine', 'Rochester' or 'Hale's Early'.

6 Are poplars unstable?

We were intending to plant three or four fast-growing Lombardy poplars to fill a gap left by a tree blown down in the gale, but have been made doubtful by friends who tell us that they are unstable. Is this true, and is there anything else we can plant instead that will grow as quickly?

It is a simple law of physics that a long pole or tree will exert more leverage pressure on the soil than a short pole or tree when identical side pressure (wind), is applied. Clearly, the total sail area is also involved but, in theory at least, a tall poplar is more vulnerable than a short tree. However, having regard to the numbers growing in potentially dangerous positions alongside roads, especially in Europe, it is evident that they do not blow down all that often, as the gale in October 1987 demonstrated. On wet soils, poplars are rather liable to develop canker and internal rotting, and they are also subject to attack by boring beetles which, although serious for young trees, is not so critical as they grow older.

On the evidence of the trees that we can observe around us, healthy poplars are quite root firm and there is no valid reason for regarding them as inherently unstable. However, I would remind you of the law that says 'if something can happen, no matter how unlikely, one day it will' and you should always consider future size and attendant risks before planting near to buildings, and where they could cause damage and injury. (See also question 7.)

7   Are poplars a risk to buildings?

Five years ago, just before we moved here, seven 'Robusta' poplars were planted 13 yds (12 m) from our bungalow. Our attention has now been drawn to the risk of damage to the foundations and drains. Could you say how likely this is, and how tall the trees are likely to grow?

Populus 'Robusta' is a hybrid and, as its name indicates, is a vigorous and fast-growing tree. Apart from sheer speed of growth, poplars also have very extensive root systems that are inquistive and invasive, seeking out drains and damp areas, anything that they can turn to their advantage. A drain run is a potential source of moisture and nutrient and, given half a chance, the roots will become positively invasive and damaging. So, as a general rule, do not plant poplars near buildings and drain runs.

Certain other factors may increase the importance of adhering to this advice. Clay, for instance, shrinks drastically as it dries, and a poplar can absorb and evaporate off an amazing amount of water from the soil, causing foundations to move, walls to crack and expensive bills as a result. A vigorous type of poplar will explore a considerable distance away from its own main stem. *P.* 'Robusta' can easily reach 60ft (18.5m) high, and you are running considerable risk with these trees only 13yds (12m) away. I feel that you would be wise to consider having them removed before any damage is done. They are still young and will be relatively easy to move, and you can then replace them with other subjects that will not present the same risks – flowering trees or shrubs, perhaps.

8   Converting a drab hedge

When visiting the gardens at Inverewe in north-west Scotland we saw a plant climbing through and over a hedge and up into trees. This plant carried a lot of orange-scarlet flowers and turned a drab hedge into something beautiful but unusual. Have you any idea what it is and would it be likely to succeed in the south? We would like to try the idea.

It so happens that I know the hedge well – the plant that caught your attention is *Tropaeolum speciosum*, the 'Flame Flower', and a perennial climbing species of the same genus as the familiar garden nasturtium. It is propagated by root cuttings, and unfortunately is not found offered for sale very frequently. This is a pity because the idea of encouraging flowering climbers to wander through hedges is very attractive. Of course, nature thought of it first, as we can see in the hedgerow with honeysuckle, wild hop, dog rose and blackberry.

Something similar could be tried with the yellow-flowered annual species *T. canariense* or 'Canary creeper' – the seed is stocked by most seedsmen – but it is not so vigorous and tall-growing as the perennial kind. Many of the show gardens around the country nowadays seek to augment their income by running nurseries selling many of the plants in the garden. It just might be worth writing to Inverewe.

9   Not such a heavenly tree

I was given an 18-inch (46-cm) high young tree which I am told is called 'Tree of Heaven'. It doubled its height in this, its first summer, and I am apprehensive as to its eventual height. My garden is small, and I would appreciate your advice on how and when to prune it to restrict its growth to no more than 4ft (1.2m).

This tree is not for you. Although the large 3ft (1m) leaves and autumn colouring are attractive, and the tree is widely planted, the Chinese 'Tree of Heaven', *Ailanthus altissima*, should not be grown unless it can be given plenty of space to develop. Its main method of reproduction is to put out spreading invasive roots – suckers – which are quite strong enough to work under and push their way up through paths and patios. When that happens, removal becomes much more difficult. In your small garden stop it from occurring by rooting it out now while you have the chance.

10   Holly Queen – the wrong sex

Our large 'Golden Queen' holly has grown into a fine tree but it was originally planted for berries as well as its coloured leaves. It has never had even a single berry. Is there a reason for this?

You are in good company – a lot of gardeners fall into the trap of thinking that a feminine name must mean a female berry-bearing tree, whereas your tree is just the opposite. 'Golden Queen' is male and cannot bear a berry – the same problem occurs also with 'Silver Queen'. The moral is never to assume anything. If you want berries, check from a good reference book or catalogue whether the plant in question has a sex problem like holly (for examples, different sexes, or perhaps both male and female flowers on the same plant, but which reach viable maturity at different times). You may have to plant more than one plant for fertilization to occur. You need a thoroughly reliable check list, such as *Hillier's Manual of Trees and Shrubs* or the *Hillier Colour Dictionary of Trees and Shrubs* (see the Bibliography on page 219).

11 Wanted – an absence of conkers

We had a nice conker tree in front of the house, but it was blown down in the storm. We want to replace it because it was so attractive, but we would like to avoid the annual attention of children from the village who would persist in throwing sticks and other objects to knock down the conkers. A number of these objects always landed well inside the garden and damaged other plants. We have been told that there is a tree which does not set conkers. Can you tell us anything about it please?

The common 'conker' is invariably regarded as, and is often cited as an example of, an English native tree, planted in avenues in parks and estates and round cricket fields. In fact, it originates from the south of Albania, and was not introduced to Britain until the seventeenth century. Since then it has been adopted and is now so well-known and extensively grown that it is understandable how it has acquired 'British nationality'. One of the most handsome of large trees, the 'conkers' can be a problem for the reasons you describe. However, your information is correct. *Aesculus hippocastanum* (in botanical nomenclature *hippo* means 'big' and *castanum* 'nut', thus 'big nut') has a double white-flowered form, *A.h.* 'Baumannii' that does not set seed, and is a disappointment to all local children.

As an alternative, you might like to consider the North American 'Indian Bean Tree' *Catalpa bignonioides* (described on page 43). Very similar in form, this is perhaps not quite so large as the 'conker', but is equally attractive in flower, both from a distance and in the orchid-like flowers (if you can get close enough to look right into each of them). The smaller Chinese species *C. fargesii* is undoubtedly one of the best midsummer flowering trees grown in Britain. The flowers are lilac-pink, with dark red-brown spots, and there are up to 15 flowers to each truss, profusely borne over the entire tree.

[99]

12 Ideas for a small front garden

My front garden is the typical small suburban type and has partial shade for most of the day. I would like to grow a small tree – but it must be small because I would not want to obscure light from the windows. Suggestions please.

Assuming that even a small tree will reach room ceiling height, the foliage will need to be light, and not so dense as to obstruct light as the tree grows and reaches maturity. You do not express a preference for flowering or for autumn colour, but look up the following in the Tree List section – I'm sure that you will find one or other of these will excite your imagination.

Laburnum 'Vossii'
Prunus × *blireana*
Prunus sargentii
Prunus subhirtella 'Pendula Rosea'
Prunus 'Kiku-shidare Sakura'
Pyrus salicifolia
Robinia pseudoacacia 'Frisia'
Salix caprea 'Pendula'
Sorbus aucuparia (various).

13 Suggestions for a silver anniversary

We have a silver anniversary next year and think that it would be nice to mark it by planting a silver foliage tree. We know Cedrus atlantica glauca *but it would have to be very much smaller than that as our garden is not large. We would be grateful for any suggestions.*

A nice thought. The 'silver' appearance of foliage is due either to very fine hairs on the leaf and stem surfaces or to a waxy film. Both the hairs and the film limit the air's direct contact with the leaf surface cells, thereby reducing evaporation and loss of moisture. This is a natural means of self-protection for plants that have evolved in very dry and well-drained areas that cannot always ensure a constant moisture supply.

So that is the first clue in your quest for 'silver'; the choice of plant is important, but so is the soil condition to encourage and maintain the silver effect. If you are on a well-drained soil, all well and good, but if your soil is heavy and inclined to be wet, you are at a disadvantage at once and will need to work gypsum into the soil at the rate of 2 ozs (57g) per square yard (square metre) every three months. Make sure you do not exceed this rate. The gypsum will help a heavy soil take on a more crumb-like, less solid, structure.

Of the broad-leaved species *Pyrus salicifolia*, the 'Willow-leaved Pear' is a small tree that is most attractive with a pendulous weeping habit, but the most spectacular and intensely silver trees undoubtedly come from among the conifers. This is not surprising, since most conifers originate from frequently inhospitable and windswept places where plants only survive if they are able to retain water. *Cedrus atlantica glauca*, which you know, has a very much smaller weeping form *C.a.* 'Glauca Pendula'. You will find some suggestions for attractive settings in the description of it on page 81. *Picea pungens* 'Koster' is a small to medium-sized tree with perhaps the most intense silver effect of all, but if you have to go smaller than that, have a look at *Pinus koraiensis* 'Compacta Glauca', which has dense glaucous foliage and a compact habit.

For such an important purpose as this, do try your hardest to visit a pinetum or a garden where conifers are grown – the National Pinetum at Bedgebury, Kent, just off the A21 Hastings road, is ideal – and see the trees growing.

14 Withstanding sea spray

The garden of my house at Angmering backs right on to the seashore on to which, although private, the public often stray – and we and our neighbours have a security problem. Rather than raise the height of the wall, which would cut off our view, we have tried several shrubs and trees but none have been able to withstand salt spray. Can you suggest anything, please?

Tamarix will stand up to sea spray and any amount of wind, and provide attractive bloom, but it is not particularly good as a physical barrier. Much better and a real toughie is the 'Sea Buckthorn' *Hippophae rhamnoides*. This has grey-green narrow leaves, not especially notable bloom, but clusters of orange berries on the female plants, which have such an acrid bitter taste that birds leave them alone to remain attractive throughout the winter. A tough wiry habit and sharp thorns make it a formidable barrier. Plant a male plant to every three or four females to ensure good pollination.

[101]

15 Golden-leaved elderberry?

In a park nearby is a small tree with glorious golden foliage, and the keepers there cannot tell me its name. It looks very like, and has flowers and berries very similar to, the common wild elderberry, but the gold colour is so very different. Could it perhaps be an elder and some freak of nature or soil that is causing the gold colour?

The common elderberry of the hedgerows has several very attractive close relations that deserve to be better known and more widely grown, including a variety with green foliage margined with cream and yellow, others with fern-like leaves, and golden forms that are among the very finest of all golds. All are easy to grow, and the colour variations are more than useful for putting colour contrast into shrubberies and for underplanting. Just imagine the brilliant yellow-gold of these elders set against the deep purple of *Cotinus coggygria*. Stunning! There is no other word for it.

Of the several golden varieties, it is not possible from your description to be positive in naming the specimen in your local park, other than to say that, if it looks like an elder with flowers and berries to match, it is unlikely to be anything else. I would hazard a guess that it is *Sambucus nigra* 'Aurea', the 'Golden Elder'. Nice enough, but you can go even better than that with the lace-leaved form of the 'Red-berried Elder', *S. racemosa* 'Plumosa Aurea'. It is slower growing than most other elders, and is often listed as a small shrub. This only goes to show how variation can occur from place to place, soil to soil, and the way the plant is treated. Our stock trees at Avery Hill were every bit of 12ft (3.5m) tall – hardly a small shrub – and they were cut unmercifully for propagation. However, they seemed to thrive on it because the never-failing result was a mass of very deeply divided fern-like golden leaves, contrasting with the grey-green leaves and mauve flower heads of *Buddleia davidii* on each side of the group. The red berries in autumn are another delight. Elder and buddleia, elder and cotinus: there are a couple of suggestions to grace any garden.

16 Identification of fruit tree stocks

We see fruit trees in a garden centre with labels that say 'MIX' and 'M26'. Can you tell us more exactly what this means because the staff at the centre can only tell us that 'if affects the way they grow – big or small'.

Part of the original purpose of East Malling Research Station in Kent was to determine the cause of, and indicate how to correct, the serious deterioration of soil structure in the Kent fruit orchards. The soil scientists were able to show that this was caused by the old method – thought at the time to be clean and therefore tidy and healthy for the trees – of ploughing and harrowing the orchard floors clear of any other growth whatever. Modern practice is to grass right up to the trees, to mow and return organic matter to the soil (see also page 25). Another vitally important job done by East Malling was the standardization and classification of the stocks that choice fruit varieties were being grafted on to.

I can remember seeing the gypsy fraternity coming around the nurseries 'flogging' wild rose briar stems that they had dug and cut from hedgerows. The nurseries would plant these out and bud them for their standard roses. The practice was so widespread at one time as to be virtually the usual way that many nurserymen obtained their standard stems. Heaven only knows what the ancestry was, what the vigour was, what effect it would have on the way the implanted bud would grow, and what kind of standard rose the customer was buying. Good nurseries do not go in for that sort of thing now, but several places were still at it to my knowledge, only a few years ago.

It had been very much the same with the stocks used for grafting apples and other fruits, and it was quite normal for an orchard planted with one particular variety to have big trees, little trees, good croppers, poor croppers, trees that bore fruit early in the season, others that would be weeks later, trees that bore fruit in the first few years of life, old veterans that had scarcely started. Some trees bore fruit that tasted fine, and some fruit that even the pigs refused. How on earth could the growers decide what varieties were good, bad or indifferent when every tree in the orchard, although ostensibly of the same variety, was behaving differently?

The first task in sorting out the mess was to vegetatively reproduce the stocks so that more could be produced that would be exactly the same, and to graft on one variety to compare the results. There were so many stocks that only one top variety could be used at first, Lane's Prince Albert. The test comparisons were all grown in as near identical conditions as possible, and gradually, by process of elimination, hundreds were whittled down to dozens, and as time passed, to fewer still, so that now we have relatively few, but each with a reliable pedigree and a known performance.

[103]

The letter 'M' relates to Malling, and the number – sometimes in Roman numerals, more often not – to the identity of the stock pedigree. In more recent years, stocks have been bred specifically for special purposes, such as early fruiting, ripening within a very short period to assist the pickers, resistance to disease, and so on. M9 or MIX, one of the first to make its mark, produces a small tree, but which comes into fruiting early on. It is eminently suitable for small gardens, but its primary use was in revolutionizing orchard practice all over the world to produce smaller trees, and more to the acre, which would yield early, and did not need great tall ladders for pickers to waste time moving from tree to tree and climbing up and down. In many parts of the world, ladders are no longer used – what cannot be reached with two feet on the ground stays where it is – and a great proportion of these trees are on M9 stocks.

Other numbers have different properties, such as being able to deal with various soil conditions and climatic conditions, which are of more interest to commercial growers. Other fruits also have their own classified stocks, although not so many as apples. By and large, and without getting too involved in the niceties, apples on M9 stock fulfil all that the amateur gardener will want in the private garden. Being one of the earliest, it has been around for a long while – and it has stood the test of time.

17   Harry Lauder's Walking Stick

Can you please tell me if the corkscrew hazel flowers? I would like to grow more of them to make walking sticks.

Corylus avellana 'Contorta', also known as 'Harry Lauder's Walking Stick', because he used to come on stage with a grotesquely twisted stick like a corkscrew, allegedly made from this tree. I have never heard that this is a proven fact – in the pictures I have seen of him, his sticks look a little too regular and evenly twisted to be *C.a.* 'Contorta'. I think it much more likely that his sticks were twisted into shape by quite an old 'country trick' of 'winding' and tying in a young stem around a pole or stout stick so that it takes on the corkscrew shape as it grows. Then, when it is stout enough for a walking stick it is simply cut out, cleaned, dried and varnished. All manner of different shapes used to be grown in this way, including the conventional walking stick and the 'rat catcher's' stick which, instead of a curved handle, has a straight handle length turned at an angle so that, when held upside down, the handle lies flat on the floor and provides a much better weapon with which to hit and break the backs of rats running for safety.

As the botanical name indicates, *C.a.* 'Contorta' is merely a form of the common hazel that has a strangely contorted growth habit. The catkins in spring may have a curious attractiveness, hanging from the twisted branches, but the tree produces very few nuts. The only reason for growing it in the garden – if you have room for this sort of thing – is as a curiosity. If you want walking sticks, you will do much better to use the common type, and train the stems as described.

18   An acacia by another name

A friend who used to work in a park gave me some seeds of a tree that he said was called Albizia. They have germinated and I do not know what to do with them – the name does not appear in either of my gardening encyclopaedias. I would be pleased if you can tell me anything about this tree.

Look again in your books under *Acacia lophantha*, the old name. It comes from western Australia, where it can reach 50ft (15m) but in this country it will be lucky to reach half that, and outdoors is only hardy in the mild south-west. Maturing plants will bear the sulphur-yellow bloom associated with acacia, but as this is produced early in spring – when you see the imported stuff in the markets – you will be very lucky to see much without glass protection.

The main attraction is the ornamental deeply lobed foliage. It was a favourite idea in days gone by to use young seedlings as 'dot' plants in massed bedding and floral displays, much as you can still see silver-leaved plants used. That kind of gardening is heavy on labour and, having become much too expensive in a cost-conscious world, has consequently gone out of fashion. It was a work of art, and the only places where it is seen now are in south coast holiday resorts and tourist places with a reputation for floral displays.

19   A reminder of Canada

I am a Canadian domiciled in the UK and would like to grow a Canadian maple to remind me of home. Is it possible to grow the maple here?

There is no reason why not. Several maples that are native to Canada can be grown successfully here, and might very well be described as 'Canadian'. However, if you have in mind the red maple leaf as depicted on the national flag, then strictly you should be looking for the true 'Canadian Red Maple' *Acer rubrum*.

The early spring and summer colour of the characteristic deep palmate leaves is dark green with a grey-green glaucous colour underneath. The dark green indicates a high chlorophyll content and is a clue to the tree's need for plenty of all-round light to manufacture the anthocyanins which turn the characteristic scarlet red as the chlorophyll breaks down in autumn. The tree is tolerant of a little alkalinity but, like most of the highly coloured trees from North America, it is not happy and does not colour well in chalk.

A. rubrum will ultimately make a large tree, and this could put it out of court if your garden is not large. Fortunately, it has two forms that have smaller dimensions, and which are suitable for average-sized gardens. Neither are easy to find, and you will probably have to rely on the specialist nurseries which you will find listed on page 221. *A.r.* 'Schlesingeri', a medium-sized tree, received an Award of Merit in 1976 for its consistently fine autumn colour. *A.r.* 'Scanlon' has very similar colouring, but a narrower, more columnar form, making it even more suitable where space is restricted.

20 Ornamental crabs for clay

We would like to plant an ornamental crab apple, but our soil is clay and we wonder if this would be unsuitable. The garden is fairly exposed, with little protection from cold north-easterly winds. Can you possibly suggest a variety or varieties tough enough to cope?

For the most part, the *Malus* species are reasonably tolerant of heavy soils and chalk, so that is not such a problem. Furthermore, they are generally hardy and resilient enough to 'come back' if and when they are knocked back by a hard winter, but an exposed and windy position does present an extra burden, which narrows the choice somewhat.

Prudence suggests that you pay heed to the reason why some leaves take on a grey-green, grey, or even silver appearance. The two basic causes are either a thick epidermis (skin) to the leaf, sometimes waxy and 'glaucous', or a hairy, even woolly, fur-like growth. The purpose in each case is to reduce moisture evaporation (transpiration) from the leaf by insulating its surface against the air. For this exposed windy position, therefore, varieties with grey-green foliage (and a cold, exposed windy place of origin in their ancestry) will have a big advantage. Take your pick from the following:

Malus hupehensis This small tree from the Hupeh area of China has soft pink buds opening white, which are fragrant and borne in great profusion on stiffly upright branches. It is a good tree for a small garden. The fruits are yellow tinted with red. An attractive tree, it took an AGM in 1930. *M.h.* 'Rosea' is a pink-flowered form which is not so upright, but more spreading and a lovely tree in bloom.

M. ioensis comes from the central USA where it is known as the 'Prairie Crab'. The branches are downy and the leaves woolly. It has large 2-inch (95-cm) fragrant flowers, which are white flushed with pink, and grow in groups of four, five or six. A semi-double pink form, *M.i.* 'Plena', is arguably one of the very best of the flowering crabs. It took an FCC in 1950, and that is praise indeed. Unfortunately, however, it has a weak constitution, and definitely upholds the general North American aversion to chalk soils.

Another Asian species is the true 'Siberian Crab' *M. baccata* (not to be confused, as is often the case, with *M.* × *robusta*, a larger and rather variable hybrid tree that has two forms 'Red Siberian' and 'Yellow Siberian'). The true species from Siberia is extremely hardy, as you might expect from such a place. Its variety *M.b. mandshurica* eventually makes a round-headed tree about 30ft (9m) high, with white fragrant flowers in April (earlier than most other crabs), followed by small berry-like red and yellow fruits. It took an FCC in 1969, and is generally regarded as the hardiest crab of all. With Siberian origins, it is as tough as old boots and should easily shrug off your windy position.

21 A yellow cherry?

At the Chelsea Flower Show a few years ago, there was a stand – I forget which – exhibiting a yellow-flowered cherry. Now that we have moved and have a larger garden with several pink cherries, we would like to grow that unusual yellow one – not only for its curiosity, it was truly beautiful. However, I can find no mention of a yellow cherry in my books. Can you tell me anything about it, please?

Not much doubt here, because there is only one really good yellow cherry – there are some that are creamy and leave too much yellow to the imagination and wishful thinking – just like the blue rose, and the blue dahlia. The cherry that you saw was *Prunus* 'Ukon' and, while it is unusual, and undoubtedly very attractive when seen as a young specimen at a big show, you will need to be very careful on two counts. First, the true *P.* 'Ukon' is rather robust and can make a spreading tree that will merge into other cherries if you merely assume that it will be of average dimensions – you will have to give it quite a bit more space than most others. Think in terms of a 30–35ft (9–10.5m) high spreading form, and not less. Like all the cherries, these Japanese hybrids are easy to grow, and not fussy about soil types unless they are badly drained and swampy. They are quite partial to a little chalk or lime around their roots.

The flowers are semi-double, and, depending upon the clone that the nursery is using, can vary from a yellowish cream to a more definite primrose-yellow, occasionally with a slight tinge of green or even pink – clearly reflecting a complicated ancestry which it is very doubtful if even the modern Japanese can understand! The flowers are freely borne, and what makes this tree so attractive is the perfect combination of the flower colour with the brown-bronze young leaves. But that is not all, for in autumn the foliage turns a rich rust-red then to a deeper purple. After all that you may think that the AGM awarded in 1969 is richly deserved.

Now for the second reason for care – take note that the flowers are semi-double. *P.* 'Ukon' is botanically very close to another Japanese variety called *P.* 'Asagi'. This is another 'yellow', but with less justification, being much more pale and insipid. However, I have seen it in a nursery garden centre, with a *P.* 'Ukon' label on it. The giveaway is that the bloom in this case is single. Now you know – either see your choice in bloom before you buy it, or order from a really reputable nursery.

22   The connection between oak trees and cooking

On holiday in Greece I saw a small shrub with leathery, probably evergreen, leaves, in shape something between a holly and an oak, and with 'fruits' like flat acorns. I brought some home. How should I germinate them and will the shrub grow in UK?

This is an interesting question. The plant is a shrubby oak, commonly called the 'Kermes Oak', and botanically *Quercus coccifera*. Found growing all around the Mediterranean littoral, its origin is actually the more arid plains of Portugal. In these areas it will sometimes reach 12ft (3.5m) or a little more, but in Britain seldom more than 6ft (2m) high. The evergreen leaves are borne very densely, and if you had looked longer and more carefully, you would probably have found and remarked upon some of the leaves having prickly thorns – the leaf form is quite variable.

Keep your acorns dry and cool until mid-March, at which time sow them 2 inches (5cm) deep and 3 inches (7.5cm) apart in deep boxes or pots of John Innes seed compost, with at least 5 inches (13cm) under them, transplanting them at one year old into their final positions. We found that this plant does not like root disturbance after this – the parks were always complaining about planting failures and it was not very popular with them!

A point of interest, with which you will most likely not be familiar. In the warmer Mediterranean areas this plant is host to the 'Kermes insect', which gives the plant its common name. The crushed body of this small bettle-like insect is the source of cochineal, the red colouring dye used in cooking.

23 A hardy palm

When visiting Torquay and Newquay I noticed many palms growing outdoors – some were quite large trees. Can you tell me of any varieties which would grow outdoors in other parts of the country?

Normally, with a question like this, it is necessary to distinguish between what is meant by 'the rest of the country' and 'other parts', that is, to be a little more specific. Some plants will be hardy in some southern coastal parts, but not in the rest of the country as a whole. With palms however, although there are isolated protected climatic pockets where the odd specimen contrives to exist outdoors, the only really rational answer to this question is not to try growing palms if you wish to avoid disappointment.

There is only one palm that is hardy in the UK, and that must have mild 'Cornish Riviera'-like conditions – and, ideally, protection to prevent the large 3–4ft (1–1.2m) fern-shaped leaves from being shattered by wind. *Trachycarpus fortunei*, the 'Chusan Palm', comes from central China. Starting as no more than a shrub, the central shoot grows, and the fibrous remains of old leaf bases form woody trunks with a typical palm-like cluster of leaves at the top, which, over the years and in favourable positions, can reach a surprising tree-like height.

Like a maize or sweet corn, with which you may be familiar, the flowers are monoecious – that is to say, the male and female flowers are borne separately, but on the same plant. Usually yellow-cream in colour, the flowers are borne in long panicles in early summer followed, if you are lucky, by very dark fruits.

24 Thuja, a cure for warts?

Could you tell me something about a tree known as thuya, which produces small round green cones, and leaves that smell strongly when cut or crushed? The boiled leaves are an excellent cure for warts, and I was able to remove a number of them by bathing my hands in a solution made from this tree.

Correctly spelled thuja (the 'j' is pronounced as a 'y'), this is a relatively small genus of evergreen conifers that could hardly have a wider range of origins, from North America through Europe to the farthest east of Asia. With unusual and strongly aromatic – but not unpleasant – foliage, it is perhaps not so surprising that it should have a place in the folklore of many lands, and various medicinal qualities have been ascribed to it. By their very nature, warts have always been high on the list of things to be rid of, and with their cause somewhat obscure and for long the subject of speculation and guesswork, it is only natural that thuja should turn up as a cure.

Before scientific diagnosis became the rational and accepted procedure in the treatment of ills, medicine was very much a case of trial and error – error was hard luck, and improvement or cure, because such knowledge at once conferred privilege and power in a community, became a matter for mystery and secrecy. However, folklore and 'old wives' tales' are not to be dismissed out of hand. The effects often ascribed to herbs and plants are invariably the results of observation, even if not understood at the time, and have not infrequently been borne out by modern scientific analysis. Various concoctions of thuja have been used successfully in the treatment of scurvy, fevers and rheumatism. Who knows? It may well have a curative effect on warts, and it would not be the first time that such a claim turned out to be true.

Until it is scientifically disproved, holding your hands in a solution is hardly likely to do you harm, and all the time that you feel it works – coincidence or not, some other explanation or not – you go right ahead and believe it. No doubt, after reading of your experiences, there will be many others who will try the same cure.

You ask for a little further information. Although a genus of no more than ten species, there are literally dozens upon dozens of varieties and forms from enormous trees to small shrubs, darkest green to brightest gold, and every shape in the book – it is very diverse in habit. It is commonly called 'Arbor-vitae', often interpreted as 'wood of life' – a name singularly appropriate to its medicinal attributes.

Problems of cultivation

25 Acers hate winds

During the autumn of 1985 I planted an Acer palmatum *'Atropurpureum' which died during the winter. This was replaced the following autumn, and although the new plant appeared to have become established with leaves appearing, by the following July they began to shrivel at the edges and eventually dropped. The young tree is now quite bare and looking poorly. Can you please suggest what I should do?*

The ornamental maples do not like wind at the best of times, and newly planted juveniles – like most other new plantings – are even more at risk. These fellows do not like their roots being disturbed, and they are rather slow to make new osmotic root hairs (which are the parts of the root that absorb moisture and nutrients from the soil) but that is just what they have to do if they are to live and become established. This is a case that proves the dictum that preparation has to be before planting – you cannot do it afterwards. Read the section in this book dealing with planting (pages 10–13), feel the sense of what it is trying to say, and another time, make sure that you get plenty of organic 'sponge' under the roots.

As plants evaporate moisture from their leaves (transpiration) this has to be replaced by intake at the roots (osmosis). Your maple made leaf on the sap already within itself and began to transpire, but its as yet inadequate root system was incapable of absorbing moisture fast enough to keep pace. Even under normal circumstances, it is problem enough to get maples established in the first year or two – they need more help and care than most to get going and you will not help matters by not getting enough moisture-retaining matter under the root area. Add to that another physiological factor. Maples have soft leaves with no glossy shine, hairs, or waxy surface, and so they do not have much inbuilt ability to 'fend off' air movement across the leaf surface cells that contain the sap liquid. Consequently, even a slight breeze can 'force dry' leaves, and put a heavy demand on the moisture supply coming up through the trunk, branches, twigs and leaf stalks. When the moisture supply cannot keep pace, the inevitable result is that the leaf cells become limp (flaccid) and collapse, beginning at the edges, and when the walls fall in, there is no way of putting them up again. The damaged cell area dries out completely, and if the problem continues, the plant has to do the only thing it can to try to save itself – shed the load, by dropping the remaining leaves.

That explains what has happened, but what can you do? It is too late now to get under the plant, but you must get organic matter down there somehow. So, mulch plenty of compost, leafmould, moss peat, or the remains of old gro-bags around the plant, and put any earthworms you uncover in the garden onto the mulch and let them get to work at taking it down. If you try anything more drastic, you will only disturb the roots – worms will do a better job now than you can.

Put up a wind-deflecting screen around the plant for a couple of years while the root system develops. There is a small mesh plastic net obtainable especially for the purpose. In the evenings, when it has been windy or sunny and the inside liquid pressure is bound to be a bit low, spray the plant over with clear water and get the leaf surfaces well wetted so that during the night, with photosynthesis stopped, they have a chance to take moisture in and plump up again. Of course, it goes without saying that you should not let the soil become dry.

26 *Propagating an acer*

I have a four-year-old Acer palmatum *and would like to know how to propagate it. I have tried cuttings in sand and peat in a propagator at 70°F (21°C) for the last two years without any success at all. I have just installed a mist unit and hope that this will be the answer.*

The odds are very heavily against cuttings rooting without mist, and even with that extra encouragement you will probably find the proportion of cuttings that do root will be very small. You could try aerial layering, but you will have to be very careful indeed how you handle your knife. Make an upward cut through a half-ripe leaf joint – it will be something less than pencil thick. Dust the exposed wood with hormone rooting powder, use a little moist sphagnum peat to keep the cut prised open, pack a small handful of wet peat (soaked with rain water and the excess squeezed out) around the cut area, wrap a few turns around with polythene film, and seal the ends and side with insulating tape to prevent any drying out.

You will have to be patient, rooting is slow. When the moss is permeated with root and you judge that there is enough to support the tip away from its parent, it can be severed and potted into a 3-inch (7.5-cm) or suitable pot, using John Innes No. 1 potting compost. Do not use a stronger compost, because the young plant has to work to make root. If the nutrient supply is too generous the roots do not have to search and develop.

Another alternative you could try is budding – like you would a rose – in August, or grafting in early spring just as the sap is rising, onto a rootstock of the common sycamore. Remember, acers are vulnerable to moisture evaporation, and budding and grafting are therefore best done in the humid atmosphere of a closed frame or greenhouse.

27 Splitting its sides – not a laughing matter

A split has developed about 1ft (30cm) long in the trunk of my Acer cappadocicum *'Rubrum'. The split is 5ft (1.5m) from the ground and pronounced. Can you suggest the cause and a cure, please?*

Apart from the effects of badly-made ties (see the section dealing with staking and tying) the usual cause of bark splitting is a long spell of dry weather or seriously inadequate moisture supply, followed by a sudden deluge when there is still growing period left and the roots take it in. It happens with all kinds of plants from cabbages that split their hearts, and roots like carrots and beets that burst open, to trees. Usually, it does not happen within the first few years of planting because the root system is still developing and has not yet reached full absorbing power. But when it has been growing a few years and become established, then comes the danger period. This is another reason for getting plenty of organic sponge under the roots when planting.

A dry summer means that the new annual outer cambium and bark layer – the last outer ring seen when you cut across a trunk – is deprived, thin and not elastic. A sudden surge of sap then builds up internal pressure to a point where the inelastic constricting outer layer bursts and the trunk splits. By the nature of their physical structure, some trees are more prone than others to this problem – cherries and plums are notorious – and of course, when it happens, you have to make quite sure that other troubles do not get into the open wound and cause infection. There are plenty of problems ready and waiting to jump in.

As soon as possible, make sure that the exposed surface inside the wound is clean and has not already collected debris. Clean off any adjacent dead bark, make sure all is clean and dry, and apply a protective coating of Arbrex. The lower end of the split is easy enough – you can run the Arbrex down where the split is too narrow to reach in. The top is another matter and you will have to press and work it in as best you can. I suggest that you keep a wary eye open; examine the Arbrex coating to see if it is moving to reveal that the split is still opening. Apply a second coat in two weeks in any case.

If the split has gone deep, it will be easy for leaf and other debris to enter and collect. Reduce the likelihood of this by wrapping the trunk or branch with fine gauze or plastic, but if the latter, make sure it is not airtight. In any case, take it off every couple of months to make quite sure that there is no sign of decay in the split.

Look to the stakes and ties – the trunk now has a weakened area that could be vulnerable to wind blow. With luck, a young tree will gradually be able to grow over and cover the split, but it will need lots of patient care, and you will have to be a good nurse.

28   Acer not colouring

Two years ago I purchased an Acer palmatum *from a reputable nursery. The leaves are a pale green, and in autumn they turn yellow and brown, but they never turn the bright red which I believe they should do. Is there anything I can do to make them turn red?*

The extent and the intensity of autumn foliage colour inevitably vary from year to year because weather, rainfall, duration and intensity of sunlight, soil conditions and availability of nutrients all play a part, and of course all are variable. First, however – and in my opinion the most likely reason – let us be sure of something else. Was the plant that you purchased a named variety? Should it be red – or was it simply *A. palmatum* and you are assuming that it would be red? You mention 'a reputable nursery' – well, if it was, they will have used a label that resists decay and will still be clearly legible. If that label indicates a varietal name that should be red, a really reputable nursery will prefer that you draw their attention to it.

Acer palmatum – if that is what it is – could well be the colouring you describe. If you really want red enough to buy another, I suggest that you buy one clearly labelled *A.p.* 'Heptalobum Osakazuki' which you will find described on page 37. The only other thing left that you can do is to ensure that the tree is not short of potash and not in avoidable shade. The red colouring in autumn foliage and fruit is caused by the presence of substances called anthocyanins. These are produced during the summer in sunlight, the longer and brighter the better, and in doing so the plant pulls hard on the available potash in the soil. As autumn arrives, it is part of the breakdown process for green chlorophyll to decline and its masking of other colouring pigments to subside as they intensify. If the anthocyanins have developed well, they will be turning red, but if there was insufficient potash and they were not made, you will not see much red. You can make sure there is no shortage by putting down plenty of compost mulch and spread into it 2oz (57g) to the square yard (square metre) of Humber Compound (see page 10) in spring and again three months later. That will take care of the potash – or if you are using other fertilizers that are not NPK-balanced like Humber, put down the same amounts of sulphate or muriate of potash.

29 Filling a cavity

When we moved to our present address four years ago, we noticed a hole on the trunk of a horse chestnut tree. This has steadily become worse, and now goes deep into the trunk with dead soft wood all round. We have been told that we should fill the cavity with newspaper and cement, but do you think this will stop the trouble?

No! I think you have been told utter rubbish! Newspaper is organic, will decompose and add more trouble to what you already have, without doing anything to cure it. You first have to decide how bad the damage is – you know that it is getting worse – and second, is it already bad enough to imperil the safety of the tree? How big and old is the tree? A big tree is potentially dangerous – does this wound significantly weaken the trunk? Other questions you should ask are can the tree be saved? Do you want to save it? Is it a risk to buildings and drains? Would it be safer to take it down now, or wait for it to fall? Would you rather have something better to look at?

If you decide that you would prefer to keep the tree, you have to find out if that is possible by discovering how far the trouble has gone. That could very well take the decision out of your hands. Every vestige of decay has to come out, and there will be a lot to be removed – it has been going on for four years to your knowledge. You have to use chisel, pick, gouge, whatever to explore as far and as deeply as you find necessary. Every morsel of discoloured wood has to come out. You will need a torch to see into the depths and a lot of time, patience and care. You may quickly reach the decision that the tree is so weakened that it is unsafe for you to be inside digging further. I suspect, on the history of the trouble, that this is what will happen, in which case this is where you hand over to an insured professional firm of tree surgeons to remove it.

However, if the trouble is not that bad and you can keep the tree, every, repeat *every*, vestige of decay has to come away. Remove all dead bark near the wound edge. Cover the entire exposed wound with Arbrex, and fill the cavity with a mixture of three parts of horticultural vermiculite – which is inert and sterile – and one part cement. This concrete mix has to take weight and stress – the entire cavity has to be filled, up as well as down. Force it in little by little, until it is tight and firm with no air pockets. Finish off with the concrete overlapping the lip at the bottom of the cavity hole – if you leave a ledge for rain and debris to collect, the trouble will start again.

Is it worth it? You will realize, after all this, that the job has to be done properly, or it is all a waste of time.

30 Purple birch turning green

I have a purple birch about eight years old. This year two of the new branchlets high up have small green leaves and there is also a group of green leaf shoots from the stump of a pruned branch. Can you confirm that these green shoots should be removed?

(above left) Laburnum anagyroides 'Vossii' (see page 55). The very free flowering of this hybrid form, here shown to good effect, is much better than the common type. It is magnificent as a solo specimen, and glorious as a flowering tunnel.

(above right) Fraxinus excelsior 'Pendula', the 'Weeping Ash' (see page 49). Already attractive, this young specimen pictured here will later develop a 'flat top' and a pronounced weeping habit.

(left) Acer palmatum 'Heptalobum Osakazuki' (see page 37). The brilliant fiery colour of this maple seen here in the conditions it likes best – sunlight shafting on to it in a light woodland setting.

(opposite) Nyssa sylvatica (see page 60). The 'Tupelo' from North America is seen here in an ideal setting against a contrasting colour backdrop at the R.H.S. Gardens, Wisley.

(above left) Thuja occidentalis 'Rhein-gold' (see page 91). Often described and sold as a dwarf shrub, this glorious old-gold evergreen is quite capable of becoming a 16-ft (5-m) tree.

(above right) Sorbus aucuparia kewensis (see page 74). A smaller tree, with darker green foliage and deeper red berries than most other rowans.

(right) Malus 'John Downie' (see page 59). This photograph shows the large, highly coloured fruits that make this the most popular and widely grown of all crab apples.

(above left) Cupressus sempervirens (see page 85). The 'Italian' or 'Mediterranean' cypress – where its tall, slender shape, breaking the skyline, is a familiar sight.

(above right) Cupressocyparis leylandii (see page 83). Usually clipped and constrained as a hedge, this is the handsomely shaped tree it makes when allowed to grow naturally to maturity.

(left) Calocedrus decurrens (see page 80). Another tall (eventually 100ft – 33m) evergreen conifer, so useful for providing shape contrast and breaking the skyline.

(opposite) Cedrus atlantica glauca (see page 81). A close-up photograph of the silvery, blue-grey needle leaves that clothe this most majestic of all trees. The only drawback for most gardens is the eventual size of the tree – it becomes very large.

(opposite) *Cotinus coggygria* 'Flame' (see page 44). Usually regarded as a shrub – albeit a large one – the 'smoky sumach' can easily reach tree proportions in favourable conditions. The 'smoke' is due to the effect of feathery blooms seen against this fiery colour.

(top left) *Catalpa bignonioides* (see page 43). Not unlike the well-known 'Horse Chestnut' in size and appearance. However, the blooms are followed, not by 'conkers', but by tresses of 'beans'.

(above left) *Halesia carolina* (see page 50). A close-up view of the 'snowdrop' blooms that smother this beautiful tree from southern USA.

(top right) *Magnolia soulangeana* 'Lennei' (see page 58). This photograph shows the rich and more deeply coloured form of this popular tree.

(above right) *Prunus subhirtella* 'Pendula' (see page 65). One of the most beautiful of all small flowering trees, pictured here in Kew Gardens.

(top left) Pinus montezumae (see page 89).
The long, shaggy needle leaves of the
exotic 'Montezuma Pine' from the hills
of Mexico.

(above left) Picea brewerana (see page 88).
The long, weeping tips of the branches
make this small tree one of the most
striking and beautiful of all conifers.

(top right) Juniperus virginiana 'Skyrocket' (see page 86). The aptly named
'Pencil Cedar' on the left of the photograph is a good illustration of how
variation in shape, colour and distance
can be used to provide contrast and
interest.

(above right) Chamaecyparis lawsoniana
'Pembury Blue' (see page 82). The
finest grey-blue of the evergreen 'Lawson' conifers is small enough to be
accommodated in all but the tiniest
gardens.

(opposite) Picea pungens 'Koster' (see
page 88). A fine young specimen of the
'Blue Spruce', giveing a foretaste of the
splendour to come.

(opposite) Fagus sylvatica 'Dawyck' (see page 48). This is the golden form of the upright growing or fastigiate beech.

(above left) Escallonia 'Donard Seedling' (see page 48). The prolific blooms, borne on long, arching sprays, follow hard pruning of this vigorous hybrid.

(above right) Prunus sargentii (see page 65). One of the most graceful of the flowering cherries, and regarded by many as the very finest of all.

(right) Cercis siliquastrum (see page 43). The neat form of this young specimen belies its later tendency, as it grows older, to flop about and become ungainly – but then even more curiously attractive.

(top left) Prunus 'Kiku-shidare Sakura', often called 'Cheal's Weeping Cherry' (see page 66). Probably the most popular of all weeping cherries, and a 'natural' for small gardens.

(above left) Cedrus atlantica 'Glauca Pendula' (see page 81). One of the smaller cedars. Imagine this beauty mirrored in a pool, with a waterfall nearby!

(top right) Garrya elliptica (see page 49). The long, silvery grey-green tassels borne during winter months show up well in this photograph.

(above right) Syringa josiflexa 'Bellicent' (see page 76). This photograph shows how it is well worth seeking out the more unusual forms of the common lilac.

(opposite) A close-up view of the apple-blossom-like blooms that smother a well-grown *Escallonia* 'Donard Seedling' (see page 48).

(top left) Liquidambar styraciflua (see page 56). A tree of changing colours: amber in spring, green in summer and the rich reds of autumn (shown here).

(above left) Carya ovata (see page 42). The common name 'Shagbark Hickory' may not be pretty, but the tree's appearance certainly is!

(top right) Quercus robur 'Fastigiata' (see page 69). Not all oaks are as wide as they are tall – as this handsome upright form of the 'Common Oak' clearly shows.

(above right) Robinia pseudoacacia 'Frisia' (see page 71). This has glorious yellow-gold ornamental foliage and is a much smaller tree than the better-known type; it deserves to be more widely grown.

(opposite) Pinus sylvestris 'Aurea' (see page 88). The bright cream-yellow of the young growth shows up well against the green of the older foliage below – a most eye-catching effect.

(top left) Populus 'Serotina' (see page 64). This has copper-red foliage in late spring, which turns a pale green, and an open-branch system with minimum light impedence. A better tree for drive and roadside planting than those often seen.

(above left) Metasequoia glyptostroboides (see page 87). The long-lost fossil tree. Early spring foliage is bright pink before turning this shade of bright green. A romantic story befitting a handsome tree.

(top right) Taxodium distichum (see page 90). A conifer that thrives in damp, swampy conditions. The foliage turns orange-bronze in autumn, before falling.

(above right) Sorbus aucuparia 'Joseph Rock' (see page 74). The cream berries, seen here, contrast strongly with bronze-purple foliage in autumn.

This is not unknown in a purple birch – there used to be one in a garden adjoining Dulwich Park that was half and half! Whenever there is a deviation from the type (called a 'sport' or a mutation – a genetic accident that is quite unpredictable, and one of the ways that evolution occurs) it is by no means certain that the variation will continue into the next generation. Even when propagated vegetatively in order to avoid the influence of another parent, it is quite possible for the variation to 'sport back' or 'revert' to the type, or it can sport again into yet a further variation.

Very often it is necessary for several generations to pass without reversion before a variation can be said to have settled down and become reliably 'fixed' (see *Cupressocyparis leylandii* 'Castlewellan' on page 84). Even then, the possibility that something could trigger a reversion lurks deep down in the genetic make-up. Perhaps the most frequent cause is cutting, when the cell division involved in the production of healing scar tissue or callus leads to adventitious shoots with the genetic make-up thrown out of gear. I have seen trees and shrubs, cut too regularly and repeatedly for cuttings, 'revolt' in just this way, and settle back again when allowed to rest for a few years. This is not to be confused with the different habit, leaf, flower or colour that we see when a rootstock breaks out from below a graft.

It is not uncommon for this birch to throw out an odd leaf or shoot. They should be removed when as young as possible by rubbing or pulling, but not by cutting which creates callus tissue, and no doubt is the cause of the 'groups' of green shoots from the cut-off branch stump.

Usually, sported growth is not so vigorous, and when a reversion back to normal occurs, its extra 'normal' vigour enables it to grow faster and to overpower the weaker sport. The classic example of all this is the golden privet which frequently throws out green shoots and will revert completely if not stopped.

31 Care of Judas Tree seedlings

I have grown some 'Judas Trees' from seed sown last spring. They are now about 3 inches (7.5cm) tall and seem quite fragile. How do I look after them from now on?

This tree comes from Asia Minor, and when new-born babes like these young seedlings are exposed to the rigours of our winter you cannot expect them to live through it regardless. They will need the protection of a covered cold frame and careful watering – don't let them dry out, but overwatering will be fatal. If you have germinated the seeds in the greenhouse they will still need to be moved to the cold frame, but you must try to avoid a sudden drop in temperature by making the move gradually – put on ventilation in the greenhouse during a mild day and move the seedlings near the fresh air, then out to the cold frame kept closed for a few days. In the spring, as the embryo leaf buds begin to swell, pot up the seedlings singly or plant them out under the protection of an open-ended cloche.

32   Bladder Senna seed

I picked up some large pods that had fallen from a senna tree in a garden that we visited. The seeds inside these pods are still green. Will they ripen and germinate if I sow them? I would appreciate any help you can give me.

This tree-like shrub is 'Bladder Senna', *Colutea arborescens*, a member of the pea family that is tolerant of chalk and dry soils, and in this country reaches 10–12ft (3–3.5m) high. Its yellow flowers are followed by the fat seed pods that you picked up. The 'Bladder Senna' is native to the Mediterranean littoral of southern Europe – and this is important because factors like temperature and sunlight intensity and duration are vital for pollen ripening and fertilization, and affect the viability of seed. In this country, it would take a warm Mediterranean-like summer for seed to be fertile. The fact that the seed you picked up was green and soft shows that it was infertile. The tree therefore had no further use for it and so aborted it, as do many other plants in the same circumstances.

When the seed is viable the pods ripen, become thin, dry to a straw colour and inflate like a bladder, hence the common name. When shucked, the seed will have become brown and hard. The easiest way to propagate this tree is to insert cuttings of the current year's wood in a cold frame during autumn.

33   Cotoneaster pruning

I've just purchased a Cotoneaster *'Hybridus Pendulus'. Can you explain the pruning method to be followed please?*

[118]

Pruning depends how big the plant is at present and the form you want it to take. This is a pendulous small tree-like shrub, and its shoot tips and branchlets will have a natural weeping habit. If you want it to become a weeping standard, choose the strongest and straightest stem, removing the others and so concentrating the plant's efforts into making height. Tie it to a stake, take it up to 5–6ft (1.5–2m) and then top it to produce side shoots which will weep.

Other than this kind of forming, no routine pruning is necessary. If you want it to adopt its natural shrub form simply remove dead wood, badly positioned and crossing stems during March–April to produce and maintain a good shape – you will find an open shuttlecock-like form is most satisfactory.

34 Seedling thorn not true

After waiting two years, I have managed to germinate some seeds from a very pretty May tree that grows near here. Its flowers are white with a pink-red edge. How long shall I have to wait for the seedlings to flower?

There can be no guarantee that your seedlings will 'come true' and have the same flowers as the tree from which you collected the seed. Named varieties with particular flowers, colours and characteristics have to be propagated vegetatively, either by rooting cuttings or, because this is not entirely satisfactory, by grafting shoots on to the more vigorous rootstock of the common wild type. The shoot growth then exhibits its inherent flower colour, normally in about four years, sometimes three. The seedlings that you have germinated will need six or seven years before the first flowers appear and show how much of the parent colour they have inherited.

35 Handkerchiefs from seed

How long will it be before seeds of Davidia involucrata *('Handkerchief Tree') germinate? I sowed them in a pot of John Innes potting mixture and set them outdoors last autumn.*

Davidia is one of many tree subjects whose seed is slow to germinate and may even need weathering first. This is usually achieved by putting sand in a clay pot, sprinkling on a thin scattering of seed, another layer of sand 1 inch (2.5cm) thick, and more seed and sand in layers in a method called 'stratifying', and standing the pot in an open

[119]

frame where the weather can get at it. We used to do this in late autumn soon after the seed had been collected. Eighteen months later, in the next-but-one spring, the pots were emptied out and the seed sown, not into potting compost, which is too rich, but into seed compost in deep trays or pans. The seedlings the following spring were very carefully potted up just as the swelling leaf buds indicated sap movement.

If you do this on a reasonable scale, as in a nursery, you will in effect be putting out a fair amount of food that will attract the attention of mice and shrews. It is a good precaution, therefore, to wrap the pots in small mesh mice-proof wire netting.

36 Why no hankies?

My Davidia *'Handkerchief Tree' is twelve years old. It came from a reputable nursery and has been well looked after, yet it has never borne any handkerchief blooms. If I cannot hope for any flowers, should I replace it, or is there anything else I can do?*

The handkerchiefs are not blooms – which are in fact quite inconspicuous – but bracts or modified leaves, which turn white. In much the same way, the individual flowers of hydrangea are very small indeed, and what are often thought of as petals are not petals at all, but coloured bracts.

The bracts are, however, part of what might be called the flower complex in the sense that, if there is no flower, there will be no handkerchief bract. Left to itself, your twelve-year-old may produce next year, or it could be several years more before it does. If it is thriving, why should it bother? It is doing very nicely, and there is no reason why it should hurry to go through the procedure of reproducing – putting up flower as the precursor of seed. I suggest, therefore, that you do what is often done to a reluctant fruit tree to make it come into bearing; frighten it, make it think that its life is in danger! The tree's natural reaction is 'perpetuation of the species'. It will try to ensure that another generation is created before the threatened death occurs. You can threaten the tree by seriously wounding it – cutting through some of its roots (root pruning) would do the job. Dig a trench about 1½–2ft (46–61cm) away from the base of the stem, two spits deep and about half way round the tree, and cut through every root you meet. That should scare the living daylights out of it! I would be inclined to do the job at any time other than springtime when the sap is rising fast, and you could expect your first hanky a year or so later.

About 1950, I remember, it became necessary to prepare to drain the lake in Dulwich Park. The 'plug' should have allowed it to be emptied into a stream, but when it was broken out nothing happened, and it was necessary to trench back along the drain run to find the blockage. The trench went quite close to a fine 'Handkerchief Tree', which carried a nice display every year. The trench was 6ft (2m) deep at this point and a lot of roots had to be cut through. The job was started in the New Year, the *Davidia* flowered as usual in the spring – but the following year it was an incredible sight! The hankies were so numerous that they obliterated the foliage completely.

37 Snapped eucalyptus

Hearing on Radio 4's Gardeners' Question Time *that eucalyptus was the fastest-growing tree, we planted one at the far corner of our garden to block out the sight of a window in a house backing on. It certainly grew fast, but in most winters the leaves turned brown as though scorched, and although new leaves grew each time, it was not a pretty sight until they did. In the October 1987 storm – by which time it was over 30ft (9m) high – it blew over against an old concrete fence spur alongside and snapped. A friend says that, when cut down, these trees will send up fresh growth. As the root has not actually lifted out, is there a chance it could do this? How long would it take, or should we have the stump removed and plant afresh? If so, is there anything that would grow as quick and not turn brown in winter?*

I would guess from the height quoted that this is *E. gunnii*, which is a fast grower, and although liable to scorch brown in winter, is hardy enough to come back. It is also the variety most widely grown to produce the blue-grey foliage used so much in floristry. This is produced by coppicing – cutting the main trunk back to 18–24 inches (46–61 cm) from ground level – and so forcing a lot of young shoots. The main question is whether the tree bole suffered root breakage, although it did not turn over. You can cut back, and see by the shoots next spring whether there is any chance of carrying on.

For replacement, you will find several suggestions in the tree lists here, but I wonder if you need go much further than the evergreen conifer *Cupressocyparis leylandii*. This is fast-growing and hardy

[121]

enough to stand up to the cold winds of an evidently open and draughty position.

38 Why no spindle berries?

Why does my spindle tree fail to bear any berries? I have had it for four years and it is covered with greenish-coloured flowers each spring. It had lots of pretty berries on it when I bought it. Is it necessary to have male and female plants to get berries?

Unlike the hollies, the spindle berries – *Euonymus* – do not carry male and female flowers on separate plants, so there is no need to get another for that reason. Whenever you get a problem like this, with no obvious reason, the first thing to do is to go back to basics and see how the plant grows 'wild' in its place of origin and try to spot the differences in the way it is growing in your garden. Consider the climate, temperatures, soil, habitat and so on.

The native spindle, *E. europaeus*, grows widely in hedgerows and light woodland where it gets partial and dappled shade. Banstead Heath in Surrey – 2 inches (5cm) of soil on top of solid chalk – has some fine examples growing quite wild. Bloom is borne on two-year-old wood, so pruning should consist only of shortening back long straggly growth to promote side shoots which will eventually carry the berries. In addition to dappled shade, another effect of hedgerow and light woodland is the annual carpet of leaf fall. If your plant is in a position where it is not getting this, you can make up for it by a thick layer of mulch each autumn. Probably, with roots restricted at the time you bought it, the plant was 'fighting back' and trying to produce another generation. Now it has been getting itself established, making root and top growth, its mind has been on other things. If it does not bear berries in the next year or two, I would 'frighten' it by root pruning (see question 36).

39 An impenetrable barrier from seed

For security purposes I need an impenetrable hedge around my large garden and small orchard. Will you please tell me if it is possible to grow the Honey Locust, Gleditsia, from seed in this country, and how it is done? I need so many that it will be very expensive to buy plants, and the few seeds that I have obtained from a local park have not germinated.

We were faced with a demand for hundreds of this shrub, and I can tell you how we did it. During the Second World War, all the park railings were sacrificed for melting down, and for a long time after, intrusion and vandalism after dark became a serious problem in several places. This was combated by planting masses of thorny barriers like berberis and quickthorn. *Gleditsia triacanthos* with its vicious 2–3 inch (5–7.5cm) barbed thorns became in great demand, and initially the poor seed germination presented problems. How the solution squares with natural processes I am not sure, but this is how it was done.

In March, heat water to the point where you can just bear your elbow in it, soak the seed in this for about 20 minutes and then allow the water to cool. Sow the seed spaced out singly into deep trays of John Innes seed compost rather deeper than usual for seed of this size – about ¾–1 inch (2–2.5cm) – firm the compost, water by immersion until the water just shows through, and place in a warm propagating frame. We had to use a thick bed of fresh stable manure – there were no soil warming cables in those days – weaning off gradually to an open greenhouse bench as the heat subsided. You can translate that as a temperature of about 65–70°F (18–21°C). When the seedlings are 2–3 inches (5–7.5cm) high, harden off gradually and move to open cold frames, and then to lining out in open ground at the second spring. Two years there, and they will have become big enough for replanting to their final positions. Some reference books indicate that the seed should be stratified like quickthorn and holly, but it never worked for us.

40 A leafless witch hazel

I bought this tree growing in a pot in May. It is planted in a sunny position with lots of compost under it. The leaves began to turn yellow and orange at the end of July and a month later had all fallen off. Isn't this a bit early? And does it mean a shortage of something? I bought the tree because I understood that it blooms in winter. Do you think that it will do so?

The salient clue here, I feel, is 'in a pot, planted in May'. The potted root ball could well have had plenty of time by May to have become dry. This is one of the problems with pot-grown, ready-to-plant material, when the garden centre or nursery are just a little neglectful or too busy with the seasonal rush of business to keep all the pots moist. The sap rises, the new leaf forms, but the dry root ball puts a brake on things.

Witch hazels – *Hamamelis* – are slow growing, and slow to get off the mark at the best of times. When they are dry and thirsty, they are slower than ever to move away from the root ball, the moisture absorption ability does not develop and the initial leaf growth cannot be sustained and so it falls earlier, like your tree. This is very unfortunate for a young plant because it means that a couple of months' photosynthesis elaboration in the leaves has been lost.

When a root or pot ball dries, it can take a long time and a lot of rain and watering before enough can soak back into it from the surrounding soil to avoid damage. Water from above merely runs off like water off a duck's back – try it and see. It is always wise to soak a ball before planting, whether or not it feels damp.

What to do now? I would even be inclined to see if I could carefully lift the plant – if it has made little root, there will not be much to damage – and give the ball a good soaking. As it lifts clear I would not be surprised if a lack of new root action confirmed this diagnosis. Failing that, or even when you replant, sink four or five 3–4 inch (7.5–10cm) clay pots to rim level as near to the edge of the root ball as you can. Plug the drainage holes of the pots with newspaper so that water drains out slowly, and make a point of filling them every day, keeping this up until autumn. Your task, now that the leaves have dropped, is to prevent further drying out of the stems and twigs. Mulch the soil surface heavily after a good rainfall to retard drying, and with fortune on your side you should be able to save the plant and have normal leaf growth next year – but don't be disappointed if there is no bloom this first winter. Your plant has had a nasty ordeal so early in its life.

41 Why no holly berries?

Our holly was ten years old and had not had any berries. We were advised that only females bear berries, so we bought a 'Golden Queen'. That was five years ago and although there has been what appears to be bloom we still have no berries!

If you mean that you have never had a berry, even from time to time, then the first tree is a male – but so is the second! Despite its name, a 'Golden Queen' cannot ever bear berries (see also question 10). The advice you were given is quite correct, but you chose the wrong sex again. Hollies are not fast growers, and even if you plant a known female variety, you are not likely to see berries for a few years until she matures and comes of age. So whatever happens, I am afraid that you will not be seeing berries for some time yet.

You can confirm this diagnosis for yourself by carefully looking at the bloom next time it appears – you may find a magnifying lens helpful. If the small white flowers have four tiny stalks in the centre, these are the pollen-bearing stamens and the tree is definitely male. On the other hand, if the flowers have a single club-headed stalk, this is the pollen-receiving pistil, the tree is female, and there is no reason why it should not bear berries. Look down the list of trees in this book, or in a good catalogue, choose a female, and in time your patience will be rewarded with a 'berry happy Christmas'.

42   Rooting holly cuttings

Could you tell me when and how to take cuttings of holly – I have tried and tried without success. It does not much matter whether they are male or female as I want them for a hedge.

Holly is difficult to root from cuttings, and is not worth attempting without bottom heat from a soil-warming cable, the enclosed atmosphere of a frame to reduce transpiration from the leaf surfaces and, advisedly, a mist unit. You must expect a lot of failures, and if you only want a few plants, you may have to put down a couple of dozen or more to get just one or two rooted. You will stand the best chance by pulling or cutting away 3–4 inch (7.5–10cm) side shoots with a good ½ inch (1cm) or longer heel. Do this in August when the cuttings are full of sap and plump. Trim the heels smooth with a sharp knife or razor blade, lay aside for an hour so that the cut surface dries, dip them in hormone rooting powder and insert into sharp sand over a bed of peat. Keep the cuttings moist (if you do not have a mist unit), closed and warm.

Rooting can take anything from one to three months. If you lift the cutting very carefully and find the cutting tip swollen, this is callus tissue and it is at least trying. Cut a small piece away with a sharp blade, repeat the hormone dip, and try again. Rooted cuttings can be potted up singly, but leave them in the same propagating case for a few days, and remove them slowly step by step to the colder outside –

weaning at this stage is more important than you might think. As you want so many, and are not too bothered about the type, why not stratify some seed, and try propagating that way?

43 Autumn-flowering in spring

A few years ago I bought a laburnum which was supposed to be an autumn-flowering variety. The first year it did flower in the autumn, but since then it has flowered in the spring. I prune it but still it does not bloom in autumn. What else can I do?

An interesting question. This is a case where a common name, based on a reputation or tendency, exceeds the performance and is therefore a misleading misnomer. *Laburnum anagyroides* is the common and popular spring-flowering tree, whose masses of yellow bloom is one of our springtime glories. *L.a. 'Autumnale'* is simply a particular clone that tends to bloom a second time – albeit less intensively – in the autumn.

An occasional bloom out of season is not uncommon with many plants. Why and how it begins is not always clear and, indeed, there is probably more than one cause. One likely explanation is weather, such as a highly destructive late frost, or a very favourable summer leading to an abnormally heavy fruit crop, or a heavy production of next year's flower buds. Such things can throw a plant's timetable out of gear. A heavy crop taxes a tree's strength so that it has a rest next year with little or no bloom or fruit. The following year, with strength built up, it goes mad, then a rest again – an alternate year cropping pattern called 'biennial cropping' that is very common with some apple varieties.

On the other hand it could be something in the genetic make up. Slight variations are occurring all the time and are one of the ways that evolution takes place. In nature, a variation may be to a tree's advantage, and it can be carried over to following generations giving them an advantage over others. On the other hand, there is not much chance of seed from an autumn-flowering apple – or laburnum – being able to ripen before winter, so that whenever that kind of variation occurs, it usually is soon stopped again by natural forces. However, if we can imagine a plant being thwarted in spring, and trying again in autumn, drifting into a wrong timetable that persists and becomes a habit, the next biological step is for the habit to become part of its nature. Even if nature does not think much of it, we may find the variation attractive and desirable, so we make sure that it perpetuates by propagating it vegetatively – apart from physiological variations like colour, shape and form, there are variations in timing that become 'fixed', and there are many examples in addition to the laburnum. Some plants have gone the whole hog and changed drastically from the original pattern, but for the most part, out of season flowering is secondary and additional to the main springtime flush, and this applies to your laburnum. If true autumn flowering is what you expected when you bought this plant, then you were under a misapprehension or were misinformed.

Finally, you remark that you prune it – what on earth for? Laburnum does not need pruning and it is quite likely that you have been pruning away much of the wood that would have borne bloom. Leave it alone to do its own thing in its own out of season time.

44 Propagating magnolia

I have a nice Magnolia soulangeana *and would like to know how to propagate it.*

There are four methods of propagation open to the amateur, of which three – seed, cuttings and grafting – will put you to not a little bother, as satisfying as it may be to succeed, while the fourth is relatively simple. At any time of the year, but preferably in autumn, select a low branch that can be pulled down easily to ground level – this should not be difficult as the tree is wide-spreading and there are likely to be several such branches. At a point where the current year's growth grows on from the last year's, the 'semi-ripe point', make a short upward cut through a leaf joint to make a 'tongue'. You will have to be very careful how you do this because the wood at this point is quite brittle. Using a small paint brush, dust the wood inside the cut with hormone rooting powder, and insert a small wisp of damp sphagnum peat to hold it open. Peg the cut area down into a 4–6 inch (10–15cm) deep excavation in the soil under the tree, again being very careful in case the brittle shoot snaps across the cut. You may find it helpful to place a peg either side of the cut to take the strain of the branch trying to spring up.

If the branch will not come down easily, you will have to take the soil up to the branch by heaping up a mound. Stock trees in the

[127]

nursery often have so much of their lower growth taken for propagation that mounds are heaped up in complete circles round each tree just like craters! One distinct advantage of this 'clone layering' (another and different meaning of the word 'clone') is that it is easier to dig your hand in and under to carefully explore how far rooting has gone. That this is happening is usually apparent by the tip showing obvious signs of vigour and growing away.

At this stage I much prefer to make haste slowly by carefully exposing the original cut without actually disturbing anything, and only partly severing the young plant's dependence on the mother tree. If you cut the plant off before the new root system is up to the job, you will lose the youngster. Give it another 3–6 months before you take it off completely, and remember, magnolias do not like to have their roots disturbed. This means that you will have to lift the young plant with its root ball kept intact by passing a sheet under it, and letting the sheet take the weight of carrying the soil ball – somewhat easier from a mound than digging down into level ground (see question 64).

The alternative to layering into soil is aerial layering, which is described in question 26. You will find soil layering the easiest, however, and the most reliable. It will take at least a year, probably nearer two. You may simply pull a branch down and encourage it to layer itself unaided by the cutting, by throwing a spadeful or two of soil over. This will take twice as long to root, but it could hardly be easier.

Finally, ensure that the rooting area – especially a mound – does not dry out. Use lime-free rain-water, and keep the spot well mulched with spent tea leaves or bags.

45 Transplanting magnolia

Three years ago I bought a Magnolia soulangeana, *and after a slow start it has at last shown signs of growing away. However, when I planted it I think I positioned it too close to a wall – about 2ft (0.6m) away – and I think that it would be better to move it to a better position before it becomes too big. What is the best time to do this?*

Unless you absolutely have to take the enormous risk in moving this tree, my advice would be not to. Magnolias do not like their roots disturbed, and although your plant appeared to be standing still for three years, it was clearly making root and becoming established. Of course the tree will grow lop-sided at least until it reaches the top of the wall, and you may one day have to prop it with a support, but that is better than the likelihood of losing it altogether.

You could have a blessing in disguise. I have not been there for some years now, but at one time I had a very good customer and friend who, out of sheer admiration and worship of the lady, had bought the house and garden – Munstead Wood, Godalming, Surrey – that had belonged to Gertrude Jekyll. At the side of the main lawn, on the outside of the kitchen garden wall near a great sweet chestnut, was planted a magnolia. I have a photograph of it now, made into a Christmas card and sent to me by my friend, and I have never seen a magnolia carrying so much bloom. I do not know the origin of this particular specimen, nor which particular clone of *M. soulangeana* it is (see page 58), but it is clear that the competition of the chestnut and the restricted root run caused by the wall were making it fight, and it was responding by putting up this mass of bloom. Now you can take a leaf out of Gertrude Jekyll's book – and leave your magnolia where it is.

If, notwithstanding, you are determined to take a chance, February is the best time to try, just as the sap is on the move – and don't be surprised if the shock affects the bloom a few weeks later. You will have to start well away from the tree, dig deep, move in slowly, and get right under without any more disturbance than you can possibly help, and lift it, root ball and all, into an already prepared planting hole (see question 64). Keep the soil moist and use every tea bag or morsel of pot drainings to mulch around it. I would not use artificial fertilizers or extra feeding – the roots have to work to get established all over again, and they will not go far if you put nutrient on their doorstep. I wish you luck – but I would leave it where it is.

46 No flowers in 18 years

I have had a magnolia for 18 years and it has not flowered. We feed it well and make sure that it never becomes dry. It has made a lot of growth and is now very big – at least 25ft (7.5m) tall – but does not have any flowers. Would you say it is a rogue (I think it is called) and should we replace it, or is there anything we can do to make it bloom?

You do not say which species this is, but to reach this height in the time makes me sure it is our old friend *M. soulangeana* again. I say again, because this problem crops up as regular as clockwork. There are literally hundreds of different clones of this one variety – look at

[129]

the description in the tree list on page 58. Some of them are notoriously slow to come into flowering – I have heard complaints of 30 years, so you may have some way to go yet!

That is a possible reason, but a much more likely cause is that you are being much too kind – it sounds like your tree is living the life of old Riley! Why should it bother to start going through the process of reproducing itself if it is doing very well as it is? Read question 36, which, although dealing with *Davidia*, also applies here. This magnolia needs a good scare. Stop the feeding, get in among the branches and thin out any that are crossing and badly positioned (see question 47), and prune a few of its roots – if it is ever going to flower at all, this should get it going.

Incidentally, you may be interested to know that there is a direct connection between this principle of wounding a tree to make it bloom and the old, old custom of going round orchards and fruit trees and beating them with sticks, like beating the bounds of the village. The trees were beaten not with silly little wispy wands wielded by choir boys as is the modern way, but were given a good bashing with sticks and cudgels. The wounding and bruising to the trunk's cambium layer – where the sap flows – made the tree fight back and try to perpetuate its kind by making lots of seed or fruit. Some of these old country customs are not as foolish as they seem. I can just imagine an old yokel losing his temper and bashing the hell out of a tree that refused to fruit! He would not have understood why it worked – but he would have reasoned that he had to do it again and again. In a more sophisticated way, go and clout your magnolia, and watch what happens.

47 *Magnolia pruning is different*

When is the best time to prune a magnolia? I have an old tree that has become very congested.

Most deciduous trees are pruned in late autumn and winter when the leaves have fallen, the sap movement is at a standstill, and the tree is dormant. Pruning or cutting back a magnolia is different.

Magnolias have thick fleshy twigs and branches, and the thick leaves hang on until the frost puts paid to them, so the sap movement has kept going, and the wood is soft, plump and sappy. Open wounds at this time, exposed to cold and wet, can quickly take harm and rot.

The job is best left till late June or July, after you have enjoyed the springtime flush of bloom. You would be wise to have a protective like Arbrex ready to seal all cuts, so that the wounds then heal quickly, without the risk of rotting back.

Begin pruning by taking out congestion in the centre. This is secateur work to start with; you should not move on to bigger cutting out with a saw until the congestion and confusion has been cleared enough for you to see what you are doing. Proceed slowly, and before beginning any saw cut, trace out where the branch's offshoots and smaller growths go, and what will be the effect if the branch is removed.

The golden rule of this kind of progressive cutting back is: 'slowly, slowly, catchee monkey'. Small pieces are easier to move safely without splitting, crashing and doing harm. You can always take out a bit more, but you cannot stick it back on again when you go too far. Always visualize what it will look like as every piece goes, and try not to leave great gaping holes or the tree lop-sided. Done by early July, there is still time for young shoots to develop and to clothe the tree again. Of course, the tree may well be smaller, but the key factor that decides if this kind of job has been done well is if you are able to stand back and not be able to see where the removed growth has come from.

48 Soil conditions for Lily-of-the-valley Tree

I have a Pieris *'Wakehurst' form which has been planted for four years, but it has grown only about 2 inches (5cm) during that time, and remains about 15 inches (38cm) high. It looks like a picture in the spring with its red leaves, but I would like to see it growing more quickly towards its full height of 6ft (2m). Our clay soil overlays chalk but has plenty of peat worked into it, and a liquid feed is given during the summer, so what else can be done?*

The 'Lily-of-the-valley Tree' – which, incidentally, can reach to considerably more than 6ft (2m) – does not like lime, so you have taken a risk in planting a subject that is incompatible with the sub-soil in your area. However, all is not lost, but you will have to decide how far you want to go in following two courses of action. You will often see the advice to dig out a hole and fill it with peat before planting lime-haters, and although this may work for a while, inevitably lime seeps in from the sides and up from below, so that, depending on the susceptibility of the plant, it will become progressively more unhappy.

The second and safer course – and I have had many correspondents who have done this with success – is to build up above the lime soil with a raised bed separated from the soil below by an impervious layer like a plastic sheet or a pool liner. If you can make a shallow depression that will tend to hold moisture under the bed, so much the better, but do make quite sure that excess drains out above the sheet edge, and there is no possibility of excess outside seeping back. You could even build a retaining wall of peat blocks, logs, or even loose-laid bricks around the bed to increase its depth. The larger you can make the bed, the more it will be able to resist drying out, which is the big enemy of this method.

Everything you do must be in the direction of preserving acidity and excluding chalk and lime. Never use water straight from the tap: it is almost certain to contain some lime, if only a little. It is not a difficult job to intercept rain-water coming off your roof, and to divert the down pipe into water butts. Peat tends to oxidize slowly and this, plus settling for the first few years, will mean that you will have to make sure that the plants do not get their roots exposed. Mulch every autumn and spring with peat, and if you use soil or compost, make quite sure that it is the ericaceous lime-free kind.

Foliar feeding and spraying over occasionally with Epsom salts are often recommended to ensure that critical deficiencies of magnesium do not occur. This can be helpful – it is unlikely to do any harm – but you should never regard foliar or liquid feeding as a substitute for the natural process of nutrient assimilation via a natural and vigorous root system.

One important thing you can do is never to empty the teapot down the sink or throw away tea bags. Collect the tea leaves and bags into a bucket and use them to water and mulch around the *Pieris* and other lime-haters. Lime tends to lock up iron in a chemical combination that makes it unavailable to plants. *Pieris* and similar plants such as rhododendrons and azaleas need a lot of iron in their leaf make-up, and this is one reason why they dislike lime. The iron and acidity of the tannin in the tea leaves – which come from a species of camellia – is enough to counterbalance the lime in all but the most heavily limed tap-water. It is the only time that tap-water should ever get near your *Pieris*.

This may seem a lot of trouble to go to but, once set up, a raised bed virtually looks after itself and there are many acid-loving bulbs and short growing subjects that can also be underplanted. The idea works very well and you can always add to it and make the bed bigger.

49 *Propagating* Pieris

The soil in this area is sandy and acid so that we are able to grow rhododendrons and other lime-haters quite well. Advice I was given in answer to a question put to a gardening magazine made it sound so easy, but I have tried and tried to propagate my Pieris *'Forest Flame' from cuttings without the slightest sign of success. Now I am trying you to see if you can tell me how to do it.*

The soil in sandy, quick-draining areas invariably tends to leach out soluble nutrients and lime so that a tendency to acidity is quite normal. Therefore, unless you are in an exceptional position, there should be no difficulty in growing this lime-hater, and in propagating into the natural soil where the plant is situated. If it is big enough to have branches low down near the soil, you may be able to layer in the same way as magnolias (see question 44). Failing that, or if you want to persist with cuttings, follow the procedure as outlined for holly in question 42.

You will need the influence of rising heat that derives from a soil-warming cable, and the humid atmosphere of a closed frame or case or a mist propagating unit. This immediately creates a problem: where does the water come from? If you rely on mains water for the pressure to create the mist spray, it probably will contain enough lime to make pieris cuttings root shy. That means collecting rain-water, and obtaining a pump to create the pressure, which results in a lot of expense that puts the cost out of proportion.

Without a mist unit, however, I would say that your only hope with cuttings is to imitate one by lightly spraying several times a day with a hand-held fine mist sprayer, and keep the cuttings inside a closed frame in the greenhouse and with bottom heat. Such advice is not very practical when you have to go to work each day, but that is what is involved. Perhaps a friend or neighbour may be able to help.

However you try to meet these requirements, it will be a challenge – but this is all part of the satisfaction you feel when the first roots appear! It is all very well to keep trying, but unless you can go a long way to providing these special conditions for a very difficult subject, I doubt that you will ever enjoy that satisfaction of glueing roots onto *Pieris*. You will stand a much better chance by layering.

50 Cutting back a cherry

When is the right time to cut back a large overgrown flowering cherry?

There isn't a right time – it should not be cut at all! However, if needs must and you really are forced to carry out such sacrilege, the first thing to do is realize the risk you are taking and to have the right precautions ready to hand for immediate use. Cherries, like plums, are liable to be infected by the dreadful 'silver leaf disease'. This is a fungus, and at certain times of the year the spores are in the air in abundance. As soon as they get into a tree, normally through a break, a cut or other open wound, the disease quickly runs through the twig, into the branch, into the trunk and throughout the tree. The first sign that you usually notice is that the leaves turn a silvery hue, even whitish. It may just be restricted to one branch, when a severe amputation might save the remaining body, but it is more likely to have gone too far and the whole tree become infected – and there is then no hope.

That is the risk you take, but if the job has to be done, do it on a dry windless day in July. If the weather is dry during April, May and June, give the soil around the tree a good soaking so that there is no shortage of sap when it comes to cutting. This is important because rising sap exuding from wounds quickly coagulates in dry air to form a natural barrier of gum. Assist the exclusion of any fungus spores by painting all cuts with Arbrex as soon as they are made – literally secateurs or saw in one hand, Arbrex in the other.

The spores of this fungus are most active during mild spells in winter and spring, and these peak periods are avoided by accepting the risk of bleeding while the sap is rising – it is the lesser of two evils. Be thorough with the Arbrex protective, and examine large cuts every day for a few weeks to make quite sure that there are no cracks in the paint cover. At the slightest sign of opening, repeat the protection.

51 Cherry with two colours

Our cherry tree usually has copper-coloured foliage and pink flowers, but this year a few small branches at the bottom had white flowers and light green leaves. What is the reason for this? Does the tree need feeding?

This question is typical of a very common problem – it occurs regularly and repeatedly. Evidently, this is a tree that was 'top worked', which means that the pink variety was budded or grafted on to a stem of the common wild cherry or 'Gean', which has white flowers. The same thing happens with roses and all manner of trees and shrubs when a vigorous rootstock is trying to push its energy into a less vigorous top – the 'scion' – that has been worked onto it. You can liken it to a pressure that builds up in the rootstock, and which bursts out by forming shoots of its own.

In a rose, this is called a briar, and it is normally easy to see when it happens because the colour and form of the leaves are quite different. With other subjects it is not always so noticeable – the leaves may be very similar. Shoots that appear down the length of a standard stem you know are in the wrong place, and so they usually get rubbed off when very young and soft. However, when the shoots are high up in the vicinity of the graft, they may easily be mistaken for graft wood and allowed to grow, until they become mature enough to carry bloom and the trouble comes to light. The problem then – as the question indicates – is that the shoots have become 'branches' and, instead of being rubbed off when infantile, they will have to be cut away with secateurs. Even rubbing away with finger and thumb should involve painting the spot with Arbrex, but with a much larger wound the risk of infection is that much greater, and from this point on I suggest that you take very much to heart the subject matter of the previous question.

You should also appreciate that in removing a 'branch' you are removing a sizeable safety valve with the result that the stock may well try to break out again elsewhere. You would be wise, therefore, to study and compare the leaves so that you can more readily recognize differences in future early enough for them to be removed before they need the knife.

52 A Prunus triloba *that will not flower*

Please can you tell us how to get the lovely pink flowers on a Prunus triloba *growing against a wall at the back of the vegetable border. We have had it for ten years – in the first two years it flowered quite well, but since then, very little.*

This was one of the cherry varieties in greatest demand in London parks. We propagated hundreds every year, and never had this problem. It is one of the most beautiful and reliable of all the cherries, so we are looking for a clue in your cultivation of it. I think that we may have found it in 'growing against a wall at the back of the vegetable border'. The tree is in the wrong place, not for growing, but because it gets in the way.

Whether bush, half or full standard, it really needs all-round space to grow and develop as a balanced specimen. The flower buds form on wood produced the previous year, mostly on shoots but sometimes on little spurs on older wood. With a tree growing against a wall, new shoots will break away from the wall at more or less right angles and into the working area of the vegetable border. I reckon that you pruned these shoots out of your way.

If you let the tree grow unpruned, as you should, very soon all the weight will be on one side, and you may have to prop it up to stop it leaning over. This is all you can do, unless you want to risk losing it altogether by digging and lifting out what is by now a well-established tree. I would suggest that you lose a small part of your vegetable border, leave the tree alone and let it grow.

[Note: This diagnosis was confirmed by the questioner, who later reported what a marvellous tree it had become.]

53 *Amanogawa suckers*

Lots of young shoots are sprouting from the soil around the base of my 'Amanogawa' cherry tree. Are they young 'Amanogawas' and would they be worth lifting and planting in other parts of my garden?

Prunus 'Amanogawa' is always bottom-worked from near ground level because of its fastigiate upright growth, and not top-worked like most standard trees. The feather shape then starts just above ground level, and not from the top of a standard stem, which would make it look distinctly odd. It is not all that unusual for suckers to form – the root-stock does not even have the length of a standard stem in which to spread its energy, so the roots try instead and put up shoots that may be near the base of the stem, or more distant from it, as when suckers come up in the lawn.

Root-stock shoots are useless to you, but if you cut them away you will only be pruning and more will grow. Instead, pull the suckers away – use pliers if you cannot get enough grip with your hands. A jagged wound does not produce the callus tissue like a clean wound, and the chances of adventitious shoots (more suckers) is reduced.

However, don't forget to paint the wound with Arbrex protective before replacing soil.

54 Upright-growing weeper

I have a tall straight-growing branch growing from my 'Cheal's Weeping Cherry'. At first I thought it would turn over and weep like the other branches, but there is no sign of it doing so. What should I do about it?

First, read question 51. Flowers of a different colour are one thing, but when the shoot that breaks out from the stock has a different conformation to the scion – which it is bound to in the case of a weeper – you very soon have a pig with one ear down and the other standing up. The leaves in this case are also quite different, and if you see a shoot like this in future, don't wait to see if it will weep – take it out at once. The danger in waiting is that the stock pours more and more energy into the upright 'briar' and progressively ignores the graft, which suffers, becomes starved, and eventually, if left unattended, will fail altogether and die.

Suffering growth is weak growth, unable to resist ever-present pest and disease attack. You can see how, if you do not keep an eye open for little things that go wrong, you can soon have a can of worms. Adjacent questions give plenty of detail on cutting out, and the need for protecting open wounds. This cherry is not a long-lived tree at the best of times and is particularly vulnerable to silver leaf disease.

55 Pruning a weeper

I have a couple of 'Cheal's Weeping Cherries' that have grown very well, and the long branches have now reached ground level. Some say these should be pruned just short of the ground, others tell us to leave them. What is the correct procedure please?

It would be interesting for you to go back to those offering the advice and ask them why! 'Cheal's Weeping Cherry', more correctly named as *Prunus* 'Kiku-shidare Sakura' is not a long-lived tree, and I have seen a great many with their lives made even shorter by diseases like silver leaf and canker that have entered through untreated wounds. The frequent and serious point of entry with this tree is where the long weeping stems reach ground level and blow about in the wind. When the ground is lawn, the abrasive effect is not serious, but a concrete or

[137]

gravel path or a rockery are bound to cause laceration and abrasion, and that is enough, the door is wide open to infection. It is wise therefore to carefully prune the stem tips just clear of the ground – and at once to paint the wounds with Arbrex protective.

56 Transplanting oaks

Having lost some particularly fine oaks in the storm, I would like to replace them with some of their own acorn seedlings. I don't think there would be any problems in finding enough as there are a number of 6–9 inch (15–23 cm) self-sown seedlings germinating where they fell in previous years and we have been careful not to harm more than could be helped when clearing up. However, I read somewhere that there is a special problem with transplanting oaks – and come to think of it, I don't recall seeing oaks very often in garden centres and nurseries. Could you tell me anything about this and how and when to move the seedlings?

Your apprehension is well founded. A germinating acorn very quickly puts down a long tap root of 1ft (30cm) in its first year when the top is little more than 3–4 inches (7.5–10cm), so your second year 6–9 inch (15–23cm) seedlings will have penetrated to perhaps twice as deep. There is little fibrous root at this stage; the absorption ability is mainly in the growing tip, and if the tap root is broken, the seedling is in for a hard time. This is why it is difficult to transplant self-sown oaks unless they are very young and small. If the seedlings were growing in containers it might be easier to transplant them, but only might, because it is not natural for a tap root to coil round the bottom of a pot. Oak seedlings just do not like their roots being disturbed, nor do they like being transplanted, so they are not very good subjects for garden centres.

The best way is the natural way, to sow the acorn where you want it to grow. If there are no seedlings near enough to where you want, and you have to move one or two, accept before you start that you will have to dig deep to lift the tap root without breaking it, and replant to the same depth, again without harm. Do the job in late November or early December when the seedling has gone to sleep.

57 Pear leaves in curlers

I planted a willow-leaved pear earlier this spring and its leaves are now curling badly. Also, several of the small branches seem to be dying back from the ends. Is this a disease of some kind?

Well, it is a bit early yet for it to have picked up disease. The problem could be sap-sucking pests, but if they are present, it is more likely that they are aggravating the main cause. Take a careful look under the curled leaves for any sign of insect pests – most likely sap-sucking aphids. If they are about, clean them off with an insecticide.

You do not make it clear whether the tree was bare root or pot-grown – *Pyrus salicifolia* is sometimes sold bare root – but in either case, spring was much too late for planting. Four or five months earlier, the roots would have had time to move and develop some absorbing ability, and a dry root ball would have had more time to soak up some moisture from the soil around it. The tree has put out leaves on the strength of the sap within it, and been unable to support them. It is in a bad way if branches are dying back as well, and you will have to be very lucky to save it.

However, it is worth a try, so sink half a dozen 3–4 inch (7.5–10cm) clay pots in the ground to the rim, as close as you can to the original soil ball or, if it was bare rooted, about 6–9 inches (15–23cm) from the base of the stem. Stuff some newspaper into the drainage hole of each pot to allow a slow leak. Give the surrounding soil a good soaking and leave the pots full of water, topping them up each day for at least a month or until autumn, whichever is first. I would also spray the foliage lightly each day with clear water, to try to get the leaves to absorb a little water and delay falling, but make sure you spray very lightly in case you knock off the leaves. If you are too late and they have shrivelled dry or they fall off, then you have to try to prevent any more moisture loss from the twigs and branches. See if you can get some S600 transplanting spray, and give the remaining growth a coating with it. If you have difficulty in obtaining S600, contact the manufacturer (Synchemicals Ltd) direct – the address is on page 221.

This is a lovely tree, and I hope that you save it. If you do lose it, try again, but next time read the chapters here on planting and do the job properly. Prepare well, buy well, and plant well – in autumn.

58 *Removing* Rhus *suckers*

Is there any way that I can stop a Rhus *tree sending up strong suckers all round the base? They are an awful nuisance, and if there is no way to stop them I think I will have to get rid of it.*

This is evidently *Rhus typhina* and, as suckering is the plant's natural method of reproduction, there is nothing you can do to stop it. If you decide that the attractive foliage is worth the price you have to pay to get it, removal of unwanted suckers will be a constant job, and you will need to be careful how you do it.

With a spade or trowel, clear soil down to the root from which each sucker arises. They will need to be long enough for you to grasp each firmly and pull it away – avoid cutting unless you have to, as this is more likely to encourage yet more suckers. You will also need to be wearing a stout glove to tug at these suckers because, if you stress your skin when in contact with this plant, you will be quite likely to develop a nasty rash. Some people are very allergic to even touching the plant, and grasping and tugging with bare hands greatly increases the chances of finding out that you are one of them.

59 Rowan seed needs special treatment

My mountain ash has produced an enormous crop of berries this year, and it looks so nice that I would like to grow some more trees just like it. I have tried before but never had any luck. Can the tree be grown from seed, and if so is there any special way to do it?

The berries of mountain ash, like those of holly, hawthorn and many others, will often be seen germinating and seedlings growing quite naturally where they have fallen. This can be a bit off-putting to say the least, when you sow them, give every encouragement, and nothing happens! The difference is that the seed that germinates naturally has been exposed to weather and frost, and you have been too protective and kind.

Collect the berries, preferably those that have fully ripened and fallen – but don't let the birds gobble them first. Put a layer of sand in a tray or pot, scatter berries on this, then another layer of sand about 1 inch (2.5cm) thick, then more berries and more sand in alternate layers. This process is called 'stratifying', that is, seed and sand in strata. Wrap the tray or pot in wire netting to keep mice or birds away and place it in an open cold frame or similar protected position in a border, where rain and weather can do their work.

If you sow the berries as soon as they are ready to fall in autumn, they should have had five months or more of weathering by spring, and if this has been severe enough to have done its job, much of the seed will be ready to germinate, although some of it may require another year. Tip out the sand and rescue the berries, but be very careful how you do this. We often used to find seed already on the move, with embryo roots forming, and they should not be damaged at this stage. Handling them with care, you can either sow them into John Innes seed compost in deep pans or trays, singly and about 2 inches (5cm) apart so that those that germinate can more easily be lifted in autumn without too much root disturbance to any adjacent but slower seed, or you can sow them direct into 3-inch (7.5-cm) pots. In either case, seed that does not germinate the first year will often do so after a second year's weathering.

Keep potted-up seedlings exposed outside but protected from heavy snow and very severe freezing. An open cold frame is best, as if conditions become really bad, you can put the covers on for a time until the worst is over. Naturally, under the parent trees, seed will invariably have weathered for perhaps two or even three years in the accumulating leaf litter before it is ready to germinate.

60 Willows from cuttings

Is it possible to strike cuttings from a weeping willow tree?

Willow wands 2–3 ft (60–90 cm) long are the easiest things to root. There are two usual methods. During October, make a slit trench by driving in the spade to about 9 inches (23cm) deep, levering it slightly, just enough to open a slit, and lift the spade out, repeating alongside to form a slit trench as long as required. Trim the wands with a sharp knife just below a leaf joint – you probably will not even need hormone rooting powder, they root so easily – and simply push the wands into the slit until they 'bottom' firmly, about 6 inches (15cm) apart. Drive the spade in again 2–3 inches (5–7.5cm) away and lever the soil over hard against the cuttings, closing the first slit but leaving the second open. Go along the row and give a firm tug to make sure that they are all tightly held. They will have grown away by the following autumn, and you can lift them for transplanting to where required or into nursery rows 2ft (60cm) apart for growing on or training up as whip stems.

The other method, often done where large numbers are involved (as in a nursery) and where space is a bit limited, is to tie the wands into bundles of 50, and to heel in the bundles in trenches. In spring, when they have weathered over the winter, the bundles are lifted, and planted out singly into rows.

[141]

Rooting is very easy. I once had a know-it-all neighbour on an allotment. He was not going to pay good money for pea sticks, but instead gathered a great bundle from where trees – willows – had been cut back near the lake across the common. His peas were not so good, but we all had to admire the biggest and finest willow hedge for miles around!

61 Useless lilac suckers

I have potted up several suckers from my Charles Joly lilac tree, and they are growing well. Is there any special treatment they will need before they are planted out in the garden?

Yes! Your young plants will need to be thrown away! Sorry to dent your pride and satisfaction in growing these suckers, but they will only give you great disappointment when you see the first flowers.

The named cultivars of *Syringa vulgaris*, of which the double dark red 'Charles Joly' is one, are propagated by grafting onto the more vigorous wild *S. vulgaris* stock, and the suckers that you have potted up will therefore only have the small flower spikes of the wild type. The alternative to throwing them away would be to use them as stocks, and to try your hand at grafting.

Another way would be to bend down lower branches of the tree, and layer into the soil in the same way as for magnolia (see question 44). Rooting should not be very difficult, but the resulting plant can never be as good as the parent because it will be on its own roots and lacking the vigour of the wild type being pushed into it which the parent enjoys. That is why we go to all the trouble of budding and grafting weaker onto stronger growing types.

62 Wisteria as a standard

We have been given a 2-ft (60-cm) tall wisteria as a present and would like your opinion as to whether it can be trained as a standard. I asked about it at a radio programme in our village society, and was told that it could not be done, but somebody got up and said he had seen it done. He didn't go down too well, I thought, for contradicting the experts, and I missed him after the meeting to find out more. I thought I would ask what you think.

Why on earth shouldn't it be done? I have seen standards several times, and I have grown one myself – all that is needed is a little imagination and a little understanding of the plant.

First, the natural habit of wisteria, like many other plants, is to clamber rather than climb over and into other shrubs and trees, or our cultivated garden equivalent – fences, pergolas, walls and, perhaps where most often seen, the fronts of houses. All it needs is something to hold it up! It will not stand by itself as a standard tree, as that is not its habit, and even when old and having a substantial trunk, it is really too brittle and top-heavy to be safe. But it can be trained over a suitable support to take that form, and is frequently grown over pergolas and up into other trees, so why not a tree-like support?

Many years ago, I was shown what to me at the time was a novel way of growing blackberries – like hops – on the farm of a well-known soft fruit grower near Maidstone, Kent. He grew them that way for another reason, and I am sure that his heavy crops were something of an accident and not entirely intentional! However, some time later when I learned the botanical explanation of the heavier crops, I extended the principle into an improved method of cordon fruit growing, to a different kind of pergola for roses and, more than successfully, for a wisteria. The wisteria is not very fast growing, but the early results were very encouraging. I have not seen it for several years now, but the last time I heard from my correspondent, he reported that it gets better every year.

You are going to train a large umbrella that is not altogether sure on its own stem or trunk, and will therefore need support throughout a long life. A wooden post will decay in time, so you will have to erect a stout concrete post of the kind used for chain link fencing, or build a brick pillar with a steel rod core to a minimum height of 6ft (2m) – 8ft (2.5m) would be better, to leave room for you to walk under with the bloom hanging. Arrange two or three long pole or tubular supports, approximately 12–14 ft (3.6–4 m) long cross-wise across the top to form a large cross or a six-point star on top of the post like the spokes of a wheel. Connect the ends with wire or rods to form a rim, and again at every foot (30cm) or so back to the centre so that you have a spider's web.

Train your wisteria up the central post, then shoots out along each spoke to the first intersection. Bend the soft shoot along the wire or rod to the second spoke, along the spoke to the next intersection, and so on, so that the shoots follow a zig-zag route to the outer rim, then work

[143]

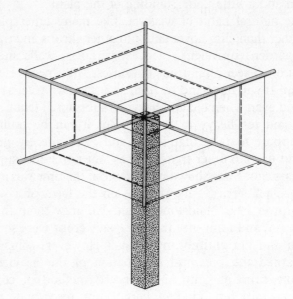

Fig. 12   An umbrella canopy 12ft (3.6m) in diameter, 8ft (2.5m) high, provides an excellent support for wisteria and other climbers – an effective and unusual feature for your garden.

your way back again. The repeated bending is important, because it restricts sap flow, and causes the wisteria to react by making more bloom than you thought possible. The only way to get a wisteria to take the form of a conventional tree is to let it clamber through one, but the method described here is an unusual and most beautiful tree-like variation. The same method can be adapted for many other subjects – the more vigorous roses are especially suitable.

63   Propagating Leyland Cypress

Can you please tell me how to propagate leylandii *conifers? I wish to grow a hedge of it but the cost of so many trees would make it very expensive.*

First, I suggest that you read the full description of *Cupressocyparis leylandii* in the conifer list section so that you know something of the troubles arising from the several different clones of the plant. Having sorted that out, you will realize that it would be wise to restrict your cuttings to one parent tree so that the progeny are identical. Commercial production uses mist units and bottom heat, but even then, the failure proportion can be high. Without mist, it will be higher still and much slower – a closed case and humid atmosphere will be vital. If you cannot provide the bottom heat, it will not be worth trying, so don't waste your time.

Make the cuttings 3–5 inches (7.5–13cm) in length. They should be pulled away from a main lateral stem, with a heel attached. Trim them smooth with a very sharp knife or razor blade, dip in hormone rooting powder, and follow the procedure described for holly cuttings in question 42.

I have tried two alternative methods with some success, but you will still need the humid closed case and bottom heat. Cut a length of plastic film 3–4 inches (7.5–10cm) wide and 6ft (2m) long. Lay this flat on the table and cover it with a ¼ inch (6mm) layer of two parts sand to one part fine sieved peat. Water with a fine rose or spray so that the peat is thoroughly wet. Lay the prepared cuttings on the mixture with the foliage overlapping one side and the cutting ends about 1–1½ inches (2.5–4cm) from the other edge. Begin rolling from one end, trapping the cuttings in the roll, and keeping it as tight as you can or the mixture of sand and peat will fall out. It should end up looking like a large swiss roll, with foliage out of one side. When it is complete, use string or stout elastic bands to hold the roll tight and firm, and stand it on wet and warm sand and peat in a closed frame. Occasionally lift the roll to see when roots are protruding, and when enough appear, simply unroll and pot up.

A clay pot is required for the second method, and preferably one that is old fashioned and porous, not the modern kind with an impervious ultra-smooth surface. Plug the drainage hole with glue, or better still, cement. Next, find another pot into which the first will fit leaving a gap of no more than ¼–½ inch (6–12mm) all round. 'Pot up' the smaller pot in the larger, filling the gap around and under with equal parts of sand and peat and, using a pencil, to make the holes, push in hormone-dipped cuttings about 1½ inches (4cm) apart. Stand the pots in the closed frame, water them well and keep the inner pot full so that water slowly percolates through the porous inner pot to the compost. Rooting will become evident when you see them coming through the drainage hole of the outer pot.

64 Moving conifers

I want to move some so-called dwarf conifers that are now over 6ft (2m) tall to a different part of the garden. I gather that it is risky to do this, but they have to be moved. I don't want to lose them and would be grateful if you could tell me how it should be done.

Decide exactly where the trees are to go, and take out planting holes about 2–2½ft (60–75cm) wide and two spits deep to begin with, although you may have to vary this as you find out the size of each root ball. Three days before you attempt the move spray each tree as thoroughly as you can with S600 transplanting spray, and again two days later – the day before the move. This will go a long way to reduce moisture loss from the foliage, which will not be replaced until new root action has developed. Have the equivalent of a couple of buckets of compost, peat, or the contents of old spent grobags ready nearby to put under each root ball as it is planted. Next, you will need a 6ft (2m) square heavy-gauge plastic sheet or a heavy sack opened out. Roll this up half way. With a trowel, or very carefully with a spade, and starting well away from each tree (the distance will probably vary from tree to tree, so you will have to treat each one on its own merits) begin lifting soil a few inches deep, then nearer and deeper. You are looking for the first signs of the roots in order to find out how far they extend, and how wide the root ball is likely to be. As soon as you find them, scratch a mark right round the tree, the same distance from the trunk. You will have to try to keep outside this ring. Dig a trench half way round the tree and throw the soil well clear. Clear out the loose soil and, from the bottom, take out a second spit at an angle, working under the tree. If you see any sign of root you will have to go deeper. If a third spit is required, you will need to widen the trench, taking soil from the outer edge.

When you are approximately half way under, push the rolled-up edge of the plastic sheet down beneath the tree, with the loose edge pulled up and around the base. Half-fill the trench under the sheet so that, as it comes free later, the tree will be supported on the backfill. Then repeat the process from the other side, digging down and under part of the tree at a time, if this is easier for you, until you are able to reach under to the rolled-up part of the sheet and can unroll it, pulling the edge out, so that the tree root ball has a stout sheet under it. You will almost certainly need help to lift and carry the tree to its new position. Unless it is light enough for you to do this singlehanded –

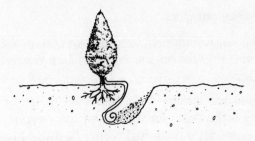

Fig. 13 *To move evergreen and established trees, first dig under from one side, roll heavy plastic sheeting to the bottom of the hole, and partly backfill (to support the tree while you dig from the other side).*

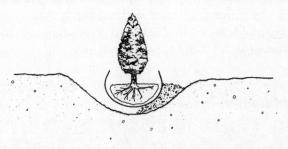

Fig. 14 *Dig from the other side until you reach the roll of sheet; pull the sheet out, leaving the root and soil ball intact in the centre of the sheet. Wrap and bind the sheet around the trunk, then gently drag the tree to its new position.*

and it will be remarkable if it is – don't be heroic and struggle, as that will only endanger the root ball, but get help. When the tree is alongside the planting position, you will see if the hole is big enough or needs enlarging. Fork up the bottom, work all the compost in and tread it firm with the bottom at just the right depth – or as near as you can judge – to let the root ball rest with the tree at exactly the same planting depth as before, not deeper, and not more shallow. With assistance, lift the tree into the hole, with the best side facing the point from which the tree will be seen, and roll or slide the sheet out, whichever is easiest and less likely to damage the rootball. Finally, back fill, tread firm, and there you are. Care at every stage is the secret of moving evergreens and conifers – there are no short cuts, unless you want regrets.

[147]

65 Trimming conifers

My five-year-old leylandii *hedge is growing fast and I feel that I should begin trimming it to thicken and shape it. Can you please tell me the best time to do this?*

Whether you are aiming for a flat-faced hedge or a loose informal screen, July is the best time to start for two reasons. First, the growth is slowing down after the initial spring flush, and cutting back is then less of a shock to the plants. Secondly, having made that initial spring growth, over-long protruding shoots can be tidied up.

From there on the ways diverge. A flat-faced hedge requires shears or clippers to cut through foliage regardless, and produce the flat face consisting of numerous half-leaves and shoot ends. Informal trimming is much more skilful and is done with secateurs. The art is to achieve the desired shape, form and size without being able to see where you have cut. No half-leaves will show, and no crudely cut straight edges – when finished, the job should look untouched.

66 Golden conifers in the shade

The only place I would be able to plant the golden conifer I like is shaded for half the day. Friends tell me it will lose most of its gold in shade – is this true?

It is best to regard all golds and yellow-golds, margined and variegated, in the following way. All plants need to convert the energy of sunlight for their own life processes and for the elaboration of their physical structure. This they do via the process called photosynthesis, in the presence of the green-coloured chlorophyll which gives leaves and stems their green appearance.

At some time in their evolutionary history some plants adapted to and learned to live with reduced amounts of sunlight, and this could have had any one of three basic effects. Not so much chlorophyll was needed in total so, first, the leaves could be smaller or not so numerous. Secondly, the leaves could remain the same size, or even become bigger, with the green chlorophyll more thinly and sparsely distributed throughout the leaf structure so that the green colour becomes pale and no longer masks other coloured substances that may be present, such as yellows and golds. The third effect is that part of the leaf remains green with the normal concentration of chlorophyll, while the remainder contains less (yellow and gold) or no (silver and white) chlorophyll at all. Such areas can be well defined like margins or large 'blotches', or the area can be fragmented into spots and mottled colouring.

Whatever form the effect takes, the basic principle is the ability to survive on reduced intensity and amount of light, translated into normal sunlight but less chlorophyll needed to convert it. It follows, therefore, that if you take such a plant and reduce the light availability by planting in shade, it can only make up the deficiency by producing more chlorophyll, with the result that the yellow and gold becomes masked by the extra green, and so do the margins, spots and blotches. That is why your golden conifer will very likely lose its good looks.

67 Conifer seed and heat

Is bottom heat required to grow conifers from seed? Or does it have to be stratified? I have lots of very nice trees and very many cones. I would like to try to propagate them.

If plants have evolved to live in certain ways, it is very seldom indeed that humans can interfere and get them to grow better in a way that is different to their nature. Very often, they can be induced to grow better than naturally but only by understanding the natural processes, and helping them to work more efficiently by providing what the plant likes, and reducing or removing what it does not like. We cannot dictate to a plant and tell it that it ought to grow a different way because we think it would be better.

Conifers seed themselves, and appear to have managed very well for millions of years without us by dropping seed to the soil, albeit in several different ways, and, with luck, finding a suitable spot in which they can germinate. If we are to improve the luck, and the chances of germination, it will consist of measures like preventing the seed being eaten, and reducing competition from other plants crowding them. Just as you like a holiday and feel better in a warm climate, they sometimes respond to a cosy temperature, but not always. Conifers don't need a soft living, they do not respond to it. Imitate nature by scattering loose seed on the surface of wet seed compost and covering them with a thin ¼ inch (6mm) layer of leaf litter – either peat, or litter from the floor under the parent trees – and leave them outside, protected from mice, squirrels, birds and other interested parties.

Some conifers have come to expect to experience really blistering winters, perhaps more than one, and perhaps some seed found it an advantage not to drop out of the cone, but to hang on for a year or two until the cone fell off the tree, or it rotted away before releasing the seed. It is no good telling a seed that wants to wait a few years for its cone to rot away that you have a better idea for it, to come and snuggle down in your nice warm propagator! You can do no better than to study and try to understand the differences and idiosyncrasies of your particular species, how they grow and germinate in their natural habitat – and try to help nature, not change it.

68 Stopping a Monkey Puzzle

I would like to stop my 'Monkey Puzzle' tree from growing any taller. It is already 10ft (3m) high, and if it gets any bigger it will block out light from our rooms. How can we do this please: is it a simple matter of lopping the top off? Is there a special time of the year to do it?

This is a classic case of not knowing or taking the trouble to find out about a tree before planting it. A 'Monkey Puzzle' wants to make 60ft (18.5m) or more – how on earth do you expect it to stop at 10ft (3m)? To top it is sheer mutilation – and what is it doing so near the house that it takes light from the rooms? The only thing you can do is remove it. Rather than killing it outright, give it to the local Parks Department, insisting that they lift it properly (see question 64), and replace it with a much shorter subject. Cutting a tree short like this is no better than this awful modern craze or attitude of 'expendability' – plant it, grow it, and when it gets too big, throw it out and start again.

69 Monkey Puzzle from seed

A friend has given me some seeds from his 'Monkey Puzzle' tree. Is there any special treatment for these? Could you tell me the best time to sow, and if the seeds should be sown in the greenhouse?

Unless we have had an unusually long, dry, 'South American' summer, it is doubtful whether the seed will prove viable taken from a tree grown in this country, so don't be too disappointed if it fails to germinate. However, there is no harm in trying – audacity has its own rewards. As a youngster, I only had to read or be told that something would not grow, to become determined to prove the clever sticks wrong! Provided that you observe nature's basic principles, and have persistence and patience, you can sometimes surprise yourself. Go with nature, not against it, find out where the plant comes from, how it grows, the conditions it has at home, and try to imitate them, and if the conditions for fertilization were favourable at the right time – the big obstacle in this different climate – you may be lucky.

The optimum sowing period is February to April. Prepare pots or trays with a fierce draining compost mix of a very mild nutrient base – equal parts John Innes seed compost and coarse sand. Sow the seed on edge, water well with rain-water, not tap water, and place on the greenhouse staging or in a propagator where a steady temperature of 65°F (18°C) can be maintained.

As seedlings emerge, slacken the temperature gradually to 55°F (13°C) and, when they are big enough to handle, pot them carefully and with the minimum of root disturbance into 3-inch (7.5-cm) pots, filled with a slightly richer mixture – two parts John Innes No.2, one part peat and one part silver sand. Water freely in the summer, but cut back during autumn so that, in winter, the watering is just enough to keep the soil moist. By all means stand the seedlings outside during the summer, but do be careful that they do not dry out. Pot on the following year, or plant out into permanent position, with two cloches stood on end around each seedling for protection until it is 9–12 inches (23–30cm) high.

Do read question 68, and realize that this can become a very large tree.

70 Trees for a windbreak

My garden is over 270ft (82m) long, and both it and the house are very exposed to biting cold winds coming from north and east – there is so little to stop them here on this coast. I want to plant a really effective wind break, but the wind is sometimes so strong that I find it difficult to imagine how a row of conifers would be able to stand up to the job. Also, why is it that leylandii *and* lawsoniana *– which look much the same to me – are so different in price? A local nurseryman tells me that they can be planted at any time of the year because they are grown in pots. Is he having me on?*

There are several points here, so we will deal with them one at a time. First, *Cupressocyparis leylandii,* to give it its full name, is different to *Chamaecyparis lawsoniana,* and is more expensive for two main reasons. It is quicker growing, so everybody wants it for the quick establishment of evergreen screens and hedges, and glueing roots onto its cuttings is a somewhat difficult and frustrating business. Nevertheless, it is so much better for the job that enough people are prepared to pay for it and keep the price up.

Grown in close proximity, as in a hedge, the lower branches of *C. lawsoniana* have a nasty tendency to wither and die. There are many front garden hedges that can be seen in this condition – plantings of *C. lawsoniana* were considerable some years ago when it had a wave of popularity as an alternative to the ubiquitous privet.

Except for one or two varieties of eucalyptus – which are not hardy enough or have the right kind of foliage for a windbreak – *C. leylandii* is the fastest growing evergreen, rivalled only by *Thuja plicata* 'Atrovirens' (syn. *T. lobbii*). The thuja is not quite so quick growing, but is a lovely bright green colour, has dense screening foliage and is perfectly hardy.

Being pot-grown you can plant it at any time of year, provided that you bear in mind that once evergreens reach 2–2½ft (60–76cm) in height, your chances of a 100 per cent successful transplant diminish rapidly, which in turn means that the risk increases that a gap or difference will result from the replacement. Exposed to strong winds, your plantings will be more prone than usual to wind drying, and the larger the leaf area of bigger plants, the greater the risk. You will need to plant well, with lots of moisture-retaining organic matter underneath, careful attention to watering and, as an extra precaution, a thorough coating with S600 transplanting spray to reduce moisture evaporation to the very minimum. It is all very well advising you that you can plant at any time if you are dealing with just a few, but with a run of 270ft (82m), it is not so easy – appearance becomes very important and gaps are going to spoil the effect.

The plants' effectiveness in deflecting winds as strong as you describe, blowing on exposed north-east facing positions, will depend upon how close you plant them, which in turn will affect how many plants you will need and how much the job will cost. Rather than plant unneccessarily close in order to achieve a thick screen, why not copy the Dutch way of protecting their buildings on the exposed North Sea polders by starting on the windward side with low growing shrubs, taller ones behind, then short trees and finally taller trees with the house in the lee. In this way, even the fiercest wind is gently eased up and over.

A row or two of green privet on the outside would be hardy, relatively cheap and probably save its cost in preventing losses to your young conifers while they are becoming established. Keep their tops clipped in a wedge shape, and, like a walled garden, you will be surprised at the change in conditions on the lee side.

71 Spruce needles dropping

Could you please suggest a reason why the needles fall from my spruce trees – which in consequence always look rather bare? We rake up the carpet of needles as we have been advised, and do not let them lie. We have tried to compost them without success, they seem so resistant. I am sure that we are doing something wrong somewhere, as the trees seem to be more and more unhappy.

It sounds as if you have entirely the wrong soil conditions. Both evergreen and deciduous needle-leaved conifers – the pines, firs, spruces and larches – tend to drop their needles for one of two diametrically opposed reasons. Either the soil is too dry, and the trees cannot lift enough moisture to sustain the needles, so they shed the load. Too much water, on the other hand, causes the minute osmotic hair roots to recede and die back. The absorption ability is reduced and again, the evaporation organs, the leaves, have to be shed. Which is it – too dry, or too wet?

If you are faced with the former situation, logic suggests that you should try to increase the organic content of the soil by letting remain what falls naturally, and not rake the needles up. Where conifers grow naturally and shed their needles, nobody rakes them up, and all that you are doing is to deny even this contribution to the soil. If it really is that dry and barren, is it not more logical to try to inject organic matter instead of removing what little there is?

All conifer leaves contain resins and other substances that make them resistant to the natural processes of decomposition, so you have to help them. Rather than rake the needles off, it would be better to merely disturb them and break up the mat so that rain can penetrate instead of being shed off, and so that air can get in to allow decomposition to proceed. If you are in the habit of mowing grass off the lawn – a somewhat questionable procedure on soil of this type, but if that is what you do – throw it out into the conifer debris so that

[153]

the rapid decomposition of the grass acts as a boost. A little light forking into the top couple of inches or centimetres can work wonders with the bacteria population. Of course if you can spare any compost at all, that also will help. It is a slow process, and can take years to have appreciable effect. As the trees seem so unhappy, you can at least try to help them by spreading around a slow-release balanced manure like Humber Compound or Growmore (see page 10) and in dry weather lay the hose out and let it slowly trickle.

If your soil is wet, boggy, and badly drained, however, you have two courses of action. Either you have to drain off the surplus, or you have to live with it. Getting rid of water can be easier said than done – excavating and laying in drains is pointless unless you have a lower position for the water to run to. If the problem is excessive wet due to something that cannot be remedied, like a stream or a pond, it might be more rational to accept that trees like spruce are growing in conditions that are unsuited to them, to accept that they cannot be expected to live much longer and to think now about planting replacements like the swamp cypress *Taxodium*. This is similar in appearance, will revel in the conditions and, if you plant now, it will have become nicely established by the time that the spruces finally succumb.

72 *Pink laburnum turning yellow*

We have in our garden a 22-year-old pink laburnum. Over the last few years more and more of it has been reverting back to yellow, and we now have a tree with flowers of the two colours. Is there any way that we can stop this reversion and return the tree to its original all-pink colour?

Thank you for a very interesting question. Your pink *Laburnocytisus* is not 'reverting' in the sense that it is a 'sport' or 'variation' reverting back to the original type, colour, and habits. What is happening is altogether more interesting, and not all that uncommon in this kind of plant.

Long ago, when the early gardeners learned the technique of grafting less vigorous plants on to more vigorous kinds, it did not take long for the more inquisitive and adventurous to try grafting together plants that were related but not of the same genus. 'Brothers' and 'sisters' could be grafted, so they tried 'cousins', 'uncles' and 'aunts', which were a bit further removed. Most often it did not work and the plants were incompatible, but in a fair number of cases it did. One such union is that of the common purple broom *Cytisus purpureus*, belonging to the Leguminosae botanical order (the pea family) onto another member of the same order, but a different genus or division of it, the yellow-flowered *Laburnum anagyroides*. Apart from the adventurous spirit of the gardener, another and very good reason for attempting this kind of inter-generic graft is that a particular genus may not have a particularly vigorous 'wild' type among members of its own family upon which to graft others, and so the gardener looks to see if he can find a close relation that will oblige.

This particular graft union became quite popular, and then in 1825, in the Adam Nursery near Paris, a most peculiar thing happened, that needed a microscope to explain it. Examination of the stem tissues showed that, instead of the *Cytisus* scion growing away as usual, the *Laburnum* root-stock had grown up inside the scion, which now existed like a glove or envelope around the *Laburnum* core. The result was a growth with the physical characteristics of *Laburnum*, but inside the 'skin' of *Cytisus*, and this was why the usual yellow flowers were 'discoloured' shades of light bronze to clear pink. Sometimes called a 'graft-hybrid' because it is like a hybrid that has resulted from a graft, botanically it is not a hybrid at all, since the individual cell structures remain separate and unaltered – as we shall see. The correct name for this is a 'chimera' (pronounced as in 'sky' and 'Vera'). Now, gloves can become thin and stretched, holes appear and your skin shows through, and when that happens to a chimera, the underlying core tissue comes to the surface, and you get a flower colour typical of the core – in this case, yellow.

You might find it novel and attractive to have different colours on the same tree, but a word of caution. Rather like a 'briar', if you let the 'hole in the skin' become too big, there is a very real risk that it will grow out and become bigger and bigger, taking energy that should be kept inside the glove. On no account prune or cut the pink parts, because that only exposes an 'edge' of core tissue at the cut, and that can lead to a surge of core shoots bearing yellow. You will have to cut out the yellow growth and, contrary to the usual advice, do not clean the rough saw cut or pare it smooth with a knife. Leave the wood 'saw rough' to discourage the formation of callus tissue, which would inevitably lead to a lot of adventitious yellow-flowering core shoots. Always paint cuts and wounds with Arbrex.

[155]

73   To grass, or not to grass: that is the question

We have recently added a 3-acre (1-ha) meadow to our garden, and intend to plant specimen trees and shrubs. What we are undecided about is whether they should each stand in an area or patch of bare soil, kept clear of competing plants and weeds, or should grass be allowed to grow right up to the trees and be mown?

Lucky you! What a wonderful prospect to look forward to! Your quandary is one which, to greater or lesser degree, concerns many gardeners and which is therefore of wide interest. In the final analysis, the method that you adopt will boil down to labour and time availability. The primary purpose of your plans is that you should enjoy what you do and what you have done. It is no good deciding on a particular standard of maintenance, if it is going to cost too much in terms of labour, money, and time to sit back, take your leisure, and enjoy it. All work and no play turns a garden into a burden.

There is something admirable and appealing in the appearance of specimens standing in smartly clipped and hoed clean 'beds' dotted about a close-mown lawn. I know of a very large garden in Hampshire that was kept to just such a standard by its late owner. It was remarkable and admirable in its smartness and, I am sure, equally remarkable in what it must have cost to keep it going. The soil in the 'beds' around each shrub and tree was kept hoed clean and the edges trimmed clean of whiskers, with nothing out of place – I know it was the apple of its owner's eye. But tastes differ – to my eye it was not only a garden, it was also a museum, like a house full of spotlessly beautiful furnishings, in which the visitor feels unable to touch, sit and relax. It is not a 'home', it is too clinical, it is not 'lived in' – and, above all, a garden is for living in.

You may prefer the more informal, natural and easily maintained approach that is followed in several arboretums. Your 3 acres (1.2ha) will require grass cutting machinery of some size and capacity, but other readers with smaller areas can adapt accordingly. The cutting height should be set no lower than 2–3 inches (5–7.5cm); a rotary mower is the most satisfactory for this purpose, and the cheapest type to maintain. Unless the grass grows too long and a lot of swarf makes it look like a hayfield, you can keep the mowing down to no more than once a week. Furthermore, a 2–3 inch (5–7.5cm) sward is long enough to accept and hide most of the cuttings, which are thus returned to the soil. You may find it a little awkward, and have to be careful working under shrubs, but you will be able to mow close to half and full standard subjects.

The whole area will have a deep and uniform grass carpet through which you can mow out paths, shorter and therefore conspicuous, which curve and wander about to open up constantly changing views, angles and distances. It will take time to reach the stage of growth and maturity that brings out the contrasts in colours and shapes, but this informal approach allows your imagination to work overtime. There are no restrictions, and there is always enough flexibility – a setting here, a glade there – in which to introduce bulbs like daffodils, bluebells, lilies and crown imperials, which, although they cannot be cut down until they wither, nevertheless do not look untidily unkempt in the natural setting.

Culturally, the advantages of the 'mown woodland' approach is that humus is constantly being returned and recycled to the soil. This does not happen where the soil is kept bare and open. You should be able to keep the whole, paths and all, under control with a rotary mower, a machine which is very much cheaper to run and maintain than the cylinder mower needed for a close-cut lawn.

74 Keeping the Christmas tree

I have managed to get a shapely Christmas tree with plenty of roots on it and would like to keep it growing after Christmas. How should I care for it so that it recovers quickly when I plant it outdoors in the new year?

The odds are stacked very heavily against you before you start. Even when they are pulled up by the roots and not simply sawn off at ground level, trees intended for Christmas decoration have no consideration whatever paid to their prospects of a future life. With at best a torn and mutilated root, the tree then has to spend a week or two in the warm dry air of your home. By the time you remove the lights and tinsel and take the fairy off the top, it will be in an advanced stage of dehydration.

If it is to stand a chance of recovery, the first and urgent step will be to get some moisture inside it. Trim any broken and ragged roots with secateurs, and immerse as much of the tree as you can in water. The roots can go into a bucket, but if you have a water butt, more of the tree can be immersed – and if the tree is small enough to go in the bath, that is better still. Soak it for 48 hours, and while that is going on

[157]

you can be preparing the planting hole with plenty of well-soaked peat or compost forked into the bottom. Plant firmly and then spray the tree thoroughly from the top to bottom with S600 transpanting spray repeated 24 hours later. This will deposit a film or sheath over the surfaces of what leaves remain by this time, and go a long way to preventing further evaporation of moisture. It will be some time before the roots are able to absorb moisture at that end, so you have to try to prevent its loss from the top.

That is as much as you can do after you have done the damage. You would have stood a better chance of keeping the tree alive by spraying with S600 as soon as you got it home, soaking the roots for 24 hours, planting in a plastic pot or bucket, keeping it watered and standing outside for as long as possible before bringing it in to the stuffy indoor atmosphere, and getting it outside again quickly – don't wait until twelfth night. Stand the tree in a sheltered position away from wind and draught, keep it watered and treat it as for a pot plant until spring, when with care you should be able to slide it gently, with the minimum of root disturbance, from the smooth plastic pot into its planting hole.

Of course it is a nice thought to 'save the Christmas tree', but if you are really serious about growing a specimen, it is much better to buy specifically for that purpose, with proper care and attention being given to lifting with roots intact. Finally, a word of caution: before planting a 'Christmas tree' do consider very carefully what you are doing, be aware of the potential size and be prepared to accept the consequences – your charming little tree will become a hulking great Norway Spruce 100ft (30m) tall!

75 Why camellias have disfigured blooms

I am very fond of camellias and have a small collection of nine, all of which appear to be healthy and flourishing. Nearly every year, however, the blooms are already damaged as the buds open by I know not what. Could it be some form of pest damage – I cannot find anything – or some form of mineral deficiency?

With a growth habit not unlike rhododendrons, camellias are most often regarded and grown as shrubs. However, in suitable sheltered conditions they will sometimes get up to a surprising height. The beautiful flowers have led to extensive hybridizing and crossing – the number of varieties available from specialist growers runs well into three figures. On the whole a little more tolerant than most rhododendrons of a little lime in the soil, they are most at home in a deep peat-like accumulation of leaf litter.

Most camellias are reasonably hardy – as much so as a laurel hedge – but their one big weakness is the developing flower bud. These are very susceptible to frost damage, which does not become apparent until the blooms open. This is why the camellia, like the magnolia, is happiest and seen to best advantage in a light woodland setting where it is sheltered from severe wind and cold.

Several years ago, a specialist nursery I used to visit regularly in Dorset simulated woodland conditions by covering the entire nursery of several acres (hectares) with screens of wooden slats mounted on supports in order to provide dappled light and wind protection. A good nursery takes no chances and cannot afford to offer or sell plants with damaged buds, and that was the extent of the effort the Dorset nursery went to in order to avoid trouble. You can hardly cover your garden in that way, but the example should help you to appreciate how much happier camellias will be nestled in among other subjects, instead of standing exposed and above or up against draughty walls, as they so often are.

If yours are already trained on walls, don't move them, as they will not like that, but make up blinds or curtains (the best ones from the front room are ideal) that can be hung over the plants in frosty weather. I had a head gardener friend at Cranleigh, Surrey, who grew the most perfect blooms of *C. reticulata* varieties in this way. Every pane of glass in the broken-down camellia house had long since gone, and all he had for protection at first was branches cut from evergreen conifers which were laid against the plants, and taken off when weather permitted. Those blooms were sold to a London florist who was quite prepared to journey down to fetch them!

At the very least, be prepared to protect your plants with straw, curtains or netting as well as you are able. Your reward will be some of the most exquisitely perfect of any flowers.

76 Feed and compost for camellias

My camellia leaves are pale green-yellow instead of dark green and I think the trees need feeding. I would be grateful if you would suggest a good fertilizer.

Oh dear! Why have you let them get into this state? Camellias like a deep peat-like accumulation of leaf litter, just on the acid side of neutral. Like rhododendrons, which thrive in similar conditions, the most satisfactory – and the most natural – leaf litter is their own leaf fall.

A very close relative of the camellia species you grow in your garden is the species you drink in your teacup. It follows, therefore, that instead of throwing them away in the dustbin, it is much better to spread spent tea leaves and bags around their relatives in the garden, and there let them rot down. The pale green colour of your foliage is called chlorosis, and is a condition with effects not unlike the pale complexion in human beings – anaemia – which is caused by a low blood count. In this case, the camellia has a low chlorophyll count in the leaves, but both conditions are caused by insufficient availability of iron. It is quite possible for there to be enough iron in the soil, but locked up in a chemical combination with lime or chalk that renders it unavailable for plant absorption.

The favourite advice for chlorosis is to apply a 'chelated iron' compound that the lime does not lock away. This is expensive, and you really need a soil test first to determine that the problem really is due to lime. If it is the cause of the trouble, the chelate remedy can often have quick results, but it is treating a symptom, not a cause. Slower, but more persistent and long lasting, is the steady application of the acid tea leaves.

With a chlorotic condition as bad as this I would certainly try to get something into those leaves by the shortest possible route. Try to get a foliar feed that contains iron in the analysis printed on the bottle. Make it up as directed, but add one or two drips of washing-up detergent so that the fine spray droplets wet and stick instead of running off the shiny leaf surface. Spray every other day if you can for a fortnight, and then once a week. If the trouble has not gone too far and the internal leaf structure been damaged too much, you should see colour begin to return.

Finally, only ever feed with a nitrogen, phosphorus and potash-balanced nutrient source that is organic in origin, and will contain at least some iron. Humber manure is the first choice, and Blood, Bone and Fish, the second choice. Use 2oz (57g) to the square yard (square metre) every three to four months, and it will work wonders.

You will sometimes see the advice to apply sulphate of iron as a remedy for this plant condition. My advice is not to: so little is needed that, if you overdo it, the chemical acts as a plant killer. Better slow and safe than in a hurry and sorry.

77 *Spraying trees*

My fruit trees are now well over 15ft (4.5m) high, and although my books say spray every year with tar oil and other substances to check pests and diseases, they don't suggest how we are supposed to reach to the top.

How right you are. This is a good question.

It is fairly evident, if you think about it, that some force is needed to 'throw' liquid up into a tree, and more still to force it through an orifice and so break it into fine droplets.

When you want to throw liquid, the most energy-efficient method is simply to 'throw it'. Mechanically, it wastes your body energy to compress air in a container, and then to use the stored energy by allowing it to expand to 'push' liquid through a small hole, gather speed and 'throw' a distance. When it is yourself that is the energy source, and you want to reach 15ft (4.5m) or more high, wasted energy has to be thought about carefully because it helps to decide the type of sprayer needed, and so avoid wasting money on gawdy packaged appliances that are not 'man' enough to do the job. The ideal, if you ever see one in a farm, jumble, car boot or other kind of sale, is the old wartime 'stirrup pump', with single-handed operation from a bucket, which is quite capable of throwing well over the height of your trees.

Why some enterprising manufacturer does not produce an up-to-date version with modern materials, instead of silly water pistols, beats me. Solo Sprayers at one time produced two or three models that operated on the same principle, and which could be fitted with an extension lance. This was very useful because, with some pests laying their over-wintering eggs deep into crevices and cracks, some force and impact is required to push the spray liquid in deep to reach them. This is better achieved from a nozzle held high than by a fine spray that has to travel some distance before it gets there.

Finally, a word of warning: your problem is a strong temptation to stand on a step ladder and gain height that way. Don't try it. Moving your arms around operating a sprayer, shifting positions to spray at varying angles, standing high on steps on soft ground is to buy a one-way ticket to hospital.

[161]

78   Coping with a tall hedge

Backing on to a golf course, our garden is protected by a tall hedge some 14ft (4m) high, which we like to keep clipped neat and tidy. This has become a problem because towers are so expensive to hire now, and the job does not get done as often as it should. Any suggestions would be very welcome.

A conventional ladder is out of the question because, being narrow, there is seldom enough firm resistance in a hedge face to prevent a ladder – and you – falling between the twigs and branches, and that is apart from the possibility of narrow ladder feet sinking into soft earth. The solution is to make yourself a ladder – I doubt very much whether you would be able to buy one these days – like those that were used in the old days in the large gardens and estates for just this purpose. The principle is to 'spread the weight'.

A typical ladder would be about 7–8ft (2–2.5m) wide, and I have seen them as much as 10–12ft (3–3.5m) high, but there must have been ladders much taller than this to reach the tops of some of the really big monster hedges. The ladder depicted in Fig. 15 is more like a large hurdle or frame and could be leaned directly against the hedge which, over this width, would be able to offer enough spread resistance to hold it up.

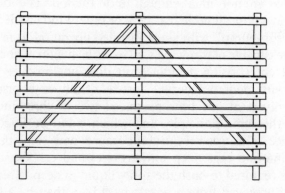

Fig. 15   A home-made ladder or frame like this allows safe access to a tall hedge; your weight is spread across a sufficient length of hedge to support you.

A better and safer improvement was to fit a long 'hold-off' board near the top (see Fig. 16). In addition to allowing cuttings to drop clear between the hedge and the ladder, this is also much safer because you are able to stand on a 'rung' with your shins leaning firmly against the next higher rung, with the work comfortably within arm's reach in front of you. Without the hold-off board, the ladder is directly against the hedge face, and so are you, and you can only clip and work while twisting your body to left or right.

Fig. 16   Add a 'hold-off' board, and you can work at a comfortable arm's length from the hedge.

An uncomfortable working position is a dangerous position, and you will have some distance to fall. Spread over this width, the legs are less likely to dig into soft earth, but even if they do, the effect is not so serious as with a narrow ladder. Fruit-picking ladders, for leaning against trees, use the same principle except that they are triangular, coming to a point at the top, whereas the hedge-cutting ladders were always square or rectangular. The only difficulty is the size and weight. This kind of ladder is rather heavy and cumbersome, and you would be wise always to get help when you want to move it along.

Fig. 17 makes the construction clear. You will need uprights of 3 inches (7.5cm) × 2 inches (5cm), rungs of 2 inches (5cm) × 1½ inches (4cm), and a hold-off board of 6 inches (15cm) × ½–¾ inches (12–19mm) all 'rough sawn'. There is no need for more expensive planed timber, but do rub the wood over with coarse sandpaper to remove splinters. Use screws to assemble it – they are firmer than nails. By all means use a wood preservative – the ladder will have to remain outdoors when not in use – but not creosote which will stain clothes, especially your shins where you lean, and make the rungs slippery.

[163]

Fig. 17 A fruit picker's ladder uses the same principle, but is designed to rest against a tree.

79 Stopping climbing cats

We have a lovely standard apple tree in our garden that has a peculiar fascination for our Siamese cats. They love to run up the trunk, clamber through the branches and, when they are not chasing birds, they chase each other and howl their curses. Is there anything we can do to stop them getting up into the tree for I am sure one will fall and be injured?

This is not an uncommon question, and apparently the trouble is not confined to Siamese moggies. The most effective solution I know is to make the tree trunk disagreeable to the cats by greasebanding, just as you would – and should – greaseband to trap migrating creepy-crawlies on their way up to bite lumps out of your apples. However, unlike crawling pests, cats can jump, and they also have considerable intelligence. If our two moggies are anything to go by, a 6ft (2m) standing jump is quite easy, especially when the corgi is after them. You will therefore need three or even four greasebands to stop them running up the trunk, and to reach high enough to prevent them jumping and clearing the lot. They will very soon work out an alternative route, and you will have to make sure that fences, cold frames, the greenhouse roof and hanging branches do not leave other doors open while you go to the trouble of closing the main entrance.

Apart from their peculiar prayers to their oriental ancestors, are they doing any real harm? Would it not be easier for you, and kinder to them, to let them carry on? They may make their prayers from another vantage point that is even more annoying to you. As for injury, of course it could happen, but it would be very unlikely because cats have the most incredible agile ability to twist themselves around so that from whatever height and in whatever attitude they start a fall, they always land on their feet.

80   The how and why of fruit tunnels

Years ago there used to be a tea garden near Eastbourne that was a favourite venue for coach trips. We remembered and wanted to enquire about a long archway of pear trees that were all joined together, but on visiting the area this year were dismayed to be told that the gardens are no more and have long been a housing estate. Would you happen to know anything about this method of joining trees, and why they were grown in an archway? Friends tell us it was just a gimmick to attract tourists, but I wonder if there is another explanation.

Well remembered – and very observant of you at the time of your visit. The late and lamented tea gardens were at Wannock, near Polegate, just a few miles north of Eastbourne, and nowadays well within that town's built-up area – and yes, indeed, the gardens have long been a housing development.

Among the many features and attractions was the fruit tunnel. In the heyday of Victorian and Edwardian gardening, when wealthy garden and estate owners vied with each other in growing rare plants and having features that their rivals had not got, fruit tunnels were quite a common feature. The idea was that your guests could stroll in the garden, pass through the tunnel, and on the way pick themselves a juicy apple or pear hanging to hand inside!

The French, who up to this time had been at the forefront of fruit growing, had developed a technique of grafting trees together, ornamentals as well as fruit, and this technique, called *plêching*, evidently arose from the wide variation in habit and performance of fruit trees at the time (see question 16). The intention was to provide a kind of mutual support along a line of trees that in fact became one

[165]

single tree. There is the suggestion also that the idea was copied from what had been an earlier practice in grafting together quickthorn bushes in the hedgerows at the edges of fields to make an impenetrable cattle-proof barrier.

However that may be, the effect often observed, and then deliberately aimed for, was to produce more flower in ornamentals and heavier cropping with fruit. It was but a short step to bend over two adjacent rows of plêched trees and graft them together to form a tunnel, and this is what you saw at Wannock. Perhaps the favourite ornamental tree for this technique is the laburnum, in which the long racemes of yellow bloom hang down inside the tunnel. There is a famous such tunnel at Bodnant Gardens, North Wales, which is a wonderful experience to walk through. (See page 55.)

81   Clearing a neglected holly hedge

We have moved into a new house that has a tall and very neglected holly hedge with elder, quickthorn, bramble, wild rose, sycamore and goodness knows what else growing through it. How can we clear out the 'weed' without harming the holly?

I had just this kind of problem when I set out to turn 18 acres (7 ha) of neglected fields into a sportsground and park, so I know just how you feel. The hedge I had to deal with was quickthorn, but the principle is just the same.

Prop up the lower branches with poles laid across boxes so that you can crawl under to reach the bases of the weed shrubs. Make up a solution of approximately one tablespoonful of SBK (Shrub and Brushwood Killer) which you can obtain quite easily from the garden centre, to a pint (0.5 litre) of paraffin oil. This mixture will be very potent to any hedging material or other plants, and you will have to be very careful how you handle it. With only a little in a tin can at any time (in case you knock it over or spill it), crawl under and with a brush, paint a 3–4 inch (7.5–10cm) collar around the stems of the unwanted plants, and repeat every two to three weeks until the plants are dead.

The best time to start the job is in early summer when there is a lot of sap movement to distribute the hormone throughout the plant. By the same token, winter dormancy, with movement at a standstill, is the least effective.

This procedure should bring about a gradual demise of the weed growth that is slow enough to allow the holly to move in and colonize the gaps without leaving unsightly gaping black holes. On the other hand, having crawled underneath, you may want to put a saw through the things and have done with it. You can do that, of course, but you will still need to paint the bared stumps to kill them and prevent adventitious growth sprouting up and starting the trouble all over again. You will also have great big holes in the hedge to remind you of your impatience.

Either way, the dead wood will have to come out and, while you are about it, make a careful inspection of the remaining hollies – from the inside – and remove any dead wood from them. This part of the job is very important, because dead wood left in a hedge is a direct encouragement to the dangerous coral spot fungus, recognizable by the small orange pustules. Take your time, be careful how you handle the solution, and be ruthless with the clearing out.

If your intention is to clip the hedge, and the dimensions are such as to require you to climb up, under no circumstances use a step ladder. Similarly, do not attempt clipping from a conventional ladder leaned against the hedge. Read question 78 – it could save you from a nasty fall.

82 Pruning a copper beech

Will you please tell me when is the best time to prune a copper beech tree?

You do not say whether there is some compelling reason for this, such as the tree growing too big for its surroundings. The proper time to prune a copper beech is never! Other than occasionally shaping and guiding early growth, just in case a leading shoot or two wants to romp away and get a bit above itself and out of proportion, a copper beech should not be pruned.

This tree is one of nature's most beautiful marvels, and it is a sad day to have to harm it. Indeed, and particularly if the tree is in a position where it can be seen and enjoyed by your neighbours, you would be well advised to make very careful enquiry of your local council or parish to make absolutely certain that there is not a bye-law or some other restriction on what you may do to the tree, and the breaking of which could land you in a spot of bother. If needs must, cut from early November to the beginning of February, and treat all wounds with Arbrex protective.

[167]

83   Planting position for the Devil's Walking Stick

I have been given a young tree called 'The Devil's Walking Stick', which a book tells me is Aralia elata or Chinese Angelica. However, no cultural instructions are given. Can you help, please?

This question reveals a common mistake, and something of a mix-up. The name 'Devil's Walking Stick' is frequently applied to *Angelica elata*, the Japanese Angelica, which is from Japan, not China. It is similar to, but has larger flower panicles than, the true Chinese Angelica *A. chinensis* from north-east Asia, which is also called the 'Devil's Walking Stick'. Both have 3-ft (1-m) long ornate foliage, very attractive white panicles of flowers and make very handsome decorative trees – but neither of them is the walking stick!

Correctly, the 'Devil's Walking Stick' is *A. spinosa*, also known as 'Hercules Club', and it comes not from the orient at all, but from the south-east corner of the USA. The bloom is green and less showy than *A. elata* or *A. chinensis*, and it has vicious spiny stems – one can easily imagine that a walking stick made from such a stem could only be handled by the Devil!

Now, which one have you been given? It is misleading to be precise about planting and culture other than to say that, in this country and climate, the tree is best planted where it can receive full sunshine, but with the protection of a building, a wall, or other trees behind it for protection – a wrap around the shoulders to keep off the draughty cold.

84   Dealing with maple seeds

Can you please help me with growing Japanese maples from seed? I need to know when seed should be sown. Does it have to be stratified? I have tried several times with seed given me by friends, but with no success.

If you mean that you are being given seed by friends who are collecting it from their own trees, as distinct from repeatedly giving you seed obtained from a reputable source, with all due respect to your friends, we can only assume that the seed is viable when collected. Then comes the question of what they do with it, because all seed from the maple family tends to lose viability rather quickly. For that reason, it has either to be sown quickly or, between collecting the seed and sowing, the seeds' living processes have to be slowed down in order to prolong life.

The first step, before any form of storage, is to ensure that the seed coat is quite dry. Any sign of dampness, especially with this seed, will almost certainly lead to mildew, mould or other fungal deterioration of the seed coat or testa. While this is quite normal in the soil where the seed embryo can germinate, it is not something that we want to happen while it is in store.

Secondly, we have to reduce respiration, the process of breathing. Although it may be stretching the imagination to think of a seed as breathing, it is a living embryonic plant, and all the time it is living, the process of respiration goes on. Some seeds have the most incredible ability to remain viable for a great many years, but the maple is at the other end of the scale, and the breathing has to be slowed right down if its life is to be prolonged. Thirdly, and another way to slow down the life process, the temperature of the seed must be reduced to keep it cool.

We can reduce the breathing by reducing the atmosphere volume in which the seed is stored – rather like being trapped in a small room with no incoming air, you prolong your life by keeping very still, and slowing down your breathing and energy consumption to the minimum. Although perfectly acceptable for 'normal' seed if it is to be used short term, wrapping seeds in paper or an envelope is of very little use for the purpose we are discussing because air can easily pass through the folds. Even with seed that has a reasonable longevity, a really good seed supplier – like Suttons, for example – sends its seeds out in hermetically sealed packets to reduce deterioration to absolute minimum.

Several plants have this short life problem with seeds, and there is a lot of sense in backing both horses in a two-horse race. Sow some seed as soon as collected and while it is still fresh, and save some for sowing later. Sometimes you will find one way will work better than the other, and at other times, it is the other way round. Dry the seed that you intend to sow later, place it in a small plastic bag, and then suck out the air so that the bag closes tightly around the seed, just like a vacuum pack. While still sucking, twist the bag neck to make it airtight, and seal it with a rubber band to ensure that the available atmosphere for breathing is down to a minimum. Then put the bag in a tin and place it in a cool place. The fridge is too cold, and if you put the tin in a shed, make sure the seed does not become frosted.

If you can put the seed into two bags, that is better still. Sow one lot in pans of John Innes seed compost towards the end of February, and the other a month later. Place the pans in a cool greenhouse, with just enough heating to make sure they do not get frosted. That is how our propagator dealt with maple seed, and one or other of the autumn batch and the two later sowings invariably produced seedlings – but he could never be sure which way was going to be the most successful.

85 Laburnums are so thirsty

Two laburnum trees about 15 years old usually produce a good show of bloom, but this year there was hardly any between them. They appear healthy enough, except several shoot tips which seem to be dry and shrivelled. Have you any idea as to the cause? There are no signs of pests, or any disease.

My laburnum usually stays green until leaf-fall in the autumn, but this July, when we had a dry spell, the foliage looked sickly and I thought it wanted watering. So I gave the ground round about a good soaking with the hosepipe, but a fortnight later all the leaves had fallen off. What do you think is the cause of this?

Two questions here with the same basic cause, and they are good examples of a problem that gets asked about more often than might be supposed. These two cases have gone over the top – usually the trouble is not so serious and takes the form of a season with a noticeable reduction in bloom rather than a serious lack of it and shrivelled leaves and shoot tips.

It is not generally appreciated that this tree is a thirsty customer, and takes a lot more out of the soil than one would expect in comparison to other trees of the same size. Indeed, this may well be a contributory cause, if not the underlying reason for the common complaint that little else will grow under a laburnum, and the suspicion that, because it is poisonous to animal life (including us), it poisons the soil for other plants. This is a suspicion only, and is not supported by scientific proof.

The bloom that appears each spring is formed during the previous growing season and exists in minute embryonic form in the buds that lay dormant through the winter. Trees have a lot more sense than we credit them with, and although perpetuation of the species – making flower and setting seed for another generation – is a basic and primary purpose, even this process can be upset. Injury, especially to roots, will often cause a plant to think it is going to die, so that it does its utmost to get through the process of flowering, fruiting and setting the seed for its succession before it meets its expected end. This is the 'plant psychology' behind the methods used to bring many reluctant plants, shrubs and trees into flower and fruit production. Dryness at roots can have the same effect, but if the dryness is long and severe, the effect on a thirsty tree with its flower buds already formed, is to make it think: 'Well, I've got my roots well down, I don't think I'm going to die, but there is no way I can sustain all these flower buds, nor will I be able to meet the surge of sap as they all burst forward.' So it sheds the load, reduces further evaporation by dropping leaf early, and cuts its own shoot length back.

Next spring is a dull time, and naturally you wonder what the trouble can be, but you have to look further back than the recent past for the cause. A dry summer can play all kinds of havoc with the following year, and there are other conditions that can influence matters. A sandy fierce-draining soil predisposes a laburnum (or any other tree) to poor flowering, which is why, if you plant a tree in these conditions, you should be more than generous with the quantity of organic matter that you get underneath. Position can also be a factor. If it is planted too near to buildings or even other trees that shield and over-protect it from rainfall, the thirsty laburnum will not even get its fair share.

With all this in mind, immediate practical steps for an established tree are fairly self-evident. Mulch as generously as you can around the tree, let the worms take it in and, in a dry spell, an hour or two with the hose running a slow dribble can prevent disappointment next spring.

86　Slow to start magnolia

My young Magnolia soulangeana *made an effort to flower this year, but could not manage it. The leaves have been pale-coloured and several of them have brown tips.*

Although the magnolia is often seen exposed to the elements in surburban front gardens, really it is not happy there. It is much better as a tree of light woodland where its access to summer sunlight is not unduly hindered, but where its roots can explore and stay cool in an annually dropped accumulation of leaf fall. They are also seen to better advantage in surroundings that hold off strong winds and protect the big showy blooms from being blown about and shattered.

[171]

New plantings are often slow to get away, especially if they do not get the organic rich condition they prefer. Exposed surface soil can dry out and vary in temperature sufficiently to hinder early root development. The flower buds are forming during the summer – you can see this quite clearly in the angle between the leaves and the stems – and although the tree slows almost to a stop in winter, as soon as the days begin to lengthen, the buds begin to swell and the tree is demanding sap from the roots long before the large flowers and leaves burst forward. If the root system has not developed enough, the flower embryos do not develop and leaves may also suffer and die back.

The early leaf of the magnolia is much more pale than the dark green it becomes during the summer. If the leaves don't darken, then clearly you have a nutrient problem as well. At this point, read question 76, which, although dealing specifically with camellias, is directly applicable also to the magnolia. Question 87 also is directly to the point.

Some varieties of *M. soulangeana* have a notorious reluctance to begin flowering (see the descriptive notes on page 58), but the fact that this young tree made the effort suggests that it is not one of the shy ones. However, shy or not, it does not encourage a young plant to get on with flowering when it has to fight so hard to get established. Give it plenty of tea leaves mulched on the soil surface, feed only with an NPK-balanced, slow-acting feed such as Humber or Growmore, and in a dry spell water well, but only with rain-water because of the likelihood of introducing lime with tap water, and I am sure it will pull round.

87   *Magnolia with a low blood count*

A small magnolia tree which I bought and planted last spring seemed to grow well at first, but during recent weeks the edges of the leaves have turned yellowish as well as the central vein of each leaf. I have also noticed that the main stem and side branches have numerous tiny flecks like some kind of blight. Can you suggest what is wrong and what I should spray with?

The magnolia has remarkably few pests or diseases that trouble it. The small 'flecks' that you can see on the surface of the stem and branches are special cells in the surface layer tissue, called stomates, through which the tree breathes. The yellowing is an entirely different matter.

This condition – a problem also with rhododendrons, azaleas, camellias, clerodendrons, pieris and many other so-called 'lime-haters' – is called chlorosis: see No. 76.

The leaves are exhibiting severe distress, so they want attention first. With a fine mist spray, apply a foliar feed containing iron and manganese (look at the analysis on the bottle). You will probably find one of the seaweed-based preparations most satisfactory.

Magnolias and other susceptible plants have a thick 'epidermis' – outer skin layer – which is often characterized by a shiny surface to the leaf, and which imparts a tough leathery feel. This thick skin makes it difficult for a spray to stick so that the nutrients in the spray liquid have time to get through the leaf surface and be absorbed. You can overcome this by adding a drip or two of washing up detergent to each container of spray liquid and so get a good wetting.

Foliar feeding is a short-term remedy for up above, and we have to look for a longer term solution down below. This entails overcoming the presence of any lime and working plenty of organic matter into the soil, without disturbing the plants. Spread peat, which will be more acid than compost, and all the spent tea leaves and bags you can salvage from the teapot.

In addition, you should ensure that the three major elements are in good supply. If you do this by putting down a slow to decompose organic manure, you can go a long way towards looking after the trace elements as well. The very best nutrient source I have used for this purpose is Humber Garden Manure – the ratio of nitrogen, phosphorus and potash is evenly balanced, and, having its base in sewage sludge and the fishing industry, the trace element content is very wide.

88 Dealing with Prunus damage

This morning I had the misfortune while mowing my lawn to hit and badly gash a five-year-old Prunus shirotae. I have replaced a piece of stripped-off bark, and tied it with string to hold it in position. Can you tell me what I should do to avoid lasting damage to my beautiful tree?

I find it uncanny how often gardeners contrive to drive their mowers with their left or right hands 'down' a bit too far, and smack into ornamental trees on lawns. Cherries in particular are at a special disadvantage, apart from the actual physical damage, because they are susceptible to very nasty and dangerous diseases like bacterial canker and silver leaf. Such diseases are perfectly capable of killing a tree, and any gardener with a cherry in the lawn where it can be snagged would be well advised not to try to mow so close, and in any case to have a first aid kit handy in the garden shed.

A repair kit should consist basically of a sharp pruning knife to pare rough bark edges smooth, Arbrex protective, and some adhesive masking tape to bind the wound, keep everything in place and prevent air-borne spores getting in. A gash or cut should be painted over at once with Arbrex, just as you would a pruning cut. If you hit a tree, stop the machine and get the protective on straight away – half an hour is plenty of time for spores to have got into a wound.

With a strip of bark pulled away, the damage is more serious. As quickly as you can, make sure it is quite clean and lay it back in position, much as you would a wound in your own skin, and bind with adhesive, masking, insulating or plastic tape, painting Arbrex over the whole. As you know with a wound to your own flesh, the quicker you get it cleaned, stitched and closed up the quicker it will heal. Then lay the hose out and let it trickle so that there is encouragement for a rise in sap, and a bridging of the cambium layer. Invasive spores are in the air all the time. At certain times – and especially if there is an infection nearby – the air is as thick as treacle with them. Speed is of the essence.

89 Dimensions of a weeping pear

We have been horrified to see an illustration in Amateur Gardening *of the weeping pear* Pyrus salicifolia *which, seen against the background of a house, appears to be a great deal bigger than we expected. Indeed, if the tree can grow as large as in the picture, it is obvious that the specimen we planted a few years ago and which is now becoming the beautiful centrepiece of our smallish garden will have to come out – it has grown quickly and made us a little apprehensive. Just how big will it grow?*

The ultimate dimensions of a tree depend upon several factors such as local conditions, soil and climate, which is why it is invidious and could even be misleading to be too specific about indicating height. The weeping pear is small compared with an oak tree or a 'conker', but in favourable conditions it can reach 20ft (6m) high – and, exceptionally, even more – and perhaps 15ft (4.5m) wide. However, compared with most other trees of its size, and especially with other weepers, it reaches full size quite quickly – perhaps it is this early speed of growth that is exciting your apprehension as to its ultimate size.

Assessment of dimensions from photographs is notoriously deceptive unless there is an unmistakable comparison close by. Perspective can play funny tricks, so rather than rely upon an inference drawn from a picture, you will be wiser to relate your garden and available space to the general dimensions above. If they are acceptable – stop worrying!

90 A galloping almond

I have had a flowering almond for four years and in that time the branches have trebled in length, and the flowers have become less and less. This year there was only one! I thinned it out last year and wonder whether I should have cut it back. Can you please suggest what I should do to make it flower properly.

This questioner does not indicate whether the almond is a conventional standard, the usual form, or a bush form. Also not made clear is whether the one flower was a deep pink almond bloom, or a white-pink single bloom.

The answer to the second point would confirm what the first indicates – that this almond was already well and truly 'briared', almost certainly beyond saving, at the time you bought it four years ago. I suspect that the vigorous root stock had already broken out below the budded almond scion which, being by-passed and ignored by sap energy rushing past into the 'easier' stock growth, has suffered and is on the point of dying out altogether. If this diagnosis is correct, the tree is almost certainly ruined.

Examine the graft or bud very carefully – you have to determine just how much, if any, of the almond scion is still alive. If you follow back from where the solitary flower was borne to this bud or graft area, it should be clear to what extent there is any bud-wood left alive and how much the stock-wood has taken over. Even if there is a little life left in the almond, and you cut away everything else, you are asking that poor remnant to take the full thrust next year of a well-established five-year-old stock. It will not be able to take it, and the stock will break out again. You can try cutting this away as quickly as the shoots appear, but having had its head once to this extent, I fear that you will be fighting a losing battle. The quickest, cheapest, most effective and

[175]

satisfactory way to have a nice flowering almond in your garden is to root out this travesty and plant another obtained from a thoroughly reliable nursery.

91 Propagating a cherry

In the grounds of the old peoples' home where I work is a very nice flowering cherry called Prunus yedoensis. *As the home is to close shortly I would very much like to keep a reminder of the happy times I have had with the old folks. Can you please tell me how to take a cutting?*

Choice varieties like this are invariably propagated by budding or grafting on to a wild cherry or plum stock. If you have ever tried budding roses, you will know what is involved, and you can try the same but more difficult procedure with a cherry. Obtaining a wild stock is easier said than done, but a nursery may supply one if you explain the circumstances, and that you want the experience and satisfaction of propagating your own memento instead of buying one of their trees.

If you had more time, you could have grown your own stock material by inserting 9–12 inch (23–30cm) cuttings with a trimmed heel into moist soil in October, or a month later around the edge of a 5- or 7-inch (12- or 18-cm) pot filled with a 50/50 sand/peat mixture. You will need to have located a wild plum growing in a hedgerow – a 'sloe' is the most likely find, and this works quite well. Dip the cutting in a rooting hormone powder, water the pot well, and place them in a cold frame where they will be protected from frost. Rooting is a considerable gamble, but if you are lucky, grow on the rooted cuttings as 'whips', allowing the main leader to grow away and make height while allowing top and side growth only for some 10–12 inches (25–30cm) from the top to pull up the sap, and cutting or rubbing out all side shoots below this to produce a clean standard stem.

Try it – nobody can adequately describe the satisfaction of producing an ornamental tree entirely by your own efforts. At 6ft (2m) high, either graft or implant a bud into a stem as thick as your little finger, much as you would a rose. Bind it in firmly, and cover all but the eye of the bud with wax or Arbrex. When the bud breaks out into leaf to show that it is taking sap from the stock, and not before, take off the top growth of the stock to divert all the energy into the bud which will thus become the new but choice head of the tree.

In the short time left available, you could try to strike cuttings of the

[176]

cherry by the above method. The rooting will be poor compared to 'wild' cuttings, and resulting plants will not be as strong as those that are budded and grafted, but at least it may give you something from which you could take budding or grafting material at a later date when you have whips ready.

Another method you could try (we used to do this at school) is to insert cuttings as above, but without the rooting hormone, into bottles of rain-water. It is another gamble, and if you are lucky, they will sprout 'water-roots'. Transplant when 2–3 inches (5–7.5cm) long into moist soil.

The chances of success are heavily stacked against you, but what better reason could you have for trying, and for trying anything, however unorthodox. If it works, it will not be the first time that initiative has been rewarded – and you will be over the moon!

92 Haircut for a weeping willow

One of my trees is the golden form of Salix pendula, *and its branches touch and lie on the ground, making it awkward to cut the grass. Shall I harm the tree if I cut the branches back so that they do not reach the ground?*

No harm should come to your willow by trimming back the long stems. If the problem is really pressing, you can do the job at any time, but given the choice, I would wait until leaf fall and then trim. You will probably find that, if you give the tree a 'pudding basin' haircut and merely cut in a straight line at ground level, this will look both unnatural and encourage a lot of side shoots from near the cut tips to cause the trouble all over again. It is much better to thin out higher up, trying to leave as natural and untouched an appearance as you can. Any new side shoots will then start from higher up and give a longer breathing space before they reach the ground. As you treasure this lovely tree, treat all cut wounds with Arbrex protective paint.

93 Training a standard

We have some seedlings growing around a particularly fine rowan and we would like to grow them up as standards both for our own use and to give to friends. We had seedlings a few years ago, but they grew as bushes more than standards. Can you tell us how to train them please?

This is a very interesting question, because so many plants can be run up as standards, and the following is generally applicable to a wide variety of plants. It is fascinating and peculiarly satisfying to train standards, whether they be soft-wood plants like pelargoniums and fuchsias or hard-wood trees. In nature, clean-stemming is usually caused by undergrowth taking so much light that lower branches are deprived, do not develop and wither. Alternatively, other plants of its own kind may grow thickly enough for the higher branches to meet and merge, forming a canopy overhead and shade underneath. When this happens – as in a wood or forest – a number of things can result.

Undergrowing plants that will survive are those that can make do with lessened light intensity or can set off very quickly in spring and make bloom and leaf before the trees above sprout leaves and pinch all the light again – a bluebell wood is a good example. If you plant trees closer than they would grow in nature, there will be a headlong rush to keep their heads up in the sunlight above the competition that would swamp them, and you can see the effect of this in any forestry plantation.

Rowans do not cast a deep shade and would have to be grown very densely for these natural rules to apply. As you are hardly likely to have a thicket of undergrowth growing around them in your garden, you will have to do the job. The principle applies to all manner of subjects, and indeed with many that are most often only thought of as shrubs – there are some novel suggestions in the tree list.

Let the plants grow quite naturally at first, tying the main central stem to a cane or stake so that it grows nice and straight. You will have to pay careful attention to these ties, letting them out to make quite sure that they do not 'cut in' to scar and disfigure the stem. As the main stem grows taller, the lowest side shoots can be taken off to begin the training. (This will provide material for cuttings with some subjects.)

Never take off more than one or two side growths at a time to keep shock to a minimum. You must leave enough foliage to make the carbohydrate for a plant that is getting bigger and whose 'head' will be getting further removed from its roots. In addition, all the time you have the central shoot tied in and growing straight, always have a second choice candidate similarly pulled to the stake, and ready to take over the role in case the main lead is damaged. As the head gets higher, the second choice itself becomes the lowest side growth and has to be removed, to be replaced by another candidate higher up.

Keep a good head going at all times. Most failures by amateurs are due to being in too much hurry to make height, removing higher side shoots too quickly, and trying to force the growing tip up so fast that the whip stem is too soft and immature for its own height. Good luck, and remember the garden rule – more haste, less speed.

94 Why a lilac scorches brown

We have a double white lilac which most years is scorched brown even before the flowers turn from the green bud stage to white. Do you think this could be due to inadequate feeding, a deficiency of some kind, or some other reason?

This is a very common problem, and although most noticeable and disfiguring with white lilac, it happens with other colours as well. Disease apart – and if it were that there would be other signs – the trouble is almost certain to be caused by dryness at the roots.

Take a careful look at your trees. Lilac is a naturally thirsty plant, not unlike a laburnum in this respect, and does not like to become dry at root level. With a lot of fleshy leaf to support, all recently made and transpiring moisture, very soon after the tree has the further burden of putting up lots of embryo flower heads. Watch as they grow quickly through the bud stage and into the burst of masses of open bloom. That bulk alone is a sudden increased demand on the moisture supply, and the bloom is very fragrant. It is not generally appreciated that fragrance entails evaporation of moisture.

You may be on a well-drained soil that predisposes your lilacs to this problem. There is not a lot you can do about that, so your two courses of action become self-evident. You can mulch heavily – all you can spare – and next time, as soon as you see the flower buds appear, lay out the hose, let it run slowly and give the root area a good long soak.

95 Beheading a bottomless cypress

We have recently moved to a new home in the garden of which are some 30ft (9m) conifers which the previous occupant tells us are 'Lawson's Cypress', and which cast shadows across the downstairs windows. The lower halves are quite devoid of any green branches and not at all nice to look at. We would like to reduce the height to 7ft (2m) and to regenerate green foliage. Can you explain the best way to do this please?

[179]

Sorry! It cannot be done. Part the foliage of any conifer hedge and look into the dark interior – you will find it leafless where the light does not penetrate. When grown in proximity as in a hedge, Lawson's Cypress has always been very ready to abort its lower branches where they meet and merge with others, a factor responsible for its decline in popularity in favour of the more accommodating *C. leylandii*.

Most subjects used for hedging will, if left to their own devices, reach heights greater than the dimensions you want, and it is the ability of some to accept trimming better than others that makes them useful for such use. However, restriction by trimming is one thing, and drastic reduction from 30ft (9m) to 7ft (2m) is quite another. Sprouting of the green frond-like foliage occurs only at the ends of younger shoots – the ability of older growth to break into green growth is virtually nil – and it is beyond hope that these trees can do as you wish. The most practical – and the quickest – way to develop a 7ft (2m) screen will be to have the 30ft (9m) specimens removed by specialist tree fellers, and for you to replant with either *C. leylandii* or thuja.

96   Wind-scorched conifers

In early October I planted 45 leylandii to form a screen for the vegetable plot section of our windswept garden. They were good even 2–2½ft (60–75cm) specimens, and I prepared very carefully with individual planting holes and plenty of organic material and sand under them, and spread on the surface after planting. Less than two months after planting all but just a few had turned an unsightly green-brown. I contacted the nursery from where they came and they said it was due to strong winds we have had, and suggested hessian screens. These were very expensive and have not solved the trouble so I have removed them. The plants do not seem to be dying, but they definitely are very unhappy. What else can I do to save them?

I believe that your nursery were quite right in suggesting screening, and the hessian screens should be put back into position at once. The next job – and I have never been able to understand why nurseries do not suggest that evergreen conifers should be protected by being given an evaporation-resisting transplant spray, or better still do the job themselves before dispatch – is to go at once to your sundriesman and get some S600 transplanting spray. You will need a fair quantity for this number of 2½-ft (7.5-cm) plants, but do it now, without waiting to read the explanation! It is more important to get this protection on.

When you have taken emergency measures and can relax again, this is the explanation. Grown fairly closely packed in nursery rows plants gain considerable mutual protection from wind and cold. Even standing in plunge beds in a garden centre is not like being planted out as a screen, where for the first time they take a kick in the face from wind and draught. Going out into a cold wind without your coat would rock you back a bit, and that is what has happened here.

In addition to colder temperatures, exposure to wind and increased evaporation rate has occurred before the roots have had time to develop and increase their absorption ability enough to cope with this demand. The result is this form of dieback, withering of the surface tissue and scorching. By covering the leaf surface with a plastic film – S600 – you are in effect providing a similar coating to that with which grey and silver 'glaucous' plants protect themselves.

The purpose of screening to deflect wind away from direct contact with the foliage is self-evident, but do be careful not to exclude light to a harmful extent. Another time, fill the planting holes with water the day before planting and let it drain away. This ensures that the subsoil under the plants will be moist, and is a strong encouragement for new root activity to work in that direction looking for it, thereby making depth and becoming established more quickly. Give the root balls a good soaking by immersion before planting – after is no good, because water will run straight round the outside of a dry ball. Mulch heavily with compost or peat and, for 2–3 years at least, until these relatively slow to establish conifers make enough new root to look after the large leaf area above them, treat them with care and kindness. They should then gradually outgrow the brown windscorch and become a uniform green.

97 Can yew be pruned?

I have trained yew trees to form a windscreen to the house, and they are growing too tall. Is it possible to cut back the tops without killing the trees?

What do you mean by 'trained'? Yew can be trimmed and shaped as you can observe by the number of hedges, and of course with examples of topiary. As with all plants treated in this way – but yew is slower growing than almost any other – this trimming develops a lot of tip and side shoots, a thicker foliage density and thus a 'face' to a 'hedge'. A yew that has not been trimmed in this way will have an open habit, not unlike the familiar Christmas tree, with the small narrow leaves being held back along the branches to quite near the main trunk until the tree becomes old and big enough for the upper branches to obscure light from lower and inner areas. In the reduced light, green leaves can no longer perform their function, so the branches and trunk become bare, and the tree takes on the bare branch configuration normally associated with an older natural tree.

This process is accelerated by the development of a light-stopping face, and if you part the foliage face of topiary or a hedge and peer inside, you will find it dark and leafless. It is in this context that you have to ask and slightly rephrase your question – can you cut it back to reduce its height?

It is clear that, if you cut a hedge face back into that dark leafless interior, you will create a leafless hole which will disfigure the hedge. Yews are slow growing, so slow that they do not require much trimming to keep to shape – which is why, if you can wait that long for them to grow, they need less time and effort than, for example, a privet which grows to form a hedge very quickly, but then does not stop and has to be cut and trimmed frequently. Consequently, even if the yew could be encouraged to sprout new green leaf from old wood, you would have to live with the hole for a long time.

But you are evidently asking whether you can cut through the very oldest wood of all – the main trunk. That would leave a leafless hole all along the top which, from an upstairs window or other high viewing point, would look pretty awful. Lawson's Cypress would most likely die on the spot, but yew can get away with it.

I remember we had to do just such a job once, in connection with a visit by Princess – to the adjacent college. Fortunately, the park authorities realized what the effect of drastic height reduction would be, and we had nearly a year's grace before the visit in which to get the job done. If you are concerned about the appearance of a hole along the top, you can minimize the effect as we did, by cutting 9–12 inches (23–30cm) lower than the intended finished height, and reaching down from above and 'pulling up' some of the branches from 12 inches (30cm) or more down, wedging and tying them so that the foliage camouflages the open top.

This will leave the top of the wall or screen looking thin in places for a while until the foliage adjusts and fills in again. Similarly the pulled-up branches will gradually fill in and clothe the top to the height you want, hiding the stump tops in the process. Spread a nitrogen fertilizer under the trees and be liberal with the hosepipe. This will encourage more sap movement and activity in a naturally lethargic subject so that the healing and filling-in takes place more quickly.

As a matter of interest, by the time of the royal visit next door, that yew hedge did not look as if it had ever been touched – it certainly did not draw any disapproving looks, and the rolls and rolls of green hessian sent in to lay along the top were not needed!

98   Felling 20-year-old conifers

How should I set about chopping down a number of Cupressus macrocarpa *trees that we planted 20 years ago, and which are now taller than the house and casting shade over the main part of the garden?*

There is a very short answer to this one – don't! Unless you have lots of time, think very carefully about what you are going to do at every stage before you actually attempt it, control with ropes every part that comes down to make sure that it falls – or, if possible, is gently lowered – precisely where you want, rope your ladder so that it does not slip with you on it, then forget it, for the job is too dangerous. Instead, call in insured tree fellers. They cost money, but you have to weigh that against your own safety.

If you are put off by the cost, or for some other reason are determined to do the job yourself, think all the time of 'what could happen, if . . .' – and make sure it does not get the chance. Take the trees down in small pieces. This may take longer, but it is safer than huge branches swinging about and sending you flying to an early retirement. You will find some helpful comment in the After-care section on pages 20–5. Do not try to remove the root balls – impregnate them with saltpetre through holes bored with brace and bit, and let them smoulder away.

Problems of pest and disease

99   Silver birch and woodworm

I am thinking of planting a silver birch, but am told that this tree is a breeding ground for woodworm. Would you please advise if this is true, and whether it would affect other trees and spread into the house?

[183]

This widespread reputation is the result of ill-informed jumping to conclusions. Birch timber shears very easily into thin sheets and is therefore eminently useful in the manufacture of plywood – vast quantities are imported to be used as backing in furniture and for making all kinds of utensils and toys. The woodworm that bores into house timbers and furniture is not interested in living wood, but it is true that birch timber – dead birch – has a special attraction for it. This is why, when the pest is observed in the house, the tell-tale holes and minute sawdust trails are invariably first noticed in birch plywood. Woodworm is most frequently introduced to our homes and buildings in imported plywood, but the controls in furniture manufacture are so strict as to make this not very frequent. Plywood salvaged and utilized from old tea chests is another matter, however, and these are quite often to be found riddled with holes.

You may observe that a fallen birch trunk or branch quickly becomes infested with the holes of boring creatures, so the reputation gains another fillip. But it is all circumstantial. Living timber is not attacked and you can plant birch in your garden with no fear that it will expose other plants – or your house and furniture – to woodworm. Keeping the garden clear of fallen birch and dead wood on the tree would be one thing, and is elementary hygiene in any case, but is no reason why not to grow it.

Incidentally, your part of Sussex is very near to the chalk of the South Downs and you should be sure that you are not planting birch into chalky soil. They prefer acid conditions to alkaline.

100 Leylandii *and woodworm*

I have been asked to move some recently planted C. leylandii *conifer trees from between my bungalow and next door 'because they harbour pests and diseases that are harmful to woodwork'. This has taken us by surprise – we have not heard of it before, and there seems to be so much of this tree planted everywhere we look. Is there any truth in the assertion?*

The evergreen conifers commonly used for screening, like thuja, *lawsoniana* and *leylandii* are resinous and contain a considerable amount of aromatic oils which repel most insect pests. These plants are remarkably free of pest and disease, which is one very good reason why they are ideally suited for screens and hedges, and why they are planted so widely.

Wood-boring beetles, larvae and the like confine their activities to dead timber, and on living trees would only be found in or just underneath dead bark. Even so, they are much less likely to attack conifers than birch, for example (see question 99).

Keep the trees and the garden clear of dead twigs and such material, and you have nothing to fear. Neither has your neighbour – if this is where the request has come from. The real reason for the request is more likely to be the common one of resentment at being screened, or obstruction of light and view – but that is another matter.

101 Holly leaf markings

Our holly tree has never shown signs of disease until this year. Now most of the leaves are affected with whitish markings which zig-zag about haphazardly. Spraying with a general insecticide has made no difference. Can you help please?

Many plants are attacked by leaf miners, in this case a specialist little blighter called the holly leaf miner *Phytomyza ilicis*. The larvae or caterpillar stage gets in between the tough top and under surface 'skins', and if you peel a leaf apart, you will find the tiny culprit. Between the tough skins is sandwiched the softer tissue and into this the pest munches, this way and that, leaving a tunnel behind it which shows through as these markings.

Where only a few leaves are affected it can be effective control to pick off and burn them, but a severe infestation is clearly more serious. Although much of the work of each leaf is damaged and prevented from making a contribution to the tree as a whole, it still represents a serious loss to remove a great number of leaves, and you have to consider other measures. The pest is no fool: it is inside a leaf with tough surfaces above and below, and its entry hole quickly seals behind it. Trying to reach it with a sprayed-on contact poison – as you did – is a waste of time because the quarry is out of reach. Similarly, a systemic poison will have equal difficulty getting through the tough leaf surface to the soft tissue inside.

The most practical step is to accept that, once inside, there is not a lot you can do, so we have to look at the creature's life cycle to see if we can find a weak spot where we can get at it. By the time you become concerned at the extent of the marks, the larva will have finished the munching – or nearly so – and be resting as a pupa. At the beginning of May or thereabouts, they will begin to hatch and break out as adults, and soon be ready to lay eggs on fresh leaves and begin the life cycle again. This is the chance to meet them coming out, and again when the eggs hatch and before the larvae get inside. We have to put on a layer of contact poison, especially on the less tough of the two leaf surfaces – the underside. BHC or Malathion or the like will be effective. Add a few drips of washing-up detergent liquid as a wetting agent to ensure a good cover and use a fine mist spray that will float up and stick. There is no point in drenching the leaves so that the spray liquid drops – that is waste. We used to spray on three consecutive days to build up a really good coating, then once a week to keep it topped up for the rest of May, then once a fortnight until the end of July.

You may think this is a lot of trouble for older larger trees – and you must be the judge as to how far you want to go – but young plants in nursery rows that were to go out to parks or to be sold, cannot have disfiguring marks like this, and so the spraying has to be thorough, persistent, and at the right time. As with many tasks in gardening, it is no good at all only doing half a job.

102   The infested oak

I am sending a leaf from one of my young oak trees. The round spores on the back of the leaf form during summer. Five years ago the trees began to develop these and also a sooty black mould during summer, and gradually the acorns began to become less and 'oak apples' formed instead. I was advised to give the trees a fungicidal spray, but this has not had any effect at all. Can you advise please?

There is no doubt that both numerically, and in variety, the oak tree is host to more insects, fungus and other forms of life than any other plant that grows in Britain. Many are parasites and do actual harm, and in total so much harm that it is remarkable that so many oaks grow and thrive as they do. On the other hand, many others enter into the tree's structure, prompting a reaction of abnormal growth, and while not symbiotically beneficial to the tree, arguably are not harmful either – at least not to any significant extent. Among these are several wasps that inject their eggs into the tissue of leaves and twigs, which results in strangely abnormal growths. The common 'oak gall' or 'oak apple' is a familiar example. There are many different kinds of these growths and many other wasps and other insects that not only cause them but also take advantage of the growths to lay their eggs inside. Such 'second stage' fellow travellers may simply be feeding on the gall, boring into it and using it as shelter, or they may be parasitic on those who initiate the gall. These parasites may have their own parasites, and those their own hyper-parasites, and so on *ad infinitum*. It is a very complicated picture, and the oak seems to put up with it.

Several of the insects have most extraordinary reproductive systems, such as parthenogenic generations (that is, live birth, or larvae developing from eggs that have not been fertilized) as well as bisexual regeneration. There are also asexual generations that take an entirely different life form, such as the fungus-looking spangles, spores or scales which were on the leaves you sent. Life takes many strange forms. In this case, you needed not a fungicide but an insecticide! If the tree is big, the advice to pick off and burn all affected leaves is hardly sensible – thousands of trees are seriously affected every year, and the problem passes, the trees live, and so will yours.

The sooty mould is a fungus that has no direct effect on the tree other than obstructing light and photosynthesis. It is living on and breaking down the sugary excrescences of aphids that absorb sap from the leaves, take what they want, and exude the rest as 'honeydew'. Again, you can take insecticidal measures, but it is a question of scale. You can hardly spray the whole of a large tree, and no tree in the wild gets such treatment, yet they live!

103 The willow goat moth

At the base of our willow tree, up to a height of 4–5ft (1.2–1.5m) there are a great many holes a little over ¼ inch (6mm) in diameter and 1 inch (25mm) or more deep. I found a white grub in one of these. Can you say what they are and what to do about them?

The grub that you found is of the willow goat moth, and if left, both it and the hole it is making will get bigger. A small infestation may be dealt with by squirting a little contact insecticide into each hole, or pushing in a couple of crystals of paradichlorbenzene (sold at Boots as moth repellant crystals) and closing the holes with clay or putty. Do this as soon as the attack is noticed and before the grubs have time to do serious damage, and a willow usually is able to grow over and heal itself.

Large and neglected infestations, and the weakening effect of so many holes (they will go much further than the inch – 25mm – you report) can even go so far as to affect the safety of the tree. I knew one at Kenwood, Hampstead, not far from the orchestral bowl by the lake, that collapsed while it was being felled – with workmen around it! Don't underestimate the seriousness of this pest.

104   Repelling squirrels

Although we used to be amused by the antics of grey squirrels in our garden, they have multiplied to such an extent as to have become a pest. They have ruined young fruit trees by stripping the bark, they have invaded the soft fruit cage and the vegetable garden, dug up crocuses and other bulbs and robbed the bird table so that we no longer get the tits and other nice birds visiting it. Is there anything that can be done to stop them?

The biggest difficulty with the grey squirrel is to get gardeners and others to see the creature realistically for what it is, and to stop letting judgement be clouded by misplaced sentiment. In listing the several crimes of the pest, this question nearly says it all, and is so typical of the many folk who learn the hard way that the delightful creature springing around the garden is really the devil in disguise. The loss of birds is more likely to be due not to the squirrels robbing the feeding table, but to them robbing the nests, for they will take both eggs and young birds.

Grey squirrels breed twice a year, producing an average of five or six young ones and, contrary to popular belief, they seldom hibernate fully or for long, but can often be seen foraging for food on a mild winter's day. They belong to the rodent family, and are really tree rats with disarmingly bushy tails. Their movements may be pretty to watch, but don't be deceived, the squirrel is a serious and damaging pest.

Whether you wish to eradicate the grey squirrel or only deter it, both courses are beset with difficulties. It is intelligent and resourceful, which is why it has been so successful at the expense of the native red. It soon learns to avoid and leap over deterrents based on smell. Poisoning is more positive, but dangerous to other garden life, to pets, and for you to handle. Furthermore, it is no good at all for you to be taking steps to keep grey squirrels out of your garden without wholehearted similar supporting action by other gardeners around you. If the pest is entrenched in the neighbourhood, as fast as you knock them on the head, others will come in from the excess nearby always looking for a space where they can get in.

The only feasible way to deal with the problem – and it will always be a continuing one until there is a squirrel counterpart of the rabbit disease myxomatosis – is to enlist the support of neighbouring gardeners, and as a body request action by the one authority with the power and ability to tackle the job on the scale needed to be effective. Contact your local council and have their professional rodent operatives do the job.

105 Clawing cats

My neighbour's cat sharpens its claws on my newly planted weeping cherry. Is there anything I can do to deter it and make it go somewhere else?

It is amazing how often this problem crops up. Once cats start on a clawing post, it is difficult to stop the habit. Break up a cardboard carton and use it to make and securely wrap a 2–2½ft (60–75cm) wide collar around the trunk – and the stake, or the cat will simply transfer its clawing to that. As the collar deteriorates with rain or the cat's claws, simply replace it.

You may say that you are soon going to get fed up with that. Now for something a little more drastic. Collect three or four small glass bottles and sink these in the soil to the rim in a ring about 4–6 inches (10–15cm) from the base of the tree stem. Carefully half fill them with ordinary household ammonia. As soon as the moggie gets a whiff of that, he or she will run like the wind and your tree will be given a wide berth.

You must be aware that the weeping cherry is very susceptible to silver leaf disease, and that entry is gained through wounds just as this cat may cause. Read question 50, and paint the stem base with Arbrex as soon as you can, before wrapping the collar around.

106 Greasebanding

Over the past two to three years I have had increasingly bad invasions of caterpillars that have attacked the leaves of my apple trees, and this year our lovely flowering hawthorns. My allotment friends say I should greaseband, but I do not want to betray my ignorance by asking them how to do it. Can you please help?

[189]

There are several nasties that spend the summer gobbling up leaves and fruit, then dropping to the ground when they have had their fill, overwintering below and crawling up again when the weather improves to do it all over again – and it appears that you have been building up a nice population of the little blighters. The idea of 'greasebanding' is to catch them at the vulnerable period when they are crawling up the trunk to get at the leaves. They can fall down, fly down, or drop inside fruit that falls – catching them that way is not very effective, unless you keep a few chickens – but they all have to crawl up the trunk, so we give them a sticky band that they cannot cross. You will have to get a tin of special grease – some people try to save the cost by using motor grease, but being petroleum-based it is harmful to the tree and, as it dries with a hard crust, it soon loses its effectiveness.

We have to make sure that the crawlies go over the grease and not under it, so with a rasp, surform or plane, smooth the rough bark over an area about 12 inches (30cm) wide completely round the trunk about 3–5ft (1–1.5m) from the ground. Smear a thin layer of grease about 2 inches (5cm) wide around the trunk at the top and bottom of this band. Wrap a 12-inch (30-cm) wide strip of greaseproof paper or plastic film round the trunk and tie it down firmly on to the two narrow bands of grease. That will stop anything trying to take a short cut up the inside. The special grease does not dry and form a crust but remains tacky indefinitely. Smear it to a good even thickness, at least 10 inches (25cm) wide with no thin patches, and the band should be impassable.

Get a band into position on every tree that you wish to protect by the end of September, and you will be surprised at what you start catching at once. You can carefully pick them off, but do check at least once a week to make sure that dead bodies and flying leaves do not form a bridge to safety. As soon as you notice the number of trappings is on the increase, take this as a sign that the big rush is about to start, and step up the inspections to daily. If you want to be on the safe side – which is advisable when there is a heavy infestation like this – put another band on above the first, as the rush can be such as to create a bridge during one night.

A further precaution in late July is to tie on a strip of rough sacking in two or three loose wraps. All kinds of crawlies will hole up in this to lay eggs and hibernate. In late autumn, when they are all tucked up, carefully remove the band and burn it.

107 Fire blight

Last year the leaves of my pyracanthas began to look as though they had been scorched; first twigs and then larger branches withered and died. I cut them back and noticed that the central core of the wood appeared to be brown and rotten. This year the trees are worse still and in a very sorry state. It is evident that the rotten core of the wood means something serious. Can you possibly suggest what it can be?

This description of scorching and internal rot is fairly indicative of a very serious disease – I think that it may well be a relatively new bacterial disease that has become known as 'fireblight', *Erwinia anylovora*. The disease was known abroad, but it was first diagnosed in Britain in 1957 on a pear tree in your county – Kent – and soon afterwards was reported on other fruit trees and a number of ornamental trees and shrubs such as *Amelanchier, Cotoneaster, Sorbus, Pyracantha* and *Crataegus* – all members of the *Rosaceae* family. It is evident that this botanical family is particularly at risk, and as it is a very large and important proportion of all the plants that we grow in our gardens, you should at once closely examine all such plants in your garden to see if any others are affected. The point of infection appears to be through the open blooms, the bacteria being carried there by bees and other insects.

You should always be observant in the garden, and as soon as a plant shows distress or abnormal behaviour, no matter how trivial, find out why. You cannot possibly spot everything, recognize every sign, or put the right interpretation on every spot and blemish – some pests and diseases leave very little sign indeed that they are inside working away. However, the characteristic leaf scorch should draw your attention, and if a trial snip reveals the rotten core you will have to act fast. The bacteria can disperse throughout a tree in days, and a rotten core shows that it is already well established. There is no known cure, nor it seems would one be feasible, because if the wood becomes rotten it is damaged beyond repair and further use, and the internal spread is extremely quick. The only cutting out that will do any good is to take affected plants right out of the garden to the fire.

After the bad news, the even more serious. If your trouble is fireblight – you don't know for certain, and it is only my suspicion from a distance – you *must* find out for sure, as it is a 'Notifiable Disease'. This means that, by law, you must notify the police at once. They may want a specimen to send for analysis, so take a piece with you, or more likely they will send somebody to call on you very quickly. In any case you will find out for sure, and the positive identification will indicate what to do next. Don't be put off – even if it is nothing to worry about, it is better to be safe than sorry.

108   Orange spots

Some of the branches of my Acer palmatum *have developed yellow and orange spots about the size of large pin-heads. There are a fair number of them and I am worried in case it is a disease of some kind. Can you suggest what it might be and the correct treatment please?*

This should be regarded as a warning not only for what it is, but also for something else that it may indicate. The orange spots are the fruiting pustules of 'coral spot' fungus, basically a saprophytic type that lives on dead and decaying wood. Particularly in the damp and muggy conditions that favour it, the spots will often be seen on bark, snags, small spurs left at pruning that have died back, and so on. It is but a small step then to pass from being saprophytic on dead tissue to being parasitic and affecting live tissue.

The dead tissue of the maple family seem to be readily attacked by coral spot. Cut and clean off affected twigs and branches, painting exposed living wood with Arbrex protective. As you do this, if, as and when you bare the green cambium layer just under the bark, look very carefully for any signs of brown staining, which will be an indication of deeper serious infection by something else and why the coral spot is getting in on the act. At the start of leaf fall, apply a liquid copper-based fungicide to the tree and again two or three weeks later. Examine the soil and area round about for dead twigs, pieces of wood, debris – anything that can harbour the fungus and provide a jumping-off base – and clean it up and burn it. The best preventive against coral spot is hygiene.

109   Soup-plate fungus

How can I cure a large ash tree which has a large soup-plate-like fungus half buried in the trunk?

This soup-plate fungus is probably a 'polyporus' developing within the living tree, feeding on it and, if allowed to go unchecked, will kill it, if indeed, it has not already gone past the point of no return. Before you do anything at all, you must consider the size and age of this tree, its position, and the damage it could cause if it comes down out of control. The wisest and least dangerous course, clearly, is to call in professional advice and tree-felling services.

If you decide to tackle the job yourself, you will have to begin by removing all the rotten wood beneath and around the fungus, and this is where the danger begins. Make haste very slowly, considering all the time how seriously the excavation is weakening the trunk. Cut, chip, and scrape smooth to sound healthy wood in every direction, no matter how far and how deep you have to go. Every slightest vestige of discoloured and affected wood has to come out, and then you should paint the entire exposed area with orthocide fungicide or Murphy copper.

The cavity that will result from a fungus the size of a 'soup plate' will be considerable and it will have to be filled. Follow the general advice given in question 29. If you judge that the tree is of such a size and weight that a 1:3 cement and vermiculite mix will not be strong enough, you will have to introduce sand and increase the cement proportion. Pay particular care to finishing off, leaving no lip and no possibility of rain and debris lodgement.

Finally, I repeat, only tackle this kind of job if you are absolutely confident that it is not beyond your capabilities – you won't be able to hold the tree up while somebody runs for help. Professional help will cost money, a crash will cost a lot more, so don't be penny-wise and pound-foolish.

110   Boot lace fungus

A green beech about 100 years old has its bark splitting vertically, and the covering of the roots comes away easily. This isn't normal, is it? Do you think it might be suffering from some kind of disease?

Not a lot of description to go on, but what there is – 100-year-old beech, vertical splitting, root bark peeling readily – suggests that it could be an attack by a particularly nasty fungus called *Armillaria mellea*. This is 'honey fungus' or, more descriptively, 'boot lace fungus' after the boot-lace-like threads that are found in the soil and by which means it can travel incredible distances, bypassing and ignoring trees that do not take its fancy, to strike at perfectly healthy specimens trees that do not take its fancy, to strike at perfectly healthy specimens for no apparent reason and without warning. The trouble could be another fungus such as canker, but the only way to positively identify the cause – and it is imperative that you do find out – is by scientific diagnosis on the spot.

Even if the trouble turns out to be not serious, you must not take chances. Contact the Forestry Commission or go to the police and report your suspicions. They will send an expert to call on you. At the very least get qualified professional help – you will need it anyway if the tree has to come down – and act quickly before the fungus has longer to attack other living trees.

111 Blotches and holes in evergreen magnolia

Can you please suggest what may be causing blotches in the leaves of my young Magnolia grandiflora *'Goliath'? First they turn brown and then break into holes. The plant appears to be growing quite well – it is planted against a warm wall for protection – but the blotches and holes are very disfiguring and I am sure cannot be doing it any good.*

Although these trees are often grown against walls for protection it does not always work out that way, and indeed can increase one of the very troubles it is intended to prevent. The large evergreen leaves are hardier than they are often given credit for, but they are prone to bruising caused by being blown about and crashing into each other and the wall. Hence, if a wall or building deflects and actually increases draught and air movement, as in a corridor passage-way or courtyard, the position could very well be self-defeating.

The bruised leaves are prone to attack by botrytis and similar fungal diseases that cause the decay of the damaged tissue, or the damaged cell structure can simply dry out. In either case the 'blotch' disfigures, becomes brittle and is knocked away by further wind blow. Young trees seem to be more prone than older tougher specimens and the problem may lessen as time goes by. I would be inclined to try to make sure that toughening is not delayed by any shortage of the one element that will have a lot to say in this respect – potash. Put down 1 oz (28g) of Humber Garden Compound or Growmore, or a quarter of a teaspoonful of permanganate of potash, to each square yard (square metre) of the spread extent of the above-ground parts of the tree, every three to four months for five to six years, by which time it should be old enough and tough as old boots.

112 Removing a wasp's nest from a tree

There is an old wasp's nest in a tree in our garden and we fear for the safety of children round about. If I knock it down, would the wasps be alive now in December, and would I have to run for it?

The only wasps that will remain alive will be young queen wasps and most likely these will have left the nest to seek out places like crevices in tree trunks, in sheds, or under house eaves in which to hibernate. Even if the queens are still in the nest, they are likely to be sleepy, especially if the nest has been subjected to cold temperature, and they will remain so until temperatures rise, and day length increases to wake them up and initiate another colony to build a new nest.

You can detach the nest easily and safely, if you can enlist some help. Hold a stout plastic bag up around it and, with a saw, sever the stalk or pedicel at the top of the nest by which it is suspended. Then as it falls into the bag, you can close it – quickly if you have any fears! – and dispose of it on the bonfire.

However, if you have to attempt the job later, when temperatures have become milder, at least take the precaution of watching for any signs of coming and going. If that is confirmed, you will have to risk some waspish interest in what you are doing or, if in doubt, call in your local pest control officer.

113 Willow leaves in curlers

Why should the leaves of my small weeping willow go all curly, turn yellow and fall off? Do you think it is a pest of some kind or a mineral shortage in the soil?

Curling leaves, yellowing, premature leaf drop – you may also see brown spots – these are all symptoms of a fungus disease called 'willow anthracnose' that is most troublesome following a wet spring. If you act very quickly at the very first sign of trouble, it is possible to suppress it almost completely – but you will only be able to keep it in check to the extent that action has been delayed and the fungus allowed to become established within the tree. A bad attack left unheeded will lead to actual die-back of shoots, by which time you will probably be able to find small blackened cankers, and then the tree is in deep trouble.

Cut out as many of the affected and damaged shoots as you can.

[195]

I know it is difficult with a large tree, but this is a measure of the problem and how you are going to deal with it. Look carefully at the green cambium ring just below the skin or bark surface, and see if you can detect any sign of brown marking. Interpret this as a sign of disease, and you have not cut back far enough. It is pointless to set out to cut out the disease and to leave wood that is affected. Having physically removed the disease by cutting out and clearing all fallen leaf and other debris to the bonfire, drench spray the remainder with Bordeaux Mixture, repeating two or three times at three-week intervals.

Next spring, just as the leaf buds swell and begin to show the very first signs of green, give the tree a drench spray with lime-sulphur. This is a very messy job, so save some old clothes or use oilskins. Don't try to be neat and tidy or avoid splashing spots of the stuff around: it is not that kind of job. Just accept that if you don't make a mess, you probably will not have done the job properly.

These may be drastic measures, and a lot of trouble to go to, but they are what is involved in getting on top of a nasty disease. If the tree is too large for you to tackle, the time will come when you have to decide that it has gone far enough and it has to come down. All the time you live with a diseased tree, you should realize that it will be a source of infection, and of course, an ailing tree is a weakening tree and at increasing risk in strong winds.

114 Dealing with lilac blight

My lilac is affected by a disease, and as the garden has been surrounded by Dutch Elm disease I think it must be that. Many of the young shoots have gone dark and look as through they have been damaged by frost. Older leaves have gone brown and shrivelled, and I can see circular spots – there is something wrong. Have you any idea what it could be?

This description reads like a nasty disease called lilac blight. There is no connection at all with Dutch Elm.

Over the years I have had a number of correspondents who have been confused by advice they had previously been given, and which had not worked. There is some confusion, no doubt, and it does not help when it is passed on as 'advice'. I can do best, I feel, by relating my experience with it. We had a lilac collection in a park, with no others anywhere near. Quite clean and with no previous hint of trouble, suddenly they all develop this disease like a plague. Where did it come from?

That park was a show place, and all dead wood was clinically cleared out with all fallen debris. As the 'guvnor remarked: 'Asking around the other park superintendents was like making enquiries in the muck heap' – rather like the observation that children who play in the streets develop immunities rather than serious illnesses, whereas those brought up in clinical cleanliness suffer badly as soon as they come into contact with a disease.

If you will read question 94 which deals with lilac scorch, you will realize that a dry spell just as lilac is bursting into bloom puts a tremendous strain on the moisture supply. An ailing thirsty tree is more vulnerable to attack. It had been a dry spring but we always mulched the shrubberies and the soil condition was excellent – there was cause somewhere, but it had not been resolved when I was posted elsewhere.

You may have neighbouring lilacs that are spreading the disease, but as you can see from the anecdote, we had no neighbours in the park. What we did then was the same as what had been done the previous year, when anthracnose developed in the willows by the ornamental lake (see question 113). All affected shoots were cut out, all fallen leaves and debris cleared up and burned. During the dormant winter, after I had left, the lilacs were spray-drenched with a half-strength lime sulphur wash.

When I returned to that park as a foreman some time later, I enquired about the lilac attack. It had been identified soon after, but had not occurred again, so I can only point to the measures taken and suggest that they may very well solve the trouble for you. The disease overwinters on older wood of lilacs and other shrubs commonly found in gardens, notably privet, and develops quickly in a wet spell following dry weather. Ensure that dryness at the root does not contribute to the problems next spring, and keep an extra special watch for the first sign of recurrence – and of course, react at once.

Legal problems

115 Can an encroaching tree be cut back?

The trouble is that my neighbour refuses to lop those branches of a tree that overhangs my garden, and of course nothing will grow in the shade. What can I do in the circumstances?

Bearing in mind that you have to go on living next door to your neighbour, make one more approach and point out that you are doing so in order to try to preserve good relationships. Point out that you are entitled by law to cut back this tree to the line of the boundary between your properties, and also to sever all roots that cross this line. Further, that if he or she is not prepared to do what you are entitled to expect from a good neighbour, then there is nothing whatever that can be legally done to prevent you protecting your property from encroachment.

You could also point out that you will endeavour to put yourself beyond any criticism by painting sawn-through boughs with protective paint, and any subsequent harm or deterioration to the tree will not in any way be your responsibility. By doing this you will at least let it be seen that any subsequent trouble will not be attributable to neglect on your part.

You could also point out that in the same way that you would not be entitled to keep any fruit that falls into your garden from an overhanging tree, you would not expect or wish to keep any cut timber, and therefore you will ensure that, as you cut the tree back, every scrap will be deposited over the fence. You may feel that you would like to have the above reinforced by being the subject of a solicitor's letter, but on the several occasions that I have known the situation to be tackled as described – especially putting all timber and debris over the fence – it has never failed to work.

116 The farmer is responsible

Our gardening is being frustrated by cattle in the adjoining meadow which lean over a barbed wire fence and chew trees, shrubs, vegetables – anything they can reach. Is there anything we can do about this? It is the farmer's dividing fence.

As a technical point of law, it does not matter whether the fence is your responsibility or the farmer's. In law, it is a farmer's responsibility to prevent his animals trespassing across the boundary line, which is precisely what they are doing by stretching their heads over, under, through or round the end of the fence. Furthermore and conversely – although you would not do such a thing deliberately – he could not have the slightest redress on you if his cattle suffered illness or worse as the result of eating something growing on your land, or indeed something they picked up like a plastic bag, piece of wire or metal.

If a poisonous plant, such as laburnum or yew, growing on your land, overhangs the boundary line or a piece falls in his field, then you would be liable if his animals browsed them. It sounds as if you have already had some discussion with the farmer, and that the trouble is continuing. If this is so, I suggest that your further contact in putting the above to him should be in writing, recorded delivery, and further indicate formally, that if he does not take immediate steps to hold the animals off, you will have no alternative but to take legal action, including claim for loss or damage. In that event, your solicitor would require a copy of your letter and evidence of its receipt – hence the recorded delivery.

117 Unlit dump in the road

We ordered several fruit and ornamental trees plus a large number of screening conifers for our new garden, and in order to be ready with planting holes and manure we ordered a load of mushroom compost. This was dumped in the road and on the pavement while there was nobody at home. We found it there when we returned after dark from business, and had to leave it there all night as we do not have a lantern. We were very worried as to our responsibilities in case anybody should run into it. Have you ever had a case like this?

You would be surprised how often this problem crops up. It is something about which suppliers and carriers should be aware, but it is an example of the present-day tendency for standards to become lax. If your road is a bus route, it is an offence to park a car unlit – but thousands are and nothing is done about it. In that sense – and with no inference as to its condition – I see no difference between your car and a load of manure! Most other roads would be governed by the provisions of the Highways Act 1959, which stipulates that any person who deposits obstructive material within 5 yards (5m) of the centre line of the carriageway is guilty of a criminal offence. Of course, loads are dropped all over the place, sometimes partly obscuring the centre line, never mind 5 yards (5m) from it. The Act regards the pavement as part of the highway, and if a pedestrian is hurt while stepping into the road to avoid an obstruction you would have something more to worry about.

As you did not put it there yourself, you would not be guilty under that section of the law, but I have known a clever counsel in similar circumstances make out a very strong case with questions like: 'What steps did you take to ensure that the load would not be delivered when you would not be available to move it and render it safe?' 'What time did you find the load – and what steps did you then take that evening to move at least part of it?' 'Realizing that you could not move it all, and not having been expecting to have to place warning lamps, what steps did you take to put out white sheets, boards or other reflective materials that would be likely to be seen in the dark by pedestrians, or in the lights of traffic?' Such questions follow each other and lead you into a difficult situation, because if your answer to the last question is 'nothing', I am sure that you, not the carrier, could most likely be found to have been negligent.

Being faced with an unexpected emergency is one thing, but leading questions like the above, put by a counsel experienced in such matters, could well and truly put you on top of the dumped load. I have been on the sidelines of litigation several times, in cases very like this, and I can tell you that the law is not only extremely involved, but also a minefield and death trap to the unwary. In the hands of a clever counsel looking for damages, anything is possible, and it would not be the slightest help to argue that you were unaware of the danger, or that you did not put it there. A shrewd counsel would tear you to pieces.

The moral is, whenever you order anything to be delivered, or have work done like tree felling, never, repeat, never, assume that the people you employ will deliver at an arranged time, or know (or perhaps even much care) about the responsibilities for subsequent trouble of this kind. Expect the unexpected, and be prepared to take action that will put you beyond criticism.

118 Tree Preservation Order – and drains

I have a large poplar tree in my garden which stands about 40ft (12m) from my neighbour's house. He has complained that he thinks that the tree's roots may be damaging his drains. As a matter of fact, we would not be averse to having it removed but the tree has a Preservation Order on it. Can you tell us what is the legal position please?

When a tree has a preservation order placed on it, you cannot cut it down, cut bits off it or harm it in any way, but that does not absolve you from liability for any damage it may cause. If you feel that a branch is dangerous, or that roots constitute danger to drains, you must obtain the consent of the authority who issued the Order before you touch the tree. They will have the tree inspected, and authorize the work or not as the case may be, but you are still liable for damage.

If you disagree with the decision and refusal to permit the work you want, you must resort to litigation and it is then a job for a solicitor. Particularly with regard to the possibility of roots causing direct damage to drains, or indirectly, such as soil shrinkage and subsidence, you will need a solicitor more than ever because the onus will be upon your neighbour in the first instance to demonstrate that his fears are well founded. That is bound to involve the collection of evidence and opinion, if not actual excavation to verify, remonstration and three-way correspondence between the authority, your neighbour and you, who are still at risk of liability! Get yourself a good solicitor and double check your property insurance.

119 Unsafe trees – liability for damage

We have a lime tree that is reputed to be 200 years old, and looked as though it would have blown down in the recent storm. Had it done so, and caused damage to neighbouring property, would we have been liable?

There cannot be much doubt that there will be a great many cases like this where trees have gone down, and where responsibility will be argued into court. I think that any householder would be wise to expect that the short answer to a question like this is yes, you are liable, and therefore you should insure against such contingencies. I suggest also that you would be wise to guard against compounding the problem, if not indeed drawing upon yourself the entire responsibility for damage, by making sure that the element of neglect could not be brought in. For example, could it be shown that you knew, or that you should have known, that the tree was in a dangerous condition? If this tree had gone down, it could have been arguable that, apart from an apparently healthy appearance, you knew it to be 200 years old and therefore, in face of this fact and its liability to cause

[201]

damage, you should have had it checked out by competent authority
– an omission that you would be wise to put right at once. In
addition, double-check your household and property insurance
arrangements.

120   Slippery leaves – who is liable?

*Every autumn our beautiful sweet chestnut carpets the public footpath with
a thick layer of leaves which become slippery as they become rain-soaked
and walked on. Would be liable if somebody slipped up and injured
themselves?*

Most probably not – there is nothing in law that is specific on the
matter, and it would therefore boil down to argued opinion.
Somebody would have to prove negligence by you – and you would
counter with 'it's up to the other party to be careful how and where
they walk'. Fallen leaves become wet, mushy and slippery – that is
commonsense knowledge – and anyone who walks on them, slips up
and falls, only has her- or himself to blame.

On the other hand, if you have allowed something to remain on the
path that you were responsible for putting there in the first place –
like mud from the wheels of your barrow – and this has been covered
with leaves, the position begins to change and become arguable, and
the swingometer of blame begins to move. I would think that if leaves
cover something dangerous that you have caused or know about, and
not cleared up or taken measures to make safe by sanding, then a passer
by who falls and is hurt may have a very good case against you. You
cannot be held responsible for what may be termed 'natural hazards',
only for what you add to such a situation by negligence, and that has to
be proven. It is generally understood to be the responsibility of the
local authority to keep public paths clear and safe.

121   Breaking a Tree Preservation Order

*We have just bought a house with several large trees in the garden.
Beautiful as they are, they cast deep shadows in some rooms – the kitchen
is so dark we have to keep the light on all the time. However we understand
that, as the trees are subject to Preservation Orders, we are not supposed to
cut them back or down. Is there anything we can do?*

When you contemplate buying a property you should wisely observe whether there are trees standing, how near they are to the building and to adjoining property, and assess their potential for causing damage and injury. You will also expect the normal search procedures by your solicitor to reveal such matters as Tree Preservation Orders, rights of way, and so on, affecting the property. Indeed, even without a search revealing such matters, there is arguably a case of misrepresentation if the vendor fails to inform the buyer of any such orders and restrictions before any expense is incurred in relation to the purchase – such as survey, searches or fees.

Breaking restrictions imposed by a Tree Preservation Order (TPO) is a criminal offence. Furthermore, any trees of consequence, size or beauty standing in front of your property, may be or have become regarded as affecting the amenities of the neighbourhood, and there may therefore be special provisions under local bye-laws or Town and Country Planning Act 1971 as to what you can and cannot do. If you do not have a precise copy of the TPO on these trees – I would have thought that they should be regarded and treated as an integral part of the house deeds – you should find out exactly what your position is from your local authority. As the trees are so large and close to the house as to obscure light to this extent, there may well be a further cause for concern with regard to danger to the drains, which you may be able to use in support of a case for the removal of the trees. I repeat, however, that you dare not lift a finger against them without the expressed permission of the authority making the Orders.

122 Dutch Elm disease – liability for injury

How would we stand in law if a dead branch from our Dutch Elm diseased tree fell on a passer-by?

I think that you would stand even more dazed than the passer-by! It is another case of opinion that would have to be argued. Liability would depend upon the extent to which it could be argued that you have taken reasonable care – or not taken any steps at all, perhaps – to ascertain the condition of any tree standing on your land which is in a position to inflict injury and damage on others.

Despite the great numbers that were growing in towns alongside roads and in places like public parks, elms are well known to have a propensity to shed a branch without warning and for no apparent reason. Added to that, there has been so much public concern and publicity concerning Dutch Elm disease that it could quite reasonably be held that you could not have failed to be aware of this, and that you have therefore been apathetic, if not negligent, in your responsibilities as a householder and landowner, since you knew that you had a diseased tree, and a dead branch, and yet you took no steps to have the tree felled or made safe. Your question reveals that you know the tree is diseased and carrying a dead branch. In the circumstances I would think it an open and shut case – and you should get the services of qualified and insured tree surgeons immediately.

123 Killing a tree

Can you tell me an efficient way of killing a red beech tree so that one cannot tell that it is not through natural causes?

I would not dare to advise how to kill a tree without the fullest information concerning Tree Preservation Orders, bye-laws, its physical condition, amenity value and so on. Why do you want to make its murder look like natural causes?

Firstly, is there a Tree Preservation Order (TPO) on the tree? Is it subject to any local bye-law? Is the tree mentioned in any legal document appertaining to the property?

Secondly, is it diseased, damaged or dangerous? Even if it is, you cannot touch it if it is subject to a TPO without the consent of the issuing authority.

Third, a red beech, especially if it is of any considerable size, may very well be regarded as having local amenity value. You could incur the enmity and wrath of neighbours if you harm it without good reason.

Apart from the above, there are also aesthetic reasons why I would not want to be party to destroying a beautiful tree. While I may be able to kill a tree in several ways that an amateur would not be expected to detect, it is hardly likely that an amateur would be able to do anything that an expert would not discern. Nor is it possible to use more sophisticated methods that would defy diagnosis by expert analysis – and that is just what could be involved (and has often been) with a distinctive tree like this.

'Slow Killing' is usually resorted to as a means of avoiding detection, and during such treatment a tree can become very unpredictable and dangerous, with consequences more serious than the original problem. Be wise and find a solution to your problem in the correct manner, through the front door and not round the back.

124   Cost of clearing gutters

My neighbour's several large trees shed their leaves into my gutters, which every year become choked. It is so expensive these days to get builders in to clear them. Could my neighbour be made to bear the cost?

I very much doubt it. If your neighbour's trees actually overhang the boundary between you, or their roots invade the soil on your side so as to interfere with your crops and plants, you can ask him to lop and restrain them. If he fails to do so within reasonable time, you can intimate that you will therefore take up your option to have the work carried out and he must pay the bill. That is as far as you can go with trees that overhang and invade, but with leaves it is a different matter.

Trees are an amenity. Planting them is legally permissible and one of the natural consequences is that their leaves are blown by wind. It is unreasonable for a tree-owner to be expected to contain them within his own boundary and prevent them being blown onto your property. Therefore, there is no way you can require that he do so and likewise no way you can compel him to accept the cost of remedying what is unreasonable and impracticable. Indeed – and this would be very apposite in the case of, say, a semi-detached house – I would expect your neighbour to have a better case against you, if, for example, you did not clear your gutters, and resulting overflow caused damage to his walls and property.

Miscellaneous questions

125   The Christmas Holy Thorn

We have been given a 'Glastonbury Christmas Holy Thorn' as a present, and understand that it has a legend or reputation about it. Other than that

it is supposed to flower at Christmas, we can find nothing about this legend.
Can you please tell us any more about it – we are quite intrigued.

This is a particular kind of 'Quickthorn' or 'Hawthorn' (*Crataegus*),
and is one of the earliest flowering trees into bloom each year. There
are famous examples at Glastonbury, Somerset, that are in bloom by
Christmas each year and, inevitably, a legend has been woven around
them.

The earliest written record of the tree with the remarkable
Christmas flowering is in 1535 in a letter or report made by a Dr
Layton, who had been sent to Somerset by the ecclesiastical ministers
of King Henry VIII to investigate the tree and the legend that already
surrounded it. Briefly, the legend – still widely believed to this day –
is that a 'Holy Thorn' had grown from a staff, that had somehow been
struck in the ground, and which had been carried and brought to
Britain by a tin merchant called Joseph, who came from Arimathea –
the very same biblical Joseph of Arimathea – who had left Palestine in
AD 37.

The tin that the Romans, Phoenecians, Arabs and other traders were
after was mined mainly in Cornwall, so what this merchant was doing
in Somerset is not clear, nor has it been explained how a walking staff,
stuck in the ground and incredibly taken root, was still alive 1,500
years later! But never mind, during the reign of Elizabeth I, some idiot
cut down the biggest of the tree's two trunks, and it remained
connected to the root by only a strip of bark. Nevertheless, it lay on
the ground for 30-odd years, continuing to bloom every Christmas as
usual. It was then separated, so the story goes, and dumped in a ditch
where, the following year, it bloomed again – and then disappeared!

Meanwhile, the remaining trunk had continued to flourish,
although by this time it had become the object of numerous pilgrims
who signified their visit by carving their names and initials all over it.
Still it continued to bloom. By this time also, cuttings from the tree
had been rooted and were growing secretly in several places –
although the reason for the secrecy is not explained unless, having
regard to the limited extent of botanical knowledge at that time, it
was inexplicable, if not miraculous, how the cuttings bloomed at
Christmas, when seedlings grown from the tree's seed flowered in
spring with all the other thorns, and not at Christmas! The original
tree had been attacked, so perhaps it was considered advisable to keep
the cutting trees hidden away for their own safety.

However, the second trunk part of the original tree was destroyed during fighting in the reign of Charles II, and reliance for continuity then rested in the secret cuttings. The examples still growing at Glastonbury and elsewhere – there is a famous one in Washington, USA – and still blooming at Christmas, are supposedly vegetative descendants of the original, albeit several generations removed.

That, very briefly, is the legend of the Glastonbury, Holy or Christmas Thorn. Historically, it cannot be proved or disproved, and you believe as much as you wish. Botanically, science originally described it as a clone of *Crataegus oxyacantha* 'Praecox', but has later revised this to *Crataegus monogyna* 'Biflora', that is, twice flowering. The genus is indigenous to Europe, North Africa and Asia Minor, so theoretically, it is possible that a stick or branch used as a staff could have been carried to Britain by a Mediterranean traveller – but whether it took root, and whether the rest of the story bears any truth, we shall never know.

126 Does laburnum poison other plants?

We have a large laburnum tree which seems to produce more bloom as each year passes. This year however, we planted out lettuce, onions, shallots and other vegetables in quite a large bed under this tree. We had not grown anything but roses in this bed before, and suddenly realize that the blossom and seed pods from the laburnum, which we understand are poisonous, have fallen everywhere in this bed. Will we be able to eat our produce?

This is an old controversial subject, with opinions falling into two opposing camps. One, that the tree has no effect whatever, the other that other plants will not grow near laburnum because it gives off 'fumes'. It is certainly true that a lot of complaints are made that shrubs and other plants fail in proximity to laburnum, and the 'fume' theory would fit in nicely, if it were not for the fact that there has been no scientific proof. Conjecture is one thing, proof another. It does not follow that, because a plant is poisonous in some or all parts, other plants nearby will be affected. After all, there are a vast number of other far more 'poisonous' plants and they are not blamed for affecting others.

Whether the tree's roots exhaust nutrients from the soil is another matter, but there is no botanical or rational reason why vegetables should not be safe to eat.

127 *Is* leylandii *poisonous?*

Is a leylandii *conifer hedge harmful to animals if they eat it? I need a good windscreen, but my neighbour's sheep and cows could reach over a small ditch.*

In its general remarks, the Ministry of Agriculture Bulletin No. 161 on British Poisonous Plants makes the observation: 'Most animals are not attracted to most of the coniferous trees grown in this country – their aromatic odour and unpleasant taste prevent them from eating sufficient to cause any harm.' I quote the extract as an example of a generalization that can be misleading – and dangerously, even fatally so.

You are perfectly right and considerate to the cattle to be concerned about the possibility of harm, but you may well deduce from the above authoritative statement that there is nothing to fear. It does say 'most animals' and 'most conifers', not 'all'. The yew is a well-known example for the proviso, because it is one of the few that are poisonous, and very definitely so. However, the Bulletin states that taste and aromatic odour are sufficient deterrent to harm.

In my experience that is just what they are not. Having spent over 48 hours without a break applying particularly horrid and distressing measures to save the life of one of my goats who had eaten rhododendron – she was lucky, she lived – I can tell you that animals do eat unusual herbage because they are hungry. You dare not risk a life on the assumption that they will be put off by taste and smell, and that goes for cows and sheep as well as goats.

Animals are lovable, curious, perverse, infuriating – and, unhappily, heartbreaking. Not all animals have the same kind of stomach and throat – goats are different from cows – and some breeds, even individuals, react differently. There is too much unpredictability. The only thing that is certain with farm animals is that one can go down and its brothers and sisters can be unharmed – but I would not trust *C. leylandii* with any cattle of mine.

Legally, it is the farmer's responsibility to fence off or otherwise protect his animals from anything that they may pick up over or through the fence or hedge that encloses them, just as he is liable for any damage that they do by stretching their necks and reaching plants on your side of the boundary. However, that does not help the animals, and I suggest that it would be kinder to them and good neighbourliness to draw the farmer's attention to your need for a windbreak, the plants that you intend to plant to achieve this, and your concern that his animals could be harmed if they do what is natural anyway. You, for your part, will ensure that branches and growth will not cross the boundary and put his animals at risk, and you would be pleased if he did his bit. It is not a big job – all he has to do is to put in some stakes a few feet (metres) away from the boundary, and run enough wire along to keep them away. I applaud your concern.

128   Does ivy kill trees?

We were advised that no harm could be done by letting an ivy grow up into our oak tree, but now the tree looks unwell. It has lost its leaves in early September, branch tips are dying and it looks nothing like as healthy as it did a few years ago. Do you think the ivy is to blame?

A lot of controversy rages around the question as to whether ivy does harm to a tree up which it is allowed to climb. Scientific investigation will have it that there is no proven evidence that the ivy does cause actual harm – and that when the tree does have ivy on it, it is dying anyway. Ivy, they say, is not a parasite, and the masses of tiny sucker-like roots that attach it to the tree are merely anchoring the ivy, and doing no harm.

That may or may not be true, say the opposing school, but is it not then a remarkable coincidence that ivy only selects those trees that are destined to die shortly, despite outward healthy appearances? The indisputable fact is that one does not see healthy trees smothered with ivy, but all too often we do see smothered trees that are dead, or nearly so. Parasite or not, smothering light or not, circumstantial or not, I suggest that it is always wise to play safe.

Cut through all the ivy stems near the ground and strip away as much as you can from the tree, as high as you can reach with safety – climbing ladders in the garden is fraught with danger. If the ivy is so thick on the ground as to constitute a risk of renewing the attack, I would clear it out by spraying it with Paraquat or selective weedkiller such as SBK.

Whether ivy has been the direct cause of your tree's trouble or is only contributory, I think that you should think carefully about the after-care implications. Is it an old tree, showing signs of final decline, or a younger one growing in difficult conditions? Is your soil sandy and too dry, is it thin and overlaying chalk, or is it quite the reverse – wet and badly drained? These are possible factors that you may be able

[209]

to do something to improve. Your tree has suffered a serious setback, and it would no doubt appreciate and respond to some extra care and attention. Over an area equivalent to the spread of the branches above, put down a dressing of Humber Garden Compound or Growmore, about 2ozs (57g) to each square yard (square metre), and repeat at three-monthly intervals for a year. In the spring, help the early rise of sap and leaf formation by laying a hose out and letting it trickle slowly, moving it around every couple of hours.

129   Preserving fallen oak timber

I have made a garden seat from the wood of an oak tree that fell some years ago. I left the timber to season, but it is now very dry. Would it be advantageous to oil it with linseed or some similar preservative oil? We had another tree down in the recent gale, and I have a lot more wood for making garden furniture.

A similar question to this crops up regularly with regard to cedar wood garden furniture. There is no doubt that oiling improves the appearance of timber by 'bringing out the grain', and it may go some way towards preservation by causing rain to shed off the oily surface instead of wetting and soaking into the wood. Oak is a hard wood and penetration would not be deep, but cracking as it dries – called 'shakes' – goes right to the heart wood, allowing rain to penetrate deeply. Add to this accumulated dust and debris, and decay can become a serious matter. The preventive measure required then is not oiling, but filling all shakes and cracks with wood filler, and this is your first job with oak that has cracked.

Cedar and teak contain natural oils, but nevertheless, proprietary oil dressings have been marketed which consist basically of oil diluted with a thinner, to aid penetration and reduce the oily sticky surface. Even with specially formulated proprietary dressings, it is advisable to leave treated timber for some time before sitting on it – hard oak that is comparatively new and unweathered is not very absorbent but your clothes are! A much better plan – after staining if you wish – is to paint the seats with clear polyurethane varnish.

130   Why chimneys on the walls?

A garden we visited this summer had a walled vegetable and fruit garden with chimneys at intervals along the top of one wall. Another interesting thing was holes about a foot square and 2–3ft (60–90cm) from ground level mid-way between the chimneys, and more at ground level. We asked, but nobody could tell us what it was all for. We have read of 'follies' and wonder if this is somebody's idea of a joke, or is there a serious purpose? We are very curious.

It just shows what you can find when you walk around old gardens with your eyes open! This is very far from being a joke. It is in fact a relic of a practice that was a feature of many Victorian walled gardens when so many of the landed families tried to upstage each other with fruit, flowers, produce or some garden feature, that their friends could not match.

Exotic fruits like peaches and nectarines come from warmer climes, and in this country appreciate protection and help through the winter, which is why they are invariably grown against walls where winds and draughts are minimized and where they can benefit from reflected sunshine and warmth. Frost and cold winds were – and still are – kept off with blinds, curtains, quilts and the like. What this questioner saw went a very big step further, by providing a warmed wall that actually radiated heat! A closer look would have revealed that the wall is hollow. Fires were lit in the bottom holes and the wall had holes along the top to let the smoke out.

Sometimes, extra draught was needed to pull the fires and to throw the smoke up higher, and so chimneys were added. Mostly these were quite plain and utilitarian, but others were not. The three twin chimneys on just such a wall in an estate at Chislehurst, Kent, that had belonged to a famous banking family were the same very ornately decorated type that were on the roof of the big manor house, and there are several other examples around the country that I have seen pictured in old gardening history books.

The fuel used was mostly cordwood and faggots, in plentiful supply from the woods and coppices of the estate – which were much larger and numerous in those days than now. This produced large quantities of ash, which had to be kept clear to stop blocking up the narrow space in the wall. The midway holes, normally kept closed, seem to have been used to help clearing the ash. The system was heavy on fuel – but that cost nothing – and heavy on staff – but that was cheap enough then. It would not do now!

131   Why apples and roses are in the same family

Referring to my gardening encyclopaedia for some information about apples, I was surprised to see that apples are described as 'Rosaceae', the same plant family as roses. Can you please explain? Apples are nothing like rose hips and apple blossom is nothing like my roses.

You are quite right in expecting members of the same botanical order to have fundamental similarities. However, there are very many cases like apples and roses where the similarities are far from obvious at first sight and, as in this case, you have to look a little deeper.

The Linnaean system of plant identification (see pages 28–9) distinguishes between plants by the systematic process of segregation according to similarity and elimination by difference. First, into major families or 'orders' by fundamental similarities, invariably direct relationships arising from common ancestry, and then by the process of elimination of less basic characteristics into the sub-divisions of genera, species, varieties, etc.

The physical construction of flowers and seed-bearing parts is an important feature of the Linnaean system. Many plants have three or (with another three borne behind the first three) six petals. You can see this quite readily in many bulbous subjects. Others have four petals, arranged like a cross, called *cruciferae*. The cabbage family, the genera *Brassicae*, is a good example. Yet others have five petals, like the single and wild rose, apples and hawthorns. The construction of the sexual parts of the flowers (stigma, anthers, etc.) and the seed-bearing parts (the container called the ovary) usually follows petal formation, and is also a basic factor of similarity within each order, but this is not always readily apparent to superficial observation.

Your rose blooms look so different from apple blossom because they are monstrosities; beautiful to our eyes maybe, but botanical monstrosities nevertheless! The full 'double' blooms that we like so much have petals that are borne in multiples of five – fifteen, twenty, twenty-five, thirty, even thirty-five – and although you may not relish the idea of pulling a beautiful bloom to bits, that is the only way to check and chart that all the many petals are in fact in units of five.

This five-petal formation is the first feature that relates apples to roses. If you look very closely at the sexual parts of the flowers – the 'single' rose bloom is much clearer, of course – you will see almost identical similarities. As you might therefore expect, the seed-bearing construction is also similar. Cut a rose-hip and an apple in halves (not

[212]

from top to bottom through the stalk, but through their equators) and you will see that, although the fruit that we eat has a massive pulpy surrounding to the seed chamber, the basic physical construction is not dissimilar to the pulpless rose-hip.

There are other likenesses too, that determine that they belong to the same botanical order of Rosaceae. It is only later in the process of elimination, when we come to comparing things like leaf shape, plant habit and formation, etc., that we sub-divide into the separate genera of *Malus* (apple), *Rosa* (rose) and, for example, *Crataegus* (hawthorn) – which many people regard as coming somewhere between, as it has many of the features of both relations.

132 Fertilizer percentages explained

I have a bag of fertilizer with 'Nitrogen 10%, Phosphoric Acid 5%, Potash 3%, Magnesium 0.5%' written on it. What exactly does this mean – and what does the other 81 per cent consist of?

Fertilizer manufacturers are required by law to put these percentage figures on their bags and sacks. For example, 10 per cent nitrogen means that 10 per cent of the product in the bag consists of nitrogen that is readily available to plants, and similarly with the percentages quoted for the other elements. Very often you will see one figure for soluble and another for insoluble phosphoric acid – simply add these figures together for a phosphoric total.

Many fertilizer products are by-products of industrial processes or are compounded from them. They may contain useful amounts of the plant nutrient chemicals in forms that plants can use, but it would be expensive and uneconomic to further refine and extract the remaining bulk proportion of the 100 per cent after the readily available nutrient values have been subtracted. In addition to some indefinable nutrient values, this bulky residue may consist of inert matter which may or may not make a useful contribution to the soil's physical structure. Some with, for example, a high sulphur content, may even have a deleterious effect, increasing acidity and making heavy soils more sticky. Others, like Humber Manure derived mainly from organic matter, contain a correspondingly high proportion of organic matter which enters into and contributes to the soil's physical structure and fertility cycle.

Many gardeners jump to the conclusion that a large residual bulk

[213]

percentage means that they are paying for useless matter that has been added to increase the bulk and weight, and done to make it look as though they are getting more for their money. While I would not say that that has never happened, there is another factor to bear in mind, which is the physical problem involved in distributing nutrient matter at so much per square yard. If only 10 per cent of a fertilizer material is readily available nutrient, and even this, at 2oz (57g) per square yard (square metre) can cause burning and scorch – as on a lawn – just consider how little you would need to spread evenly over the area to avoid scorch if the nutrient percentage was raised to 50 per cent, 75 per cent or even 100 per cent. In that case, you say, you would bulk the concentrated material with something inert – which is in effect what happens with the 81 per cent you ask about.

133 Logs for burning – an olde ditty

Following the storms, there is a surfeit of logs and timber for fuel. Some wood is better than others, and therefore better value for money. Can you tell us which is the best to buy? We used to have an old hedger living in the village who could recite a long poem about the burning qualities of a great many different kinds. Would you possibly know anything like this?

Wood has different burning characteristics to coal and, to get the best from it, has to be burned differently. Wood-burning stoves are specially designed, but if you have an open grate, place a piece of thick iron sheet in the bottom to cover as much of the bars and spaces as possible to stop the embers falling through. These are the most important part of a wood fire, because made to accumulate instead of dropping through, they build up and send out heat for a long time. As the ash collects, air flow slows, and so does the rate of burning, so that, instead of all flame and flare, you get a steady slow combustion – and great heat. Don't poke a wood fire any more than you have to.

Here is an old anonymous 'country ditty' that may be the kind of rhyme you are looking for:

> Oak logs – they will warm you well, if they're old and dry.
> Larch logs of pinewood smell, but the sparks will fly.
> Beech logs for Christmas time, Yew logs – all heat well,
> Scotch logs it is a crime for anyone to sell.
> Birch logs will burn too fast, Chestnuts scarce at all,
> Hawthorn logs are good to last if cut in the fall,

Holly logs will burn like wax – always burn them green,
 Elm logs burn like smouldering flax – no flame to be seen.
Pear logs and Apple logs, they will scent your room,
 Cherry logs placed o'er the dogs smell like flowers in bloom.
But Ash logs that are smooth and grey, burn them green or old.
 Buy all you can that come your way – they're worth their weight in gold.

A few woods are not mentioned in the ditty. Willow is a poor fuel by itself, throwing out sparks dangerously from an open fire, so it needs covering with heavier logs. Larch is mentioned, but the danger from sparks needs to be emphasized – never leave the room empty when these logs are burning, even with a fine mesh guard in position. The sparks that splutter are very small, and lethal if they get through. Walnut is excellent – and the dry twigs make good fragrant kindling. Many evergreen conifers contain aromatic resins which blaze intensely if allowed to become too dry. Burn them while still rather green and you have an incense-like odour as a bonus. Cedar is particularly good in this respect. Birch, as described, burns too fast with a bright flame – the best way to use these logs is to hold them back for brightening up a fire that has 'gone dull'.

Finally, as a matter of interest, a quotation from the renowned author G. K. Chesterton:

A queer fancy seems to be current that a fire exists only to warm people. It exists also to light their darkness, to raise their spirits, to toast their muffins, to air their rooms, to cook their chestnuts, to tell stories to their children, to make chequered shadows on their walls, and to be the red heart of a man's house and hearth, for which, as the great heathens said, a man should die.

134 Simple way to measure tree height

We have mislaid a Sunday Times *cutting in which you described a simple way to measure the height of a tree. Would you please tell us again how to do it?*

It is applied simple geometry. If you have a right-angled isosceles triangle in which the two sides containing the right angle are equal in length, the other two angles, because they are therefore equal, are each 45°. This is the method. A tree growing straight up out of the ground forms the right angle at its base. We cannot climb up the tree with a tape to measure it, so we reproduce it as nearly as we can on the ground, and measure that.

[215]

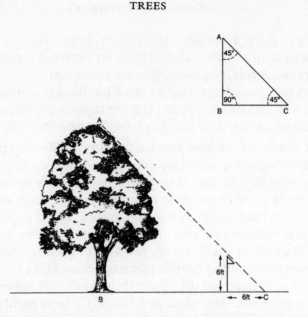

Fig. 18 Measuring the height of a tree. Sides AB and BC of the isosceles triangle are the same length. The tree height, AB, can be measured out on the ground, BC, once you have fixed the point C by using a simple 45° sight-line to the top of the tree.

Most of us are between 5ft 6 inches (1.7m) and 6ft (2m) tall, so get yourself a 6ft (2m) stake (if you use one shorter than this, you will have to bend and stoop, and probably tilt the stake over). Now make a 45° angle at one end. This is very simple – cut out one side of a cardboard carton as accurately as you can along the corners. Thin card like a cereal packet is perfect for the job, and will give you a rectangle with square corners of 90° each. To bisect one of the corners, simply fold the card diagonally, aligning the two adjoining edges, press down the fold, and there is your 45° angle. You can cut along the crease or use the card double. Fasten the card to the stake with drawing pins or tacks, keeping the 45° angle at the top like a flag on a stick, as in Fig. 19. You now have a measuring stake which is crudely simple, but perfectly ample for your purpose.

Holding the stake squarely upright with the other end firmly on the ground, move about back and forth as required so that, by sighting along the edge of the 45° angle, you find a spot where it is dead in line with the top of the tree. Put down something to mark the spot, measure the distance to the tree, add on 6ft (2m) for the height of the stake (because you are sighting at 6ft (2m), not at ground level) and that is the height of the tree. If you do not have a long measure, never mind. Lay the stake down with one end on the spot and in a straight line towards the tree, and simply fold it over end over end till you reach the tree. It probably will not be an exact full length when you get there, and you will have to estimate for the last part of the stake. Suppose the distance is eleven stake lengths and half a stake – that works out at $11 \times 6 = 66$ft (20m) + 3ft (1m) (half a stake) = 69ft (21m) + 6ft (2m) for the stake height = 75ft (23m) in total. Simple, isn't it?

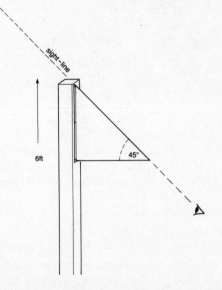

Fig. 19 *A piece of card cut to 45° and nailed to a 6ft (2m) stake is all you need. Position the stake so you can see the top of the tree along the sight-line, and there's point C, 6ft (2m) from the foot of the post.*

You can use this method to measure buildings, the town hall clock, even the church spire – the calculation procedure is exactly the same. Of course, if you use a different stake length, you will work in multiples of whatever length it is, but the principle remains the same. Remember always to do the sighting with the stake as upright as you can, and you will be surprised how accurate you can be. On sloping ground, make the sighting not from below or above the base of the tree, but from across the slope at the same level.

Bibliography

British Trees in Colour, Cyril Hart and Charles Raymond (Michael Joseph, London, 1973)

The Commonsense of Gardening, Bill Swain (Michael Joseph, London, 1976)

The Complete Guide to the Trees of Britain and Northern Europe, Alan Mitchell (Dragon's World, Limpsfield, 1985)

Conifers, Keith Rushforth (Christopher Helm, London, 1987)

The Garden Trees Book, David Carr (The Crowood Press, Marlborough, 1988)

The Hillier Book of Tree Planting and Management, Keith Rushforth (David & Charles, Newton Abbot, 1987)

Hillier Colour Dictionary of Trees and Shrubs (David & Charles, Newton Abbot, 1981)

Hillier's Manual of Trees and Shrubs (David & Charles, Newton Abbot, 1981)

International Code of Botanical Nomenclature, Bohn, Scheltema and Holkema (Dr W. Junk BV, The Hague, 1961)

International Code of Nomenclature for Cultivated Plants, Bohn, Scheltema and Holkema (Dr W. Junk BV, The Hague, 1969)

Manual of Cultivated Broadleaved Trees and Shrubs, G. Krusmann (Batsford, London, 1985)

Manual of Cultivated Conifers, G. Krusmann (Batsford, London, 1985)

Ornamental Trees (Readers Digest/National Trust, 1986)

Trees in Britain, Brian Grimes and Eric Herbert (Webb & Bower, Exeter, 1988)

Trees in Britain, Europe and North America, Roger Phillips (Pan, London, 1978)

Trees of the Countryside, Alan Fairhurst and Eric Soothill (Blandford Press, London, 1989)

Trees and Shrubs hardy in the British Isles, W. J. Bean, 4 vols. (John Murray, London, 1970-80)

Trees for small gardens, Keith Rushforth (Cassell/The Royal Horticultural Society, London, 1987)

Useful Addresses

Nurseries

The following are first-class, nationally known and reliable nurseries, offering informative catalogues, mail order and collection facilities.

Hillier Nurseries (Winchester) Ltd. Ampfield House, Ampfield, Romsey, Hants, SO51 9PA.

Notcutts Nurseries, Woodbridge, Suffolk.

Highfield Nurseries, Whitminster, Glos. GL2 7PL.

Bodnant Garden Nursery, Tal-y-cafn, Colwyn Bay, Clwyd, North Wales, LL28 5RE.

Sunningdale Nurseries, Windlesham, Surrey.

Note: Very many 'name' gardens which are open to the public, including gardens owned by The National Trust, also offer 'garden centre' facilities and are well worth inspecting.

Fertilizer, Manure & Peat Suppliers

Humber Fishing and Manure Co., Stoneferry, Hull, Yorkshire.
  'Humber Garden Manure' and very useful literature.
Maskell's Fertilizers, 1 Stephenson Street, Canning Town, London E13.
  Useful price lists of fertilizers, manures, peats, composts, etc.
Synchemicals Ltd., Grange Walk, Bermondsey, London SE1.
  S600 transplanting spray, Hormone Shrub and Brushwood Killer (SBK), etc.

Index

DEMCO